THE MASONIC BOOK CLUB

VOL. 13

Masonic Almanacs and Anti-Masonic Almanacs

Plez A. Transou

Westphalia Press

An Imprint of the Policy Studies Organization
Washington, DC

THE MASONIC BOOK CLUB

The *Masonic Book Club* (MBC) was formed in 1970 by two Illinois Masons, Alphonse Cerza, 33°, and Louis L. Williams, 33°. The MBC primarily reprinted out-of-print Masonic books with scholarly introductions; occasionally they would print additional texts as "bonuses" (though none were marked specifically as such on the title pages); sometimes a reprint would be marked "Masonic Book Club Edition"; often an unnumbered bonus was published jointly with the Illinois Lodge of Research or the Supreme Council, 33°, NMJ, USA.

Most of the MBC volumes indicated on the title page, "Volume [*Number*] of the Publications of the Masonic Book Club," some were misnumbered, and some were unnumbered. Indeed, the numbering of the early volumes was inconsistent. For example, *A Serious and Impartial Enquiry* is "Volume Five" (1974) but *Masonic Membership of the Founding Fathers* is "The Masonic Book Club Edition" (1974). Then, *Masonry Dissected* is "Volume Eight" (1977), *The Trestleboard* is "Volume 8A" (1978), and *Anderson's Constitutions of 1738* is "Volume Nine" (1978). If nothing else, MBC books keep bibliophiles on their toes.

The first volumes had deckle-edged paper and pages of slightly different sizes, though eventually the MBC settled into a 6″×9″ trimmed-page format for their books. The books were bound in a dark blue fabric with gold lettering. Listed below are the fifty-nine MBC volumes published 1970–2010 with bonuses. N.B.: A number and letter, e.g. "Volume 8A," is a numbering for this reprint series.

The club originally was limited to 333 members, but the number grew to nearly 2,000, with 1,083 members when it dissolved in 2010. In 2017 MW Barry Weer, 33°, the last president of the MBC, transferred the MBC name and assets to the Supreme Council, 33°, SJ, USA. Under the editorship of Arturo de Hoyos, 33°, ɢ∴ᴄ∴, and S. Brent Morris, 33°, ɢ∴ᴄ∴, the revived Masonic Book Club has the goal of publishing classic Masonic books while supporting Scottish Rite, SJ, USA philanthropies.

Publications of the Masonic Book Club, 1970–2010

1	1970	*The Regius Poem*	Masonic Book Club
2	1971	*The Constitutions of the Free-Masons*	Benjamin Franklin
3	1972	*Ahiman Rezon*	Laurence Dermott
4	1973	*Illustrations of Masonry*	William Preston
5	1974	*A Serious and Impartial Enquiry into the Cause of the Present Decay of Free-Masonry in the Kingdom of Ireland*	Fifield D'Assigny
5A	1974*	*Masonic Membership of the Founding Fathers*	Ronald E. Heaton

6	1975	*The Signers of the Declaration of Independence*	David C. Whitney
7	1976	*The Signers of the Constitution of the United States*	David C. Whitney
7A	1976*	*Masonic Symbols in American Decorative Art*	Louis L. Williams & Alphonse Cerza
8	1977	*Samuel Prichard's Masonry Dissected, 1730*	Harry Carr
8A	1978*	*Trestle-Board (A facsimile of the original Trestle Board by the Baltimore Masonic Convention of 1843)*	Dwight L. Smith
9	1978	*Anderson's Constitutions of 1738*	Lewis Edward & W. J. Hughan
10	1979	*Sufferings of John Coustos*	Wallace McLeod
11	1980	*The Revelations of a Square*	George Oliver
11A	1980	*Biblical Characters in Freemasonry*	John H. Van Gorden
11B	1980*	*A Masonic Reader's Guide*	Alphonse Cerza & Thomas Warden
12	1981	*Three Distinct Knocks and Jachin and Boaz*	Harry Carr
13	1982	*Masonic Almanacs and Anti-Masonic Almanacs*	Plez A. Transou
13A	1982*	*Stephen A. Douglas: Freemason*	Wayne C. Temple
14	1983	*The Beginnings of Freemasonry in America*	Melvin M. Johnson
14A	1983*	*Bespangled, Painted & Embroidered: Decorated Masonic Aprons in America, 1790–1850*	Scottish Rite Masonic Museum & Library
14B	1983*	*Making a Mason at Sight*	Louis L. Williams
15	1984	*Masonic Concordance of the Holy Bible*	Charles Clyde Hunt
15A	1984*	*By Square and Compasses: The Building of Lincoln's Home and Its Saga*	Wayne C. Temple
16	1985	*The Old Gothic Constitutions*	Wallace McLeod

28	1997	*The Masonic Ladder or the Nine Steps to Ancient Freemasonry*	John Sherer
28A	1997*	*Freemasonry and Democracy: Its Evolution in North America*	Allen E. Roberts & Wallace McLeod
29	1998	*The Masonic Harp: Collection of Masonic Odes, Hymns, Songs*	George Wingate Chase
30	1999	*Symbolic Teachings of Masonry and Its Message*	Thomas Milton Stewart
31	2000	*Freemasonry Its Meaning and Significance, An Exposition of its Ethics, Religion and Philosophy*	Otto Caspari
32	2001	*K. R. Cama Masonic Jubilee Volume*	Jivanji Jamshedji Modi
33	2002	*Caementaria Hibernica*	W. J. Chetwode Crawley
34	2003	*A Daily Advancement in Masonic Knowledge*	Wallace McLeod & S. Brent Morris
35	2004	*The Craftsman, and Templar's Textbook and, also, Melodies for the Craft*	Cornelius Moore
36	2005	*The Text Book of Freemasonry*	Retired Member of the Craft
37	2006	*Orations of the Illustrious Brother Frederick Dalcho Esq., M.D.*	Frederick Dalcho
38	2007	*Antiquities of Freemasonry Comprising Illustrations of the Five Grand Periods of Masonry from the Creation of the World to the Dedication of King Solomon's Temple*	George Oliver
39	2008	*Diogenes' Lamp or an Examination of our Present-Day Morality and Enlightenment*	Adam Weishaupt
40	2009	*Proofs of Conspiracy Against All the Governments of Europe*	John Robison
41	2010	*The Evolution of Freemasonry*	Delmar Darrah

** indicates a bonus book*

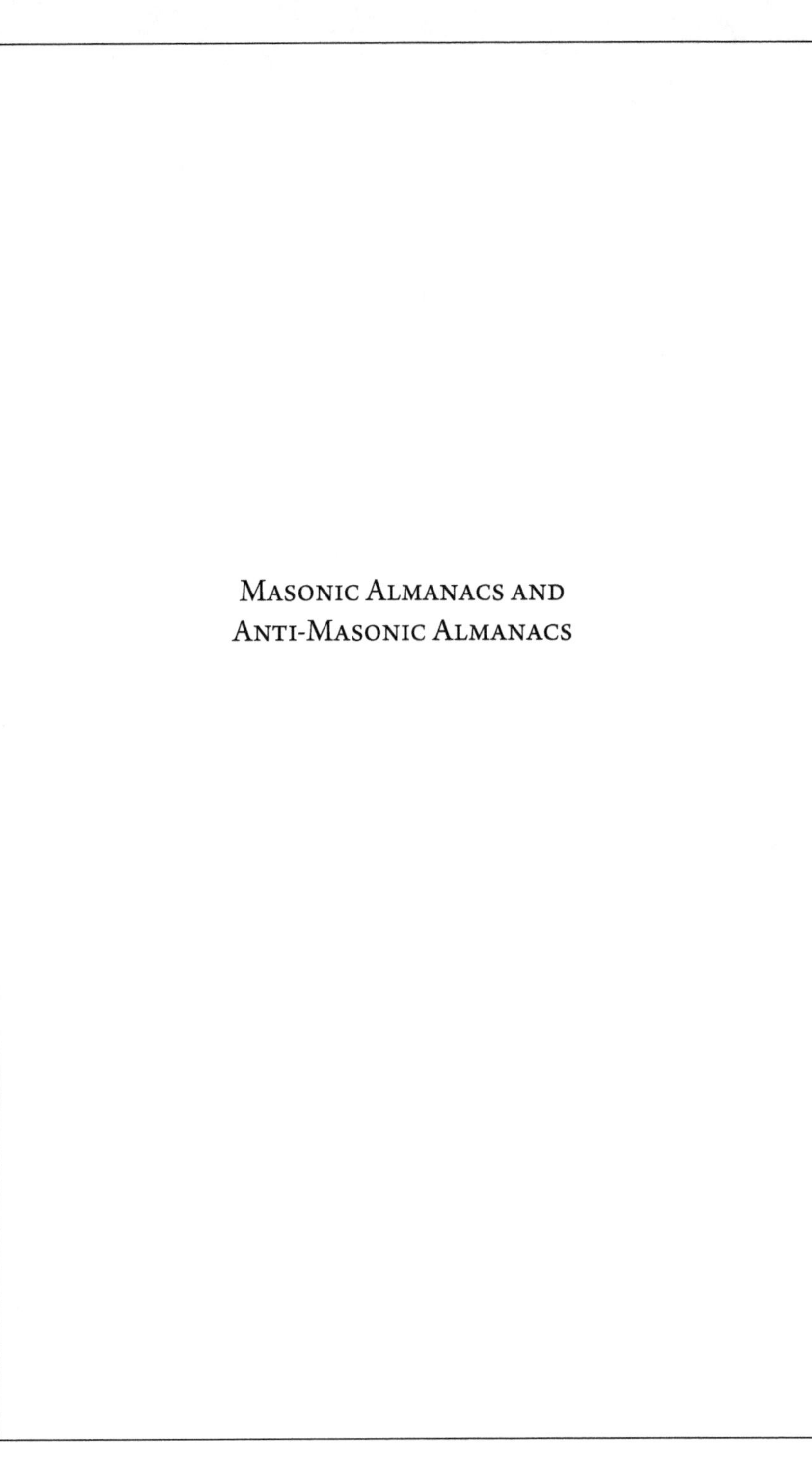

Masonic Almanacs and
Anti-Masonic Almanacs

Masonic Almanacs
and
Anti-Masonic Almanacs

MASONIC ALMANACS

AND

ANTI-MASONIC ALMANACS

WITH COMMENTARY BY

Plez A. Transou

VOLUME THIRTEEN

of the publications of
The Masonic Book Club

Published by

The Masonic Book Club
A Not-for-Profit Corporation of Illinois
Bloomington, Illinois

1982

CONTENTS

Commentary

CHAPTER

The Facsimiles

Appendices

PREFACE

Almanacs have been in existence for many years and the word is familiar to most Masons. Everyone at some time or other has either seen, read, or purchased a copy of the Old Farmers' Almanac which is sold in many supermarts and book stores. Some Masons have heard that there have been Masonic Almanacs and also Anti-Masonic Almanacs, but few of them have ever seen a copy or have one in their personal libraries. In keeping with the purpose of the Masonic Book Club to reproduce out-of-print Masonic books, your officers decided to publish facsimiles of a Masonic Almanac and of an Anti-Masonic Almanac.

For those of our members who would like to secure a broad background of the general subject of Almanacs before reading the facsimiles and the Commentary, there is an Appendix with a detailed coverage that presents adequate background information.

We were fortunate in securing an experienced, devoted, and enthusiastic member of the Craft to make a study of this subject, select the books to be reproduced, and to prepare the fine commentary contained in this book.

Brother Plez Avery Transou was born in North Carolina and received his early formal education in the public schools of that state. He then attended the Georgia School of Technology until he joined the United States Navy and served in World War Two. After the War he attended the University of North Carolina and in 1950 received the Bachelor of Arts degree. He continued his formal education at night while employed and received his Industrial Engineering Certificate from North Carolina State College in 1952. In the year 1954 he moved to Dallas, Texas where he has continued to live to the present time. He came to Texas to work as sales and marketing representative of the Myrtle Desk Company, of

High Point, North Carolina and for many years he has served the company as its District Manager in Texas.

In 1956 he was joined in marriage with Diane Parkins, and of this marriage three sons have been born: Bryan, Eric, and Scott. The family has joined the Central Lutheran Church, of Dallas.

Brother Transou was active in the Boy Scouts of America while living in High Point, North Carolina, serving on the District Committee from 1951 to 1954. He was also Camp Counselor of the YMCA. In 1951-1953 he was active in the Red Cross Blood Drive as well as in the United Fund Drive.

He has been active in a number of business groups. Among them are the High Point Personnel Managers Association, the International Home Furnishing Representatives Association, the Southwest Road Runners, Inc., the Piedmont Safety Council serving as Local Director, and he has been Program Chairman of the American Business Club.

His interest in Masonic matters started early in life. In 1942, when he was sixteen years of age, he became a member of Winston-Salem Chapter of the Order of De Molay. In 1950 he became a member of West Bend Lodge No. 434, located at Lewisville, North Carolina. The following year he joined High Point Chapter No. 70, R. A. M.

In 1956 he became a member of the Dallas Scottish Rite Bodies as well as Hella Temple of the Shrine. In 1970 he affiliated with Dallas Lodge No. 760 and became active at once in the work of the Lodge. He became a line officer of the Lodge and in 1976-1977 he served the Lodge as Worshipful Master. In 1977 he was elected a Life Member of the Lodge. He is an excellent ritualist and holds the Certificate of Proficiency issued by the Committee on Work of the Grand Lodge of Texas. In 1980 he was appointed District Deputy Grand Master for Masonic District No. 14A. In 1970 he became a member of Dallas Chapter No. 47, R. A. M., Dallas Council No. 18, R. & S. M., and also Dallas Commandery No. 6, K. T. In 1978 he became a Life Member of the Knights Templar Eye Foundation. In December, 1979 he was invested with the Rank and Decoration of Knight Commander of the Court of Honour, of the Scottish Rite of

Freemasonry, Southern Jurisdiction. In 1982 he became a member of the Red Cross of Constantine.

He has been one of the hard working members of the Texas Lodge of Research. In 1970 he was elected an Associate Member of the Lodge and in 1975 he was elected an Active Member. That same year he became a line officer of the Lodge and he served as Worshipful Master in 1979-1980. He has written papers for the Transactions of the Texas Lodge of Research and for the Texas Freemason. In 1979 he was one of the speakers at the Philalethes Society meeting held in Washington, D. C., and this talk was later published in the Society's magazine.

The officers and members of the Masonic Book Club thank Brother Transou for taking the time from his busy schedule to do the necessary research on the subject of Almanacs generally, Masonic Almanacs, and Anti-Masonic Almanacs, and then writing the Commentary. A number of persons were helpful in many ways in the production of this book and they are entitled to our appreciation and thanks for making this book possible. Ms. Inga Baum, Assistant Librarian of the House of the Temple Library, located in Washington, D. C. made available to us a number of Masonic Almanacs to examine and gave us permission to make the copy of the Rob Morris 1860 Masonic Almanac which is reproduced in this volume. Brother Harvey C. Byrd, Grand Secretary, and Librarian of the Texas Masonic Library, together with Dr. D. D. Tidwell, Assistant Librarian, helped locate various Anti-Masonic Almanacs, read the commentary and gave us many valuable suggestions. Brother Harry Carr, of London, England, while visiting in Texas on a lecture tour, had a conference with Brother Transou, gave some valuable suggestions, supplied him with the Calendar of 1812, and later supplied him with xerox copies of important material which is described briefly in the Commentary.

Louis L. Williams

Alphonse Cerza

[ix]

I

MASONIC ALMANACS

The Enigma

Of all the literary forms, the almanac is one of the most ambiguous. The word itself is not Anglo-Saxon. It is thought to be of medieval Arabic origin, meaning: first, the place where camels kneel; later, a campsite or settlement; and, finally, the weather at a specific site. Probably, the word came to western Europe from the Spanish Arabic where it meant calendar. Today, in modern Arabic, "al-manakh" means weather or climate.[1]

Therefore, any investigation of the almanac must include consideration of the relationship between the weather, the calendar, and the almanac. "Almanac" and "calendar" are both applied to the printed records of the year; and, sometimes, they are thought to be synonymous. Even though they are very close relatives, by definition they are not identical twins. As Webster defines it, a calendar is a SYSTEM of determining the beginning, length, and division of the year. An almanac is a yearly CALENDAR of days, weeks, and months, with the addition of astronomical data, weather forecasts, and other practical information. So, while a calendar is not necessarily an almanac, an almanac is a calendar, expanded to some extent by the compiler.

A study of the many different types available leads to the conclusion that there is no standard format for the almanac. The definition notwithstanding, in actual practice "almanac" and "calendar" are often used interchangeably, and this is particularly true in the case of Masonic almanacs.

---

[1] *Encyclopedia Britannica*, Micropedia, Volume 1 (1974), p. 263.

Typically, an almanac contains an ordinary calendar, astrological calculations, weather forecasts, a calendar of events, important dates, prophecy, and other useful information. However, in actual practice, an almanac might contain all, part, or very few of these basic ingredients along with any additional information of the almanac-maker's choosing.

The history of the almanac is as variegated as it is sketchy, but it probably began when man became a farmer and found himself in need of a method of determining the seasons of the year at a given location. It has been suggested tht the pyramid was, among other things, an almanac used by Egyptian rulers to insure food supplies and regulate the surplus. Wooden clogs, or notched sticks, were used as almanacs for many centuries before the invention of writing, and they remained in use in northern Europe until the 12th century and in England as late as the end of the 17th century. Handwritten almanacs appeared as early as 1150 A.D., and these manuscripts were replaced by printed versions in the last half of the 15th century. Elizabethan England saw the almanac become a monopoly when The Company of Stationers acquired the first exclusive rights from the Queen. The Company has continued in the field of almanacs, having started the historic *Vox Stellarum* by Francis Moore in 1701, and this almanac continues today under the title *Old Moore's Almanac*.

American almanacs appeared about 1630, the earliest named version being *An Almanac Calculated for New England*, and this was printed by Stephen Day, first printer in America. The famous *Poor Richard's Almanack* by Benjamin Franklin was launched in 1733, and it became the most popular publication in Colonial America. In 1793, Robert Thomas started *The Old Farmer's Almanac*, a current almanac which holds the record of the oldest continuous publication in the nation.

While early almanacs were related primarily to agriculture, as they progressed, they came to include astrology and prophecy. The manuscripts contained mostly weather and astrological information, but they also recorded religious observances. One of the earliest printed almanacs, *Ephemerides*

Ab Anno, considered the first almanac of real importance, contained navigational data, and it is thought that Columbus used this in his travels. By the 1500's, home medical advice was a popular feature of almanacs, and soon after that, other statistics and interesting facts were added. Later almanacs became more specialized. For example, in 1712, there was in England, *The Traveler's Almanac*, a feature of which was the method of calculating the time of the day by the use of a stick and the shadow of the sun. In Colonial America, the almanac was considered indispensable in the average household.

Almanacs have developed into heterogeneous mixtures of scientific, historic, demographic, and biographic knowledge. They might be literal, prophetic, and educational. Along with information of general appeal, they often contain substantial amounts of trivia. In addition to such essentials as moon phases, tides, seasons, eclipses, agricultural advice, and weather facts, many examples have the addenda of festival dates, sporting events, orations, essays, poems, verses, skits, book reviews, notes, commentaries, and advertisements. Subject matter runs the gamut and includes such oddities as topical allusions, bibliography, wit, satire, philosophy, first aid, and records—records on everything from the longest distance for catching a thrown grape to the world's longest fingernails. The almanac has come a long way from its relatively simple, original purpose.

The scope of the almanac is extensive, but as a specific literary form, it does not seem to have found great favor among those who compose reference books. However, there is a two-volume publication which lists about 1400 American almanacs known to the compiler, and it covers a period from 1639 to about 1875.[2] The listing is according to states, and each state had almanacs of local color or specific interest during a particular era. For example, Connecticut had many astronomical almanacs because of the sea ports there. During the Civil War, some states had Confederate almanacs. Texas had a *Merchants and Planter's Almanac*, a *Methodist Almanac*,

---

[2] Milton Drake, *Almanacs of the United States*, (New York: The Scarecrow Press, Inc.)

and the *Annexation Almanac of 1846*. An anti-Masonic almanac for the year 1842 was published in New York, and there were several anti-slavery almanacs. Massachusetts had an Odd Fellows almanac, and Tennessee had *Davy Crockett's Almanac for 1873*. Vermont, New York, Massachusetts, Ohio, and Pennsylvania, according to the listing, were the leading areas for Masonic almanacs, both pro and con, the anti-Masonic almanacs being the more prevalent. Both the scope and importance of the almanac is summed up in the Introduction of this book. An 1878 quotation explains that the almanac was:

> . . . the one universal book of modern literature, the supreme and only literary necessity, even in households where the Bible and newspapers are still undesired and unattainable luxuries.

H. L. Haywood says it is impossible to draw a line between almanacs and magazines in the history of American journalism, and the almanac was "the Eighteenth Century's monthly magazine, encyclopedia, calendar, a repository of literature, and what not."[3] It is the "what not" that seems to distort the standard definition and understanding of the almanac. Under the general heading of almanacs, there are some interesting variations on the classification itself. Calendars, year books, registers, annuals, digests, guides, journals, and even compendiums can be and have been called almanacs. Masonic almanacs are no exception.

The Literary Device

In his encyclopedia, Henry Wilson Coil mentions a few Masonic almanacs published in the Hague, Edinburgh, Germany, England, and France, all appearing in the latter half of the 18th century. He says the English Provincial Grand Lodges published a number during this period, but they were never popular in America. He refers to year books such as Clegg's *The Masonic Year*, explaining that unlike almanacs and

---

[3] H. L. Haywood, *Supplement to Mackey's Encyclopedia of Freemasonry*, Volume III (New York: Macoy Publishing Company, 1966), p. 1154.

calendars generally, they were often reviews or compendiums and made no prophesies. Coil says that Masonic almanacs are out of vogue today, and he implies they were not too conspicuous when at the peak of popularity.[4]

Albert Mackey, in his encyclopedia, seems to place more importance on the almanac's contribution to the main body of Masonic literature. He says that almanacs for special use of the Fraternity were published annually in many European countries, but he agrees that the custom has not found favor in America.[5]

Genealogy

As early as 1752, there appeared in the Hague the *Almanach des Frances-Masons en Ecosse*, and this or a similar work continued until 1778.[6] The first Masonic almanac (or calendar) in English was published for the year 1775. This was an unofficial publication, and it was one for which William Preston is supposed to have been chiefly responsible.[7] This unofficial version was repeated for the year 1776. The following year, the Grand Lodge responded with *The Free-masons Calendar for 1777*, "under sanction of the Grand Lodge," and, "in opposition" to the previous unofficial 1775 and 1776 versions.

Although the earliest publication dates are 1752 in the Hague and 1775 in England, publications similar to almanacs or calendars were published about three decades before. They began with the lists of lodges. Article XIII of the Old Regulations in the 1723 edition of Anderson's *Constitutions* states as follows:

> Here also the Masters or the Wardens of each particular Lodge shall bring and produce a List of such Members as have

---

[4] Henry Wilson Coil, Sr., *Coil's Masonic Encyclopedia* (New York: Macoy Publishing Company, 1961), p. 27.

[5] Albert G. Mackey, *Encyclopedia of Freemasonry*, revised by Robert I. Clegg (New York: Macoy Publishing Company, 1946), p. 53.

[6] Ibid.

[7] Albert F. Calvert, *The Grand Lodge of England, 1717-1917* (London: Herbert Jenkins, Ltd., MCMVII), p. 98.

been made, or even admitted in their particular Lodges since the last Communication of the Grand Lodge:

Rule III of the Old Regulations further directs that the Master, one of the Wardens, or someone appointed by the Master should keep a book containing:

> . . . the Names of their Members, and a List of all the Lodges in town; with the Usual Times and Places of their forming . . .

Apparently, these directives were intended to form a check and counter-check of the lodges in the town (London & Westminster) and to establish a record of the time and location of their meeting places.

The first list of names published was that which appeared in the 1723 *Book of Constitutions*, and this list contained the names of the officers of the twenty lodges that signed the "Approbation." However, the first List proper was "A List of the Regular Constituted Lodges, with the Names of the Masters, Wardens and Members of each Lodge." It appeared in the Grand Lodge minutes which began November 24, 1723. Probably, lists were made earlier, but minutes were not kept regularly until after the appointment of William Cowper as Grand Secretary in June, 1723.

Next came the Engraved Lists of Lodges which appeared from 1724 until 1778. When a new lodge was formed, an engraved card was made showing the name, number, and meeting dates of the lodges along with the emblem of the inn or tavern where they met. Eventually, these cards were mounted in a frame which became a Table of Lodges, and this table authenticated the existence of a regular lodge.[8] The first written authority to hold lodges was called a "deputation," and this gave a brother the right to form a *regular* lodge of brethren who had been meeting regularly and the right to have that lodge placed among the Engraved Lists. At that time, Engraved Lists was the "chief evidence that a regular Lodge existed."[9]

The Library of the Grand Lodge in England houses the

---

[8] Henry Wilson Coil, Sr., *Coil's Masonic Encyclopedia* (New York: Macoy Publishing Company, 1961), p. 240.

[9] Bernard Jones, *Freemason's Guide and Compendium* (London: George G. Harrap & Company, Ltd., 1965), p. 368.

earliest Engraved List which was issued in 1724. The following year, the famous John Pine, "Engraver over against Little Brittain-end in Aldersgatestreet," produced his first Engraved List and for the following sixteen years, Pine was responsible for all of these Lists.

The Engraved Lists had a frontispiece which consisted of the arms of the presiding Grand Master, and earlier versions pictured an architect explaining a set of building plans to a monarch. Then followed a list of the lodges, generally in order of their constitution, with their number on the Registry and the sign of the inn where they met. These inn signs were pictorial and typographical. As the Lists progressed, they came to include the names of Grand Officers, Provincial Grand Masters, and eventually, lodge names.

By way of explanation, until 1750, lodges did not have specific titles but were known by the name of the inn where they met. As lodges acquired individual names, it became the practice to give the lodge title and meeting place on the Engraved Lists and to omit the pictorial sign of the inn. After 1769, these inn signs disappeared entirely.[10]

After appearing regularly for over fifty years, the Engraved Lists were replaced by the calendar. The first to appear in ordinary type was the aforementioned *Freemason's Calendar of 1775*. It was published in opposition to the Lists and was not under authority of the Grand Lodge. It was prepared, "By a Society of Brethren," "Printed for the Company of Stationers," and "Inscribed, with great Respect to the Right Honorable Lord Petre, Grand Master."

In his book about Thomas Dunckerley, Henry Sadler describes Lodge No. 224, a Blue Water Lodge, which met aboard His Majesty's Ship Canceaux at Quebec, and in this is mentioned the unofficial 1775 Calendar. Sadler explains that up until 1778, both Engraved Lists and calendars were published concurrently, but in that year, the Lists were discontinued, leaving the field entirely to its modern rival, the calendar.[11]

---

[10] Albert F. Calvert, *The Grand Lodge of England, 1717-1917* (London: Herbert Jenkins, Ltd. MCMXVII), p. 97.

[11] Henry Sadler, *Thomas Dunckerley, His Life, Labours, and Letters* (London: Diprose & Bateman, 1891), p. 69.

The unofficial calendars caught the attention of the Grand Lodge, having established two facts. The calendar was less expensive than the Engraved Lists, and it could contain more information. The matter was brought before the Grand Lodge at the November 24, 1775 meeting by the Grand Secretary who informed the assembly that "a Freemasons' Calendar for 1775 and 1776 had been published by the Company of Stationers without sanction of the Society," and that he felt such a publication, "properly authorized would be acceptable to the fraternity, and might be beneficial to the charity." He moved that, "a 'Free-Masons' Calendar, under sanction of the Grand Lodge be published, in opposition to that published by the Stationers' Company; and the profits of such publication be appropriated to the general fund of the Society." The question was put and the motion passed.

The official *Masonic Calendar* was published annually in England until 1814 when it became a pocket-size book. Eventually, by 1908, the calendar evolved into the *Masonic Year Book* which continues today.

An excellent example of the Masonic almanac is *The Free-Mason's Calendar of 1812*. (See Appendix.) Considering the change in format took place shortly after the publication of this issue, it is reasonable to assume it represents a marked degree of development of the Masonic almanac. Also, this example establishes the synonymity of "almanac" and "calendar."

Year Books

Early Masonic calendars, designed to communicate with and provide information to the Craft, are a link in the chain of official publications which began in 1723 and continue today, a popular form being the year book. Although somewhat different in form and content, the purpose is essentially the same, thus year books are in the nature of the old calendars or almanacs.

In keeping with the 1723 edict and original intent, for the most part, the English Year Book is a book of lists. The title page of the current edition contains the Grand Lodge meeting dates followed by a page of calendar notes for five years. Next, there is an ordinary calendar for three years. Then there are the various lists which include:

> List of active Grand Lodge Officers
> A complete list of Lodges with the number, name, date and place of meeting, and the date of foundation (warrant)
> Alphabetical list of Lodges in London (approximately 1700)
> Alphabetical list of Provincial (and District) Lodges (approximately 5000)
> List of Lodges in English Provinces, with names of Lodges, Provincial Grand Masters, and Senior Grand Officers
> List of Prestonian Lecturers
> List of Chapters

In addition, there is a brief listing of charitable institutions and charitable grants by both Grand Lodge and Grand Chapter, plus a short financial report. The year book is more or less a roster or reference book for use in determining who's who or what's what in English Freemasonry.

An excellent year book is *The Grand Lodge of Scotland Year Book*. Beginning in 1952, this publication was edited by George Draffen of Newington, an ardent Freemason, an accomplished Masonic scholar, and a delightful personality. Editing this publication for twenty-five years, Draffen set the format for a continuously successful year book, invaluable to all Scottish Masons and of great interest to the Craft at large.

The inaugural edition begins, after a "List of Grand Office-Bearers," with a roster of other officers, representatives, and committeemen. Of interest to American Masons is the inclusion of an American on a small list of Honorary Members. It is "Harry S. Truman, President of the United States of America."

The scope of Scottish Freemasonry is astounding as proven by the listing of Provincial and District Grand Masters including those in such far away places as India, Pakistan, Barbados, Burma, Hong Kong, Natal, Newfoundland, Australia, New Zealand, Rhodesia, Transvaal, North China, and Nigeria.

There are committee assignments, and a roll of lodges (about 100 pages) beginning with the celebrated Mother Kilwinning Number 0 (Nought). The usual statistics, reviews, financial reports, law changes, rulings, Masonic events, and important Scottish dates are included. The Ancient Charges are presented, and there is a Masonic Who's Who Section. There are items pertaining to the library and museum, and a short history of the Grand Lodge of Scotland.

Compared to the English Year Book, the Scottish publication contains more than a series of lists, and the Scottish Year Book more nearly resembles the annual Grand Lodge proceedings that are so prevalent in America.

An interesting variation from the stereotype is Robert I. Clegg's almanac and/or year book which is titled, *The Masonic Year*. It was first published in 1920. It contains no monthly calendar and lists make up a less significant part of the contents. It concerned itself with recent past events, being basically a digest of reports from popular Masonic publications of the era.

In addition to information on Craft Masonry, it covers the Appendant Bodies. It has Masonic statistics, unusual events, items of general interest, building plans, and obituaries. It lists some well-known Freemasons, mentions Freemasonry overseas, and lists the time of some annual communications. There is a section on Masonic Enlightenment, some poetry, and a report on the third annual meeting of the Masonic Service Association.

Although the Engraved Lists, calendars, almanacs, and year books, each are different, there is a marked interrelationship between them, and they serve, to a degree, the same functions.

American Masonic Almanacs

Nathaniel Ames rivaled Benjamin Franklin as a practitioner in the art of almanacs, Ames being the earlier of the two. While Franklin did not direct his writing along Masonic lines, Ames, a Mason and a member of Constellation Lodge, is said to have aimed his skits and verses at the Fraternity more than once.[12] Without copies of Ames' almanacs as references, it is not possible to determine if Ames actually wrote Masonically in his almanac, but his biography contains the following lines attributed to him to substantiate his Masonic interest:

> So Masonry and Death are both the same, tho' of different name.

This quote is said to mean that man knows nothing of either Masonry or death until initiated.[13]

In her history of Masonry in Federalist Connecticut, Dorothy Ann Lipson says that the Masonic lodge acted as a conduit for all sorts of information and that lodge rosters published in various state and regional almanacs were among the first mailings of the country.[14] While this does not establish the existence of Masonic almanacs at that place and time, it does point to a relationship between Masonry and almanacs. Lipson says also that during the early years, authors and publishers used lodge rosters to announce new books about Masonry, so perhaps this is one of the earlier uses of mailing lists as a means of reaching an interested segment of the reading public.

Early handwritten minute books were kept by the Grand Lodge of Texas, and two of these old books exist today. One covers the period from 1837 to 1849, and the other from 1861 to 1868. There is no book covering the gap, the years from 1850 to 1860, but it is almost certain that such a book did exist at one time.

Printed *Proceedings* of the Grand Lodge of Texas started in 1843. In the 1852 edition, there was a reprint of the *Masonic Kalendar for 1838.*[15] Apparently, this was the first thing

---

[12] H. L. Haywood, *Supplement to Mackey's Encyclopedia of Freemasonry*, Vol. III (New York: Macoy Publishing Company, 1946), p. 1154.

[13] H. L. Haywood, ed. L. C. Cook, "Masonic Curiosa," *Transactions of the Missouri Lodge of Research*, Vol. 25, 1968. In this is mentioned Sam Bigg who wrote about the almanacs of Ames which were said to have contained "a number of rare Masonic items."

[14] Dorothy Ann Lipson, *Free Masonry in Federalist Connecticut, 1789-1835* (Princeton: Princeton University Press, 1977) p. 253.

[15] The Grand Lodge of Texas, *Proceedings for 1852.*

printed along the lines of Proceedings.[16] The title statement points to the fact that Texas came very close to losing this literary landmark.

MASONIC KALENDAR FOR 1838

Published by the Grand Lodge in 1839, republished with the proceedings of the present year, to preserve its recollection, being but few, if more than one copy in existence.

This six-page calendar begins with a statement attesting to the establishment of the Grand Lodge under authority of the Grand Lodge of Louisiana. Following that, there is a list of the Grand Lodge Officers, the Grand Master being titled "Most Worshipful," and all of the rest being "Right Worshipful," a departure from current practice. Then there is a statement that the annual communication assembled on the second Monday in November, in each year, at the seat of government. The remaining space is devoted to information on the nine subordinate lodges that make up the Grand Lodge, including the date of charter or grant, a list of officers, and the dates of meetings. It is noted that dispensation to work was granted Phoenix Lodge No. 8, not by the Grand Master, as is his prerogative today, but rather by the Deputy Grand Master. Also, Harmony Lodge No. 6, working under dispensation, was reported, "Not organized, for want of a suitable building."

There seems to be a difference of opinion as to the earliest date for a Masonic almanac in America. Writing for the American Lodge of Research, Richard Wright of New York made the statement that Rob Morris "appears to have issued the first (Masonic almanac) to support our Craft," and he cites the *Freemason's Almanac* published in Louisville from 1860 to 1865.[17] Wright goes on to say, "next came the *American Masonic Almanac*, printed by R. McMurdy of Washington, D.C. in 1864." Morris, aptly named "that indefatigable Masonic editor and publisher" by Wright, may have been the better of the Masonic almanac-makers, but he was not the first.

---

[16] Dr. D. D. Tidwell, Waco, Texas. Personal correspondence.

[17] Richard Wright, "Masonic Almanacs," *Transactions of the American Lodge of Research*, Vol. IV, No. 1 (Oct. 1942 to April 1944), p. 128.

[12]

There are several bound collections of Masonic almanacs in the library at the House of the Temple in Washington, and the earliest of these is *No. 2. Howe's Genuine Almanac for the Year 1824*. This almanac does not fly Masonic colors, but the design of the title page leaves no doubt about its Masonic relationship. The page is outlined by two columns connected by an arch. The column on the left is designated by the letter "B" and has the words "wisdom" and "order" at the top and bottom respectively. The column on the right is designated by the letter "J," and has the words "science" and "beauty" at the top and bottom. The name of the almanac is spread across the arch under which is a large letter "G" surrounded by symbols of the sun, moon, a cluster of stars, and an equilateral triangle. The author's name is "Philo Astronomie," no doubt a pseudonym of Howe. Freemasonry is not mentioned directly; however, there is an article of religious opinion, a short metaphysical lecture, and comments on virtue, charity, honesty, and common sense.

The 1826 edition of the same publication clearly establishes a Masonic relationship. "Philo Astronomie" added the initials "K.T.K.M." after his name, and the title became *No. 22. The Free-Mason Almanac*. The two columns and the arch appeared again, essentially the same, but there was the addition of the motto, "In Hoc Signo Vinces," and among the contents was an article titled, "Masonic Hints for Inquiring Minds."

In 1828, there appeared *The New England Almanac and Masonic Calendar*, published by Marsh and Capen of Boston, and this publication is mentioned in several references. It is safe to assume this was a prevalent and popular Masonic almanac, at least in the New England area. The price of 12½ cents was double the cost of Howe's almanac, but double-digit inflation was not a sign of the times back then, so the increase was probably a result of the expanded size of Marsh as compared to Howe which sold for only six cents per copy. The 1828 edition contained information of general Masonic events, specified Grand Lodge events in New England, and listed officers and meeting dates of Massachusetts subordinate lodges. A great deal of space is devoted to New England governmental agencies and officials, information on the courts, and salaries of governmental and judicial officials. An unusual feature of this almanac is a comprehensive schedule and list of fares of stage coach lines serving the New England area.

The aforementioned *American Masonic Almanac*, edited by McMurdy, is full of Masonic references and includes comments on symbolism, the equilateral triangle, Capitular Masonry, the Masonic Ladder, Masonic abbreviations, Hiram Abiff, and Masonic lectures. It has an inordinate amount of advertising, including an interesting one of a supplier of Masonic paraphernalia.[18]

At the same time Rob Morris launched his Masonic almanac, 1860 to 1865, there was another prolific almanac-maker, Thomas Adams of Boston, author of *The Masonic Register and Almanac*. His first was for the year 1860, and according to an existing copy dated 1879, he outran Morris by at least fourteen years. Adams' product was as much a register as it was an almanac, being made up, to a greater extent, of lists of officers and committeemen of the Grand Lodge and York Rite of the Commonwealth of Massachusetts. It had the meeting dates of Lodges, Chapters, and Commanderies around the state. Several pages were devoted to what appears to be direct copies of portions of the monitorial explanations of Craft symbolism, and there were small bits of Masonic data of general interest. Of the forty-four pages in the 1870 edition, nineteen pages are devoted to advertising of commercial firms and professionals. Some of these were furniture and clothing manufacturers, dentists, locksmiths, and undertakers.[19]

THE CENTENNIAL MASONIC ALMANAC OF 1876.

Masonic historians who believe that Masonic almanacs are not important research tools are missing something of value. A good example is *The Centennial Masonic Almanac*.[20]

---

[18] R. McMurdy, *The American Masonic Almanac for 1864* (Washington: 1863).

[19] Thomas Adams, *The Masonic Register and Almanac for 1879* (Boston: 1879). Adams had several printers through the duration of his almanacs and the title changed back and forth between "The Masonic Almanac," and "The Masonic Register and Almanac."

[20] *The Centennial Masonic Almanac for 1876* (Philadelphia: Issued by The Keystone, published by The Masonic Publishing Company, 1876).

In the *Transactions* of the Missouri Lodge of Research, there is a short article about Daniel Coxe, the first Grand Master in America.[21] He was appointed in 1730 by the Grand Lodge of England, and he was empowered to warrant lodges in New York, New Jersey, and Pennsylvania. The article refers to "an interesting item, which apparently has thus far been overlooked; a small paper bound volume entitled the *Centennial Masonic Almanac*, published in Philadelphia, in 1876, by that grand old Masonic periodical *The Keystone* (a newspaper), the like of which we may never see again." *The Keystone* stated that Coxe warranted a lodge named The Hoop, in Water Street, in Philadelphia, in 1730. If this is true, then The Hoop would have been the first *chartered* lodge in America.

However, historians do not agree, generally, with this. In his *Encyclopedia*, Coil has a chart of the first lodges in the Thirteen Colonies, and according to this, the date of the earliest warranted lodge in Pennsylvania is "1749/50."[22] Coil does show 1730 as the date of the earliest "immemorial rights" lodge, and he places it in Pennsylvania, but neither the chart nor the text names the lodge. However, the text does mention the oldest Colonial lodge document in existence which contains the account records of Tun Lodge in Philadelphia, and the account dated June, 1731 shows that Benjamin Franklin "paid his dues for five months back." That would have been back to February 1730/31.

Mackey feels, based on an article by Benjamin Franklin in his *Pennsylvania Gazette*, that there were several lodges established in the state in 1730 and that perhaps Daniel Coxe did have time to establish one or two lodges. However, most probably, the lodges mentioned by Franklin were "immemorial rights" lodges and not chartered or warranted lodges.[23]

---

[21] "Masonic Curiosa," *Transactions* of the Missouri Lodge of Research, Vol. 25, 1968, p. 198-99.

[22] *Coil's Encyclopedia*, s.v., "America, Introduction of Freemasonry Into," Vol. VIII, p. 34. The use of dates such as "1749/50" comes about as a result of the Calendar Reform which Coil explains in detail in his encyclopedia.

[23] *Mackey's Revised Encyclopedia of Freemasonry*, Vol. II (New York: Macoy Publishing Company, 1966), s.v., "Pennsylvania," p. 761.

The Centennial Masonic Almanac states, emphatically, that the first regular Master Mason's lodge in America was The Hoop, in Water Street, in Philadelphia.[24] Moreover, the almanac says The Hoop was chartered in 1730 by Grand Master Coxe. On another page, the almanac states that the First Provincial Grand Lodge in America was the Provincial Grand Lodge of Pennsylvania which met at Tun Tavern, Water Street, Philadelphia.[25] In still another section, it reiterates, in no uncertain terms, that Grand Master Coxe warranted the first Master Mason's lodge in America and it names The Hoop as that lodge.[26]

Regardless of warrant, charter, or "immemorial rights," Pennsylvania was convinced, in 1876 at least, the first regular chartered lodge in America was The Hoop, and it was made by Coxe. Comparing the conclusions in *The Centennial Masonic Almanac* with other documentation, the dissimilarity indicates a need for additional research on the subject.

MOON LODGES

Fifty years ago, there were over three thousand Moon Lodges in America, but with the growth of urban areas, the improved highway systems, and the availability of the automobile, Moon Lodges are almost extinct. The approximate count, in the mid-1950's, was five hundred lodges, representing thirty-six grand jurisdictions, which met "O.B." (on or before full moon) or "O.A." (on or after full moon).[27]

The custom of lodges meeting on or near a night of the full moon is an old English tradition, but it was not a practice of the Operative Masons of medieval times.[28] Moreover, it was not the result of the astronomical theme in the ritual which appeared first in the Cooke MS, c. 1410, the moon being

---

[24] *The Centennial Masonic Almanac* (Philadelphia: Masonic Publishing Company, 1876), p. 4.

[25] Ibid, p. 28.

[26] Ibid, p. 48.

[27] W. F. Mellny, "Moon Lodges," *The Masonic Service Association Digest*, January, 1954.

[28] Harry Carr, "The Full Moon and Freemasonry," *Ars Quatuor Coronatorum*, Vol. 80, 1967, p. 318.

mentioned specifically as early as 1724 in *The Whole Institution of Masonry*. Of interest, certainly, is the fact that by the time of Prichard's famous exposure, *Masonry Dissected*, in 1730, the moon was an established symbol in the ritual, the three lights representing the "Sun, Moon, and Master-Mason." However, these and other ritualistic references to the moon have nothing to do with the custom of meeting on or near the full moon. The custom had a more practical origin.

During the 18th century, the people had a common regard and concern for celestial bodies in a time when the population was more rural and there was no such things as electric lights. At the time, the almanac was a common household authority, and everyone, including Freemasons, measured their time and regulated their activities according to the full moon, for practical reasons.[29] The light of the moon was needed to light the path of the Mason on his way home from lodge.

The previously discussed Engraved Lists of Lodges showed the meeting dates of lodges. The 1734 List of 127 lodges is the earliest record of lodges whose meeting dates were governed by the light of the moon. There were two, both in Lancashire. Lodge No. 105 met in a Private Room in the town of Bolton le Moors, "Next Wednesday to every full moon." Lodge No. 118 met at the Red Dog in the town of Bury, "Next Thursday to every full moon."

Two lodges out of a total of 127 does not necessarily reflect a widespread practice of meeting on or near the full moon, but this comparison demands explanation.[30] Seven of the lodges were overseas, thirty-two were in the English Provinces, and for some reason, nine did not show meeting dates. The remaining eighty-eight were London lodges, and they usually met on specified dates. Harry Carr explains that in London and the larger Provincial towns, Masons probably had the company of other brethren on their way to and from lodge, and lacking this, it was possible to hire a torch bearer to light them safely home. The smaller country towns or villages

---

[29] Henry Wilson Coil, Sr., *Masonic Encyclopedia* (New York: Macoy Publishing Company, 1961), p. 421.

[30] Harry Carr, "The Full Moon and Freemasonry," *Ars Quatuor Coronatorum*, Vol. 80, 1967, pp. 321-322.

were a different matter. The roads were bad and there was the threat of highwaymen. The light of the moon was the only available light for use in travel over bad and unlighted roads and perhaps the most useful defense against the highwaymen.

The custom of meeting on or near the full moon was never widely practiced in England. It started in and was confined to mostly small country towns and villages, and it has been abandoned for the most part in England today. The practice of meeting on or near the full moon in America was also a matter of practicality, with lodges setting their meeting dates so the old timers could see better as they walked, rode, or drove to and from lodge.

A past secretary of Charity Lodge No. 134, meeting at Parkton, Maryland, said that in the earlier days, the horse and buggy days, many of the brethren walked from five to eight miles to and from lodge meetings. There was no train service after lodge had closed, and on several occasions, one member walked the distance of twenty-five miles to a neighboring town in order to be at work by five o'clock in the morning.[31]

A considerate Grand Lodge of Kentucky in its *Proceedings of 1874*, published an *Almanac of Full Moons* which listed the full moons each year from 1869 to 1883, showing the day of the week and the month upon which every full moon occurred.[32]

Aside from the need for moonlight to prevent a horse-borne brother from being unsaddled by an obscure, low-hanging tree limb, there were considerations for personal safety. For example, the Indians of the untamed frontier were not so likely to go undetected during a full moon. There were problems from marauding pale faces as well. The history of a Texas lodge relates that after twenty years of meeting on the first Saturday night of each month, the date was changed, resulting from an incident involving one of the brethren. Riding home on horseback, he was going down a passage that was no more than a cow trail when two riders emerged from a thicket, guns drawn. After a close look at the brother, the two

---

[31] W. F. Mellny, "Moon Lodges," *The Masonic Service Association Digest*, January 1954.

[32] Ibid.

men decided he was not what or whom they sought, so they fell behind and rode away. In all probability, the brother was scared half out of his wits, but he was not harmed. Even so, the incident was serious enough for the lodge to change the meeting date to a night with plenty of moonlight to prevent future cases of mistaken identity and any possible resulting tragedy.[33]

[33] Dr. C. L. York, "Moon Lodges," *Transactions of the Texas Lodge of Research*, Vol. IX, 1973-4, p. 69.

II

THE ROB MORRIS ALMANACS
1860—1865

Rob Morris—Life & Times

Robert Williams Peckham was one of the most prominent
and active Freemasons of the mid-19th century, however the
name is unfamiliar to most Masons today. Peckham was born
in New York City in 1818 where he lived until the death of his
father in 1825. He moved to Massachusetts and later to western
New York State to live with the family of John Morris.
Peckham adopted the surname of Morris, shortened his first
name to "Rob," and following his initiation at the age of
twenty-seven years, Rob Morris began a Masonic career that
has been matched by few. He died at the age of seventy in 1888.

Rob Morris lived during exciting Masonic times. His
contemporaries included such notables as Albert Pike, Jeremy
Cross, Albert Mackey, Robert Macoy, and Robert Freke
Gould. During his lifetime, Quatuor Coronati Lodge 2076,
the premier research lodge of the world, was formed in
England, and the Provincial Grand Lodge of the Royal Order
of Scotland, the Red Cross of Constantine, and the Ancient
Arabic Order Nobles of the Mystic Shrine were formed in
America. During this time, the Emulation Lodge of Improvement was established in England, and Gould published his
History of Freemasonry. Although only eight years of age
when William Morgan disappeared, the resulting anti-Masonic
excitement lasted long enough for Morris to join, eventually,
the defense of Freemasonry. During his lifetime, there were
nearly thirty Grand Lodges formed in America, and Albert
Pike revised the Scottish Rite Degrees.

By profession, Rob Morris was a civil engineer and a
geologist, but he spent a great deal of time traveling and

lecturing in the interest of Freemasonry. It has been said of him that he knew, personally, more Freemasons than any other man.[1] Morris was Raised in Oxford Lodge No. 33, at Oxford, Mississippi, in 1845. He belonged to all the degrees and orders of the York and Scottish Rites, and he became Grand Master of Kentucky in 1858. He authored the ritual of the Order of the Eastern Star and is considered the founder of the Order with the assistance of his friend, Robert Macoy. He was a prolific Masonic writer and a competent Masonic editor, and he was crowned Poet Laureate of Freemasonry at New York City in 1884.

During the 1800's, there were several attempts to establish a unified Masonic ritual in America, a movement that could succeed only under a central authority such as a Mother or General Grand Lodge of sorts. One of the more notable of these attempts was the Baltimore Convention of 1843 which went so far as to prepare a unified ritual titled *New Masonic Trestleboard*. Although the convention was widely respected and had considerable support, it failed.

Fifteen years later, Rob Morris headed such a movement. He formulated his own plan to re-establish the Webb-Preston ritual and solidify it into a standard working. This was to be accomplished through a secret organization, *The Conservators of Symbolic Masonry*, of which Morris was the head. He sent out confidential circulars to selected Masons to join what he called "an association of experienced and devoted Masons." Morris outlined the purpose of the association which was, for the most part, to re-establish the ritual as "arranged by Preston and taught by Webb," to eliminate innovations and errors in the ritual, to bring about uniformity of the esoteric work, to establish schools of instruction, to strengthen Masonic ties, and to improve communications with European Masons.[2] The one-time membership fee for the Conservators was ten dollars, for which there was the privilege of belonging, a Masonic degree (Conservators Degree), a journal for

---

[1] Henry Wilson Coil, Sr., *Masonic Encyclopedia*, (New York: Macoy Publishing Company, 1961), p. 430.

[2] "The Masonic Conservators," The Short Talk Bulletin, Volume XXIV, No. 1, January 1946.

members only, and a copy of *Mnemonics*, a cipher book covering the Three Degrees which was published by Morris. The plan was to last for only five years, Morris no doubt feeling that would be enough time to win the various Grand Jurisdictions over, and under a completely unified method of work, all lodges in the nation would live forever in an atmosphere of peace and harmony. However, his plan, considered "most pretentious, unique, and theoretically sound, although practically dangerous," met the same fate as previous plans, and as a result of the failure, the Masonic career of Morris suffered considerably.[3]

As a publisher, Morris made a substantial contribution to Masonic literature. His first major publication was *Life in the Triangle*, 1854, followed by *Lights and Shadows of Freemasonry* the following year. Then he published his *Universal Masonic Library*, a thirty-volume reprint of a number of Masonic books. Then came the *Code of Masonic Law*, one of the early lists of "Landmarks." By 1861, he had accumulated a large library of about 1200 volumes which suffered considerable damage and loss in a fire at his residence in La Grange, Kentucky. The surviving items, estimated at about 900 books, papers, and manuscripts, were acquired by and formed the nucleus of the present library of the Grand Lodge of New York.[4]

Considering the Masonic devotion, contributions, literary accomplishments, and reputation of Rob Morris, no better choice of a Masonic almanac for the facsimile of this volume could have been made than his first edition, the *Rob Morris Almanac for the Year 1860*.

The Series

Coil's *Encyclopedia* lists Rob Morris almanacs for each consecutive year from 1860 through 1865. The library at the House of the Temple in Washington has a bound volume containing all of these except one for the year 1864. At first, it was a disappointment to note the volume did not contain the

------

[3] Henry Wilson Coil, Sr., *Masonic Encyclopedia*, (New York: Macoy Publishing Company, 1961) p. 570.

[4] Ibid, p. 430.

1864 edition, but disappointment faded when it was discovered there was no 1864 almanac by Morris. In the opening statement of the 1865 edition, he explained, "We could not issue our almanac in 1864, owing to the conditions of the State (Kentucky) in which we lived." Morris said that the 1865 almanac was the fifth in the series, and he promised not to leave another hiatus in the series as long as the Fraternity sustained the enterprise. Several times in his almanacs, Morris expressed his intent to continue almanacs during his lifetime, but the 1865 edition was his last.

The first two almanacs of Morris were published in Louisville, Kentucky, with D. T. Monsarrat listed as co-publisher. Morris continued as compiler-author for the entire series, responsible for all the statistical matter, synopses, tables, maxims, historical items, and articles, with the exception of the few items credited to others. G. W. Hough, a professor at the Cincinnati Observatory, is credited with the astronomical calculations in the first three issues. The 1862 edition was published in La Grange, Kentucky, Morris being shown as the sole publisher, however an agent in New Jersey had been assigned to handle the general sales of the almanac. In 1863, Morris showed Chicago, along with La Grange, as the place of his publication, and in 1865, Morris had joined forces with a man named Sheville. Morris and Sheville were shown as publishers, and the address was 545 Broadway, New York City.

The price, where shown in the series, was fifteen cents per copy or ten copies for one dollar. It was explained that payment would be accepted in bank notes, draft, specie, or American postage stamps. In one edition, it was suggested that "remittances in small amounts are best made in gold or postage stamps."

Features

All of the Morris almanacs contained sixty-two pages with advertisements which were, for the most part, in the interest of Masonic literature and confined to the inside covers. The 1865 edition was an exception. It contained an appended fifteen-page advertising section, favoring a variety of business concerns. Oddly, in this section there were two pages consisting of a partial explanation and description of the Rite of Memphis along with a list of the officers.[5] Although these two pages do not resemble direct advertising, they certainly serve the purpose. Also of interest is the fact that an article by Morris favorable to the Rite of Memphis appears in the text of the almanac.[6]

In all five editions of the almanac, Morris had an opening statement to his readers which made mention of the editorial policy, general conditions, and justification of the publication, and of course there was a brief statement of content. There was astronomical data and an ordinary calendar containing a chronological list of Masonic events for each month. Also, there was a chronological list of important past events for certain days of each month.

Other regular features included items of Masonic history and custom, biographical sketches, obituaries, poetry, literary reviews, and a number of lists. These lists pertained to Lodges, Chapters, Councils, Encampments, and Consistories. There was information about the officers, meetings, dates of organization, revenue, and membership. Also, there were lists of Masonic publications and periodicals.

The intense interest Morris had in the unification of the American ritual, based on the Webb-Preston version, was reflected in his almanacs. Although this was a personal and special interest of Morris, by virtue of the fact the subject appeared in each of his editions, it must be classed as a regular feature of the Morris almanacs. Also, the comparative time frame is interesting. Remember, the Morris almanacs appeared from 1860 to 1865, exactly the same span of time Morris allotted for his campaign for uniformity to be accomplished through his group of Conservators. Morris sent out the first confidential communications in June, 1860, in which he

---

[5] The Rite of Memphis had been outlawed in France and brought to America in 1852. It is thought that the Rite had been redesigned to resemble and compete with the Scottish Rite.

[6] Showing an interest in the Rite of Memphis and having authored other degrees (Eastern Star, Conservators, etc.,) Morris seems to have favored side degrees.

explained the plan and invited support, promising that the entire operation would be terminated and the organization (Conservators) dissolved on June 24, 1865.

Another subject that received considerable space in the almanacs and one that should be classed as a regular feature was that of Masonic literature. Naturally, the publications of Morris which were for sale were mentioned, particularly the thirty-volume *Universal Masonic Library*. Also, there were two lists of general interest: one, a list of *Masonic Periodicals, 1790 to 1861*; and two, *Almanacs, Masonic and Unmasonic, 1802 to 1833*. However, the real emphasis was on the private Masonic library and collection of Rob Morris.

Soon after his initiation into Masonry, Morris started his collection which, prior to the fire at his residence, had grown to some 1200 volumes. In addition, he had manuscripts, medals, seals, engravings, correspondence, albums, by-laws, charts, paintings, relics, and photographs. Among the rare items was a first edition of Anderson's *Constitutions*. Also, there were all editions of Webb's monitor except one. There was an original minute book of a lodge in the Revolutionary Army and a rare collection of anti-Masonic material from 1826 to 1836. It is not known exactly how much of the collection was destroyed by the fire in 1861, but in the 1862 almanac, Morris made a plea to his readers to donate items to his collection which at the time numbered 50,000 (his estimate) pieces.

Morris, considered the founder of the Eastern Star, mentioned Adoptive Masonry directly only a few times. In his first almanac, he explained that the ladies' degrees in vogue at the time were the Eastern Star, the Good Samaritan, the Mason's Daughter, and the Heroine of Jericho. There was a poem about the Eastern Star in one issue, and in his last edition, there was a half page article in favor of the Order of the Good Samaritan, an adoptive rite restricted to Royal Arch Masons and their female relatives.

A special feature of the 1861 almanac was pictures of the seals of thirty-six Grand Lodges and a partial list of officers in those jurisdictions. By that time, the Morris collection contained a large number of Grand Lodge seals. There was a guide titled, "A Year's Work for a Working Mason," which listed suggested monthly objectives for conscientious Masons, and there were explanations of Capitular, Cryptic, and Chivalric Masonry along with lists of the Grand Bodies.

The 1862 edition of the almanac was more nearly a book of lists than the other issues, containing lists of periodicals, Grand Masters, Grand Secretaries, and Masonic almanacs. Also, this issue made a few general remarks about the relationship of Masonry to the "political strife" which existed in the nation at that time, a reference to the war between the states.

The 1863 edition listed the District Deputy Grand Masters of Indiana and New York, and there was a song in which some of the lines from Morris' poem, *The Level and the Square*, had been set to music.

The 1865 edition is important to the understanding of Rob Morris, the man and Mason, but about all that can be considered a special feature is the "Constitutions" of the Cosmopolitan Masonic Library Association, the organization formed to administer the Rob Morris library and collection.

Purpose

In the opening statement of his first edition, addressed to "Fraternal Reader," Morris justified his almanac. He said it had been thirty-one years since the Masonic almanacs of Isaiah Thomas, "the last publication of its kind in America," had been discontinued. Morris went on to say the storm of anti-Masonry that swept the country had discouraged Masonic writers, and consequently, much of what was said or what could have been said was "little sought after or valued." Then, he proposed that it was time to begin a new series of almanacs favorable to the Fraternity. Morris pointed out that of all the "engines" employed by the anti-Masonic forces from 1826 to 1836, "none accomplished so much evil as the antimasonic almanacs of Giddins and others," and he concluded the best countering influence would be a new series of Masonic almanacs. His choice of the almanac as the ideal literary form to counter anti-Masonic sentiment also bolsters the importance of almanacs in general. Morris, explaining that there had been a recent resurgence of Masonic intelligence by word, book, and periodical, asked, "Shall not the million-tongued *Almanac*, that whispers in every family, and hangs by every fireside, and in every workshop, give an echo to its voice?" Morris ended his statement with the promise that his almanac would be continued if successful.

Another factor in the entrance of Morris into the field of almanacs was a matter of personal objective. Apparently, he had considered publishing almanacs for a number of years. In his 1863 almanac, Morris printed, perhaps reprinted, the *Rob Morris Trestleboard in 1852*, a list of ten self-imposed Masonic objectives, number four of which was:

> I propose to revive the old plan of Masonic almanacs, discontinued for more than twenty years.

There seems to be little reason to challenge Morris' stated primary purpose for the publication of almanacs, however, as with any writer, Masonic or otherwise, there are usually underlying considerations. Among these might be the desire to impart a message or advance a cause, appealing to a specific group. Also, and understandably, there is always the matter of balancing the books.

Without question, Morris had something to say to a specific group. He was a sincere and devoted Mason. He was an accomplished author and editor. It is only natural that he would have used some literary form to express his Masonic views, and the almanac was one of these.

Also, Morris had a cause which was his ambitious plan to unify the ritual, something that had been on his mind at least as early as 1848. The plan was to be accomplished through his group of Conservators, but because this was a secret organization, it was not mentioned directly until the last issue. Even then, it was more of a whisper than an audible statement. However, Morris did use the almanac as a forum for his plan and to convince his readers of the importance of the Webb-Preston ritual.

Even though Morris was not considered a good business-man, there is no indication that he had profit in mind when he launched, simultaneously, his plan for unification and his series of almanacs. Some persons considered him to have been in good financial condition and a liberal contributor to worthy causes at the time.[7] On the other hand, it was said that Morris, during the time he was involved in his campaign to unify the ritual, was often too poor to buy transportation to a particular Grand Lodge to defend his cause, and moreover, that he "had a large family brought up in poverty and died a poor man.[8]

Without attempting, in any way, to be unfair to Morris, there are several nagging questions that arise from a conjunctive reading of his five almanacs. One has to wonder about the continuous references in each issue to the value and availability of his publications that were on the market. Also, in the 1865 (and final) edition, the appended section of paid advertising was a noticeable departure from previous policy, and Morris himself had an advertisement on the outside back cover, a choice spot in any publication. What were the "conditions" in Kentucky that prevented the publication of an 1864 issue of his almanac? Finally, the disposition of the Rob Morris Library and Collection leaves several unanswered questions.

Advertisement, direct or otherwise, that Morris may have included in his almanacs in the interest of his publications is understandable. The paid advertisements accepted for his 1865 edition is not startling either. Advertising has always been a means of producing income or perhaps defraying the publication costs. However, the personal advertisement on the back cover of his last almanac is interesting. It shows Morris to be a special agent, at that point in time, for the sale of supplies to schools, colleges, and Masonic lodges, with apparatus, books, furniture, paraphernalia, music, and musical instruments. The ad mentions that he is the publisher of the *Freemason's Almanac* and other Masonic works. All of these enterprises are related, however the last item in the advertisement shows Morris to be a special agent of the Knickerbocker Life Insurance Company, and the address (545 Broadway, New York) is the same as that of the association that was managing the Rob Morris Library and Museum.

---

[7] Ibid. p. 570.

[8] The Short Talk Bulletin, "The Masonic Conservators," (Masonic Service Association: Volume XXIV, January 1946, No. 1), p. 7.

As previously mentioned, Morris explained that an 1864 edition of his almanac was impossible because of the "conditions" in Kentucky. The conditions were not explained, but it seems reasonable to assume the Civil War was a factor, particularly in view of the fact Kentucky was a border state. We do know that the fire at his residence, a case of arson according to a statement by Morris, happened late in 1861. The 1862 edition of the almanac was published in La Grange, Kentucky, but it must be remembered that almanacs for any given year are usually prepared the previous year. The 1863 edition of the almanac indicated that both La Grange and Chicago was the "place" of publication, and it may be assumed that work on the 1865 edition, published in New York, began during the time Morris was moving from Kentucky to New York.

All of this seems tied, somehow, to the disposal of the Rob Morris Library and Literary Collection, a source of great interest and pride to Morris. It was damaged to some extent in the fire at his home, and eight months later, it was sold at auction for $750. It was held for redemption until 1864 when it was acquired by the Cosmopolitan Masonic Library Association which managed it for a time. The association offered the collection to the Grand Lodge of New York which resolved to accept it in 1865, however the actual acquisition did not take place until 1870.

The "Articles of Constitution" of the association were published in the 1865 almanac. According to one source, the purpose of this association was to raise enough money to redeem the collection and rebuild the Morris residence at La Grange. The Preamble of the constitution stated that "the calamities which led to the sale of the extensive Masonic collection of Dr. Morris afforded the Fraternity at large an opportunity at the present time of laying the foundation of a complete Masonic Library Reading-room and Cabinet in the City of New York." Membership in the association was open to Masons in good standing for the fee of one dollar. There was to be established a reading room, a system of instruction by lectures, and "such other means of improvement in Masonry as from time to time may be found advantageous."

By that time, the fourth year of his five-year plan, Morris must have recognized the impending failure of his movement to unify the ritual. In addition, Morris had suffered adverse conditions in Kentucky which necessitated the move of his residence to another area. Finally, there were those calamities which resulted in the loss of his personal control over his collection. Perhaps these adversities, to what ever extent they affected his personal life, became a major factor in his decision to discontinue publication of his Masonic almanacs.

The Facsimile

A few words about the *Rob Morris' Freemason's Almanac for 1860* are in order, although appearing as the facsimile in this volume, the 1860 issue speaks for itself. As the inaugural edition, it does establish the format for the entire series, and while there were topical and even structural changes from one issue to the next, the general configuration remained essentially the same.

As previously mentioned, the opening statement explained the principle motive for publishing the almanac which was to counter previous bad press by the anti-Masonic forces and to support the Fraternity which was, according to Morris, "riding upon the highest wave of prosperity." Even though Morris may have had other motives, his stated purpose is acceptable.

Pages 6 and 7 contained a Table of Masonic Statistics, a feature which was not continued, unfortunately, throughout the series. This type of information is valuable to anyone interested in Masonic demographics, and it touches on the conditions and progress of the Fraternity at a particular time in history.

The monthly calendars, running the length of the almanac, formed the frame of the publication. The calendar page contained the days of the month, astrological information, and the meeting dates of various Grand Bodies in the nation. On the same page, there were enclosed notes pertaining to Masonic ideals and bits of advice. There was a boxed presentation of Masonic law and custom titled, "Ears of Corn Near the Water Ford."

Opposite the calendar pages, there were articles of general Masonic interest, beginning with an explanation of the Old Charges and continuing with comments on the Landmarks and Basic Fundamentals of Freemasonry, topics which are still far too unfamiliar today. Also, there was information on the Appendant Bodies and stories designed to be supportive of the Craft.

Of particular interest is the information on page 24 about the Morris library and collection, and pages 50 through 61 express the Morris view on uniformity, both central themes of the entire series. Page 58 should be of importance to those interested in the self-esteem of Morris. There is presented the poem considered to be the best of Morris, *The Level and the Square*. It is the introductory statement that catches the eye. It begins by exclaiming that the name of Morris had become "a password in Masonic science only second to that of the 'first artificer or cunning Workman in metals'." If this was written by Morris, it says a great deal about the Morris ego.

The subtle changes in format and content notwithstanding, the 1860 *Freemason's Almanac* set the trend for the entire series. Without question, the almanacs were designed to and did support the Craft during a time when Freemasonry in America was recovering from almost three decades of disrepute. Additionally, Morris used the publication to advance his personal cause for unification, to attempt to establish the Webb-Preston ritual throughout the nation, and to enhance his Masonic library and collection, three objectives which fell, in the final analysis, somewhat short of the mark.

However, in his Masonic almanacs, Rob Morris left a substantial legacy. We can reasonably assume that there were innumerable Masonic and anti-Masonic almanacs printed in the past, although it is obvious that many were not preserved and have been lost over the years. Also, there is no question that the almanac, of considerable importance to societies of the past, was used by both friend and foe of the Fraternity. The Morris almanacs illuminate the condition of the Craft during the 19th century, an era when Freemasonry was rebounding from trying times while entering yet another period of turmoil which would test, once again, the mettle of the Order. Finally, the almanacs serve as a Rob Morris mirror, reflecting his Masonic ambitions and objectives while recording his successes and failures.

In spite of some statements to the contrary, Masonic almanacs were very much in vogue in America at one time, and they were definitely a prevalent form of Masonic literature. Moreover, the surviving copies of almanacs of the past provide valuable historical insight into the Fraternity in general and famous Masons in particular. The Rob Morris almanacs prove it.

III

ANTI-MASONIC ALMANACS

Anti-Masonry

Almost from the beginning, Freemasonry has encountered anti-Masonic activities and movements, most of which stemmed from dogmatic or frenzied types of religious convictions or dictatorial governments.[1] The stone masons of the Gothic Operative Era were involved in labor disputes with the government, but this hardly reflects anti-Masonic policy, because most of the other crafts and guilds were equally involved. The Transition Period did bring about some counter reaction in the form of mild attacks by those who, possibly suspicious of the so-called secrets of the organization, felt it was a "devilish sect" of men, made up of "evil doers."[2] Most of the anti-Masonic reaction of the Early Grand Lodge Era seems to have resulted from rival or dissenting societies. From the Grand Lodge Era forward, anti-Masonic reactions have been the result of any number of socio-economic considerations, but for the most part, anti-Masonry has been either religious or political, or a strange mixture of both.

Religious opinion has always been a factor in, if not the most consistent cause of, anti-Masonry. Before the Papal Bull of 1738, there was the suspicion that the Masons, as a body, had "second sight," practiced witchcraft, and were in league with the devil. The Papal Bull of 1738, *In Eminenti*, and subsequent Papal edicts, stipulated that the meetings of Freemasons, held in secret, gave rise to depravity and preverseness, concluding that if the Masons were not acting ill, they would not need to "avoid the light." Another strong objection was to Masonic oaths, considered by the church to have been literal rather than used symbolically as is the case. Addition-

---

[1] Henry Wilson Coil, Sr., *Masonic Encyclopedia*, (New York: Macoy Publishing Company, 1961), p. 53.

[2] Ibid.

ally, Masons were condemned for not being amenable to the discipline of the Church and for "other reasons well known to us." Of course, there was no reason why the Masons should have been amenable to the discipline of the Church, and condemnation for "other reasons" is hardly substantial argument against anything.

Religious opinion has caused problems within the Fraternity as well. Anderson's alteration of the First Charge (Concerning God and Religion), brought about considerable misunderstanding. A number of Masons failed to understand the move as one to bring about greater religious tolerance within the Order and felt the organization was departing from a 400-year-old standing belief in Christian Trinitarianism and in turn becoming anti-Christian. Since then, the religious convictions of the individual Mason, when made public, have been misinterpreted as Freemasonic dogma, and anti-Masonry among the leaders of some churches has resulted.

Anti-Masonry started in America immediately after the Revolution, but it did not intensify until much later. The disappearance of William Morgan in 1826 sparked a widespread anti-Masonic frenzy which lasted for about two decades. Eventually, the anti-Masonic forces entered the political arena, and from 1828 to 1830, anti-Masonic fever hit the high water mark. Things did not settle and the frenzy continued after 1830, covering more and more geography until Freemasonry sank to its lowest level around 1840. Freemasonry remained in intensive care for another twenty years until around 1860 when it began its convalescence and started to prosper once again.

Anti-Masonic Literature

The weapons employed by the anti-Masonic forces have been varied, but the big bomb has always been the literary device, including books, pamphlets, journals, newspapers, digests, and almanacs. Estimates vary considerably, but one source figures that at one time, there were about 130 American papers and publications in circulation with the sole purpose of fighting Freemasonry. Another source estimates that from 1826 to 1840, there were about 225 books classified as anti-Masonic on the world market, 90% of which were published in America.[3] The biggest bomb in the enemy arsenal, however, is the literary form called the "exposure," and at this point, perhaps a word about Masonic exposures is in order.

During the formulative years of the Speculative System, there was little or nothing in the way of legitimate publications, but there was a number of spurious catechisms. These purported disclosures of the ritual appeared in both manuscript and printed form, mostly by anonymous authors, and they came to light for a variety of reasons. A number were written by Masons as "aides-mémoire," and however irregular this practice was, they served a useful purpose in a society wherein the art of memorization was somewhat less than accomplished. Many were to designed to reveal or ridicule, resulting from spiteful or revengeful intent. Some were written, possibly by Masons, deliberately inaccurate, to confuse the issue. Without question, a number of them came into being as a result of the profit motive of the author and publisher alike.

Regardless of the reason, they were written, and in spite of the original intent, the exposures have had little long-term effect on the Fraternity. In the first place, they are all suspect, having been written by those who have violated, obviously, their solemn vow to the contrary. In the second place, and more to the point, any printed ritual of any organization is of little value to anyone who has not undergone the initiatory process and subsequently reached a degree of understanding.

The numerous variations and conflicting information contained in the many exposures proves them inaccurate and makes it clear that only an accomplished ritualist could possibly place a stamp of authenticity on a given exposure or portion thereof. Ironically, these exposures have actually boomeranged, serving the student as excellent insight into early Masonic practices, thus enhancing the study of the evolution of Freemasonry as revealed through the gradual but ever changing ritual.

It is widely known that Benjamin Franklin published the first Masonic book in the western hemisphere when, in 1734,

---

[3] Ibid., p. 56.

he reprinted Anderson's *Constitutions*. Not so widely publicized is the fact that three years before that, Franklin (not yet a Mason) published one of the more popular English exposures of the day, *The Mystery of Freemasonry*.

Anti-Masonic Almanacs

In 1740, there was a French publication that featured an article of anti-Masonic flavor, and it used the term *almanac* in its title. It was the *Almanac des Cocus*, an obscure and obscene magazine which circulated in Paris from 1740 to 1743.[4] In this, there was a speech which was supposed to have been delivered by Chevalier Andrew Ramsay, a Catholic and an ardent Mason, and it was presented as an anti-Masonic article.

As the story goes, Ramsay was acting as Grand Chancellor (probably a title of respect, not one of official rank) of some Masonic body, and he welcomed the candidates with an oration similar to what is called a Charge or Lecture today. The oration contained two radical themes. The first was that the purpose of Freemasonry was to unite all nations into a peaceful family with France at the center of that society. The other was Ramsay's account, presented as factual, that Freemasonry sprang from the Crusades, thereby giving the Fraternity a noble heritage, something it does not have.

The speech was printed in *des Cocus* four years after it was supposed to have been delivered. Earlier, the *Gentleman's Magazine*, April 1739, reported that the Catholic Inquisition at Rome had ordered a piece of writing by Ramsay burned, and there is a chance this was Ramsay's oration. However, there is another reference which relates to the burning of a book written by Ramsay, the title of which was *Apologetic and Historical Relation of the Society of Freemasonry*. The exact accuracy of the account notwithstanding, the *Almanac de Cocus* marks the 1740's as one of the early uses of the almanac as an anti-Masonic device.

Little has been written about anti-Masonic almanacs per

---

[4] Henry Wilson Coil, Sr., *Freemasonry Through Six Centuries*, Volume I, (Richmond: Macoy Publishing Company, 1968), p. 234. *Almanac des Cocus* translates "Almanac of the Cuckolds."

se, but they are part of the stream of anti-Masonic literature. While these Masonic lampoons look and act like almanacs, they fit nicely into the category of exposures, claiming to reveal portions of the Masonic ritual, obligations, pass words, signs, etc.

At first glance, anti-Masonic almanacs, as with all forms of anti-Masonic literature, appear insulting, perhaps damaging, to the Fraternity. As irritating as they have been, they fall short of the mark. Henry Wilson Coil put it into proper perspective when he said, speaking about anti-Masonic literature in general, "Most of them are now merely library curiosities."[5]

Without question, the ten-megaton Morgan Affair and subsequent fallout played a prominent part in the appearance of the anti-Masonic almanacs in America. As seen previously in the discussion of the Rob Morris almanacs, Morris said there was a special reason for employing the almanac in the diffusion of Masonic knowledge. Pointing to the Morgan episode, he said that of all the engines used by the enemies of Freemasonry, none accomplished so much evil as the anti-Masonic almanacs of Giddins and others.[6]

As is the case with almanacs of all types, one cannot study Masonic or anti-Masonic almanacs without becoming convinced that there were many more examples in existence than the record indicates. Almanacs were relatively inexpensive and not designed to have a long shelf life. Consequently, they have been lost over the years, and there is no way to discover the names of all of them at this late date. Also, librarians in some cases, undoubtedly failed to attach any importance to almanacs.

In an 1852 edition of a catalogue of anti-Masonic publications, there were several anti-Masonic almanacs listed under the heading of pamphlets.[7] The listing was made from reports

---

[5] Henry Wilson Coil, Sr., *Masonic Encyclopedia*, (New York: Macoy Publishing Company, 1961), p. 56.

[6] *Rob Morris' Freemason's Almanac*, (Louisville: Morris & Monsarrat, 1860), p. 4.

[7] *Catalogue of Anti-Masonic Books*, (Boston: Damrell & Moore, 1852) The compiler's name was given but listed as "A Member of the Suffolk Committee of 1829."

of various public and college libraries around the nation and covered a period of time, roughly, from 1840 to 1850. The pamphlet that appeared more often than the rest was the *Anti-Masonic Review* by Henry Ward, however it is not clear if this was actually an almanac. There were three anti-Masonic almanacs listed which were Giddins' *Anti-Masonic Almanac, The New England Anti-Masonic Almanac,* and the *Sun Anti-Masonic Almanac* which is attributed to Avery Allyn. These appeared in such places as the Vermont Historical Society, Brown University in Rhode Island, the Antiquarian Hall in Worcester, the University of North Carolina, and the University of Virginia. From this list, it is safe to assume that these three almanacs were the more popular publications of the era. Several libraries reported having what was listed as the *Anti-Masonic Almanac* (probably an incomplete title) but no mention was made of the compiler, publisher, or place of publication.

The Avery Allyn Anti-Masonic Almanac

It was not possible to obtain copies of the Avery Allyn almanac for study, however in one of the rare articles on the subject, William Hastings, did write about them with first hand knowledge of the publications.[8] According to Hastings, Avery Allyn was one of the most successful, or at least most widely read anti-Masonic authors in English. His principal publication was his exposure, the *Ritual of Freemasonry,* copyrighted on February 28, 1831. His signature bore the Masonic designation *K.R.C., K.T., K.M., etc.* According to the records of the New Haven Encampment, Allyn was a Knight Templar. However, there is no proof to back his statement that he had "been initiated into nearly all the degrees conferred (in Masonry)."

As is generally the case with most anti-Masonic writers, his famous ritual was probably not entirely his own but rather a compilation from documents already in print, and there were plenty of these from which to work. At the time, there was

---

[8] William T. Hastings, "The Works of Avery Allyn," *The Philalethes,* Volume XIV, No. 6, December, 1961, p. 99.

widespread distribution of Morgan's exposure, *Illustrations of Masonry, 1827*. Also, there was the popular exposure by Rev. David Bernard, as ardent as any of the anti-Masonic champions. The standard legitimate monitors of the era were *The Freemason's Monitor* by Thomas Smith Webb and *The Masonic Chart* by Jeremy L. Cross. With these and some degree of firsthand knowledge, it would have been fairly easy to produce a Masonic exposure of reasonable quality and reliability.

Allyn was a bookseller and author and his publisher was John Clarke who served as secretary of the anti-Masonic Convention of 1830 and was a delegate to the convention in 1831. Clarke published an anti-Masonic newspaper, *The Sun*, and because historically there has been some relationship between publishers of newspapers and almanacs, it is no surprise that Clarke published an almanac. Moreover, considering his anti-Masonic leanings, it is no surprise that his almanac was anti-Masonic. Incidentally, Clarke's publishing company folded following the collapse of political anti-Masonry.

Speaking generally about anti-Masonic almanacs, William Hastings said they "were ingenious, some would say unscrupulous, adaptations of a vehicle which was close to the heart (or at any rate, the habits) of the common man.[9] They contained grotesque caricatures showing poor blind candidates in pitiful posture and circumstance. They employed crude narrative woodcuts of the Giddins story which got full treatment in the *New England Anti-Masonic Almanac*.[10] These comic books had a sprinkle of head notes and side notes quoting purported portions of the obligations, penalties, signs, words, and a calendar of the Morgan dates, all of which was designed to ridicule Masonry and to keep the anti-Masonic fires burning.[11]

The two almanacs which Hastings attributes to Allyn were both published by Clarke, and they were *The Sun Anti-*

---

[9] William T. Hastings, "The Works of Avery Allyn," *The Philalethes*, Volume XIV, No. 6, February 1962, p. 13.

[10] Prints from the woodcuts are around today, having resurfaced as reprints in the 1980 *Year Book of the Grand Lodge of Scotland*, in an article of the Morgan Affair by R. L. Karter.

[11] William T. Hastings, "The Works of Avery Allyn," *The Philalethes*, Volume XIV, No. 6, February 1962, p. 13.

Masonic Almanac for 1831, and *No. II: The Antimasonic Sun Almanac for 1832*. Allyn's name did not appear on the first of these, but he was shown to be the compiler of the second. Even so, it is most likely that Allyn was involved in the publication of both. Allyn's ritual was advertised in both issues, and according to Hastings, who had both issues for study, the second edition had cover illustrations of drawings from other almanacs, and Allyn displayed his expertise in irony on the pages carrying the monthly calendars.

Eaton's Antimasonic Almanac for 1834

The Vermont Historical Society provided a copy of the 36 page anti-Masonic almanac published and sold by E. Eaton of Danville, Vermont, and Captain Ira White of Wells River, Vermont. In 1834, the publication sold for ten cents per copy or sixty-two and one half cents per dozen. This almanac is interesting from a comparative standpoint; and, although typically full of anti-Masonic drivel, it lacks some of the innovations and originality of earlier versions.

The title page is divided into three parts. There is the title, date, and identification of the publishers. It contains a comic drawing of three men who are supposed to be showing the manner of giving the Royal Arch word. Finally, there is presented an extract from an assumed version of the Royal Arch obligation, the accuracy of which is questionable. Pertaining to the unswerving loyalty of one member to another, this obligation implies assistance "whether he be right or wrong." The extract also says the secrets of a brother shall "remain as secure and inviolable in my breast as in his own, murder and treason not excepted."

The following four pages contain the usual information found in standard almanacs. There is weather forecasting, signs and names of the Zodiac, seasons, and eclipses. There is a short history of the definition of the year and several useful recipes include one to cure rot and scab in sheep and another to cure oxen strained by overdrawing.

Page five sets the anti-Masonic theme for the editorial content of the publication. It is a series of maledictory opinions about Freemasonry. One such opinion, objecting to the so-called secrets of the Order, states that Freemasonry is a "system of the destroyers of human virtue and happiness," and it classifies the Fraternity as a secret agency, concluding that "secret agency has overthrown *all* (author's italics) of the republics of Europe." Another opinion derides Masonry as a "numerous body of citizens trained to conceal truth and protect crime," an obvious reference to the Morgan Affair.

There are seventeen pages containing the ordinary calendar with the Zodiac and memorable dates followed by a list of court and university dates and a few jokes.

The remaining fifteen pages are devoted to anti-Masonry, the major articles being "Influence of Masonry on Jurors," and "Masonic Murders." In a denunciatory article by Ezekiel Birdseye, a suspended Mason, he told of the events which led to his removal from Masonry by his lodge. According to Birdseye, he learned of the kidnapping of a Negro by the Master of an Alabama lodge who was speculating in the slave market. Birdseye claimed to be a member of that particular lodge. Unable to talk the Master into freeing the Negro, Birdseye brought suit, but he did not proceed with the court action when he felt that Masonic influence among the jurors would prevent a decision in his favor. Requesting and receiving a change of venue, Birdseye said the case was sent to a neighboring county for trial, and that the Negro was set free. As a result of his action, however, Birdseye claimed that he was eventually charged with unmasonic conduct, tried by his lodge, and suspended. According to his story, Birdseye appealed to the Grand Lodge which decided in his favor, however in view of his conclusion that Freemasonry was a dangerous institution, he did not take advantage of his restoration, and he disavowed any future association with the Fraternity.

The article on claimed Masonic murders is extremely interesting. Of the several murders described, the account of the demise of Samuel Prichard is the most presumptuous. As a result of having authored his famous exposure, *Masonry Dissected*, Prichard is said to have been in danger of losing his life at the hands of Masons resentful of his literary efforts. According to the account, Prichard disappeared for a time, and it was reported that he had been killed. This was proven false when Prichard appeared at a later date, however the article insists that he was "subsequently cruelly murdered (by Masons) and the previous report covered the deed, the people supposing it (the actual murder) to be (another) hoax." As a person, Samuel Prichard is a mystery. Nothing is known about him, his family, social status, trade or profession.[12]

Another account is that of a Masonic murder in Belfast which was supposed to have taken place, ritualistically, in the lodge room. The victim was guilty, according to the account, of violating his oath when he proclaimed publically that *Jachin & Boaz*, a famous English Exposure, "was a true book." The man was supposed to have been duped into becoming the principal character in the ritualistic murder by the false promise of a free initiation into the Knight's Templar. At the point he was led, blindfolded, into the lodge room, he was abruptly accused by the presiding officer, told of his fate, and immediately attacked and killed by a team of assassins.

The Facsimile

(NEW ENGLAND ANTI-MASONIC ALMANAC, 1830)

Within the scope of this commentary, the earliest and one of the most widespread anti-Masonic almanacs was that of Giddins, however it has not been possible to obtain a copy for study. The facsimile, an equally popular publication of the era, is the *New England Anti-Masonic Almanac*, and it is one of three that were available. The other two are the previously mentioned anti-Masonic almanac by Eaton and the 1831 edition of the *New England Anti-Masonic Almanac*. There was an 1829 edition of the *New England Anti-Masonic*, probably the inaugural issue. It was mentioned in the 1830 edition. William Hastings said that the Giddins woodcuts received full treatment in the series of the New England Anti-Masonic almanacs, so if they did not appear in the 1829 version, they must have appeared in editions beyond 1831.[13] The almanac continued until at least 1834. This is proven by a picture of the title page appearing in the *Transactions* of the American Lodge of Research.

---

[12] Harry Carr, *Samuel Prichard's Masonry Dissected*, (Bloomington: The Masonic Book Club, 1977), p. 7.

[13] William T. Hastings, "The Works of Avery Allyn," *The Philalethes*, Volume XIV, No. 6, February 1962, p. 13.

Another question arises resulting from the name of the publisher of the New England almanacs. It was John Marsh of Boston. Oddly, the publishers of the *New England Almanac and Masonic Calendar*, a Masonic publication of 1828, the publishers are shown to be Marsh and Capen of Boston. Although the address of the publishers and the names of the printers of these two publications differ, one has to wonder if the man named John Marsh was instrumental in both almanacs.

The title page of the facsimile is dramatic even though the grotesque cartoon borders on comic relief. The emaciated candidate is kneeling upon the first of three steps, blindfolded, and he has what appears to be a hangman's noose around his neck. The Master, resplendent with top hat, is drawn with the facial characteristics of a pig, and he holds in his hand a large gavel with a three foot handle which he extends toward the candidate in a threatening manner. There is a large skull and cross bones painted on the three steps, and a real skull is sitting atop a bookcase in the background. The brethren standing around the candidate are disheveled and ghoulish in appearance. From this cartoon, one would have to feel a bit sorry, if not actually apprehensive, for Masonic initiates who are described as "poor blind candidates receiving their obligations." Under the cartoon, there is an extract from the purported obligation.

The ordinary calendar of the twelve months of the year has an unusual feature. The signs of the Zodiac have been replaced with caricatures of Masons designed to reveal all sorts of secret signs, including due guards, hailing signs, ear signs, hand signs, signs of distress, and what are called grand signs in both Craft and Capitular Masonry. The explanations and meanings are cited as being derived from Bernard's exposure, *Light on Masonry*. The incorrect terminology, incomplete and erroneous explanations, and outright fabrication of non-existent signs, all of which proves the revelation worthless, makes one wonder why there could have been any furor over Morgan's or Bernard's exposures in the first place. One humorous bit of advice accompaning these signs is the admonition that these "signs should become familiar to the eye in order that they may be detected should Masons offer them in a Court of Justice."

Beginning on page 18, there is a continuation of comment on the Morgan Affair which started in the previous edition. It consists of various claimed sworn testimony by a number of the principal characters in the Morgan drama created by the anti-Masonic forces. For the most part, objections were voiced against bribery, horrible and destructive oaths, excessive use of alcohol, and subversion in the courts, all of which was said to have been paramount in Freemasonry at the time.

If there is any truth in the charge made by the anti-Masonic forces that the Masons of the era enjoyed considerable financial gain through their Masonic association, then there is a clear case of the pot calling the kettle black. The last two pages of the *New England Anti-Masonic Almanac for 1830* show the publisher, John Marsh, was engaged in anti-Masonry for profit. However sincere he might have been in his anti-Masonic views (if in fact he actually had them), John Marsh was in the business of selling anti-Masonic literature. Marsh named more than a dozen anti-Masonic publications, including Morgan's *Light on Masonry*.[14] He mentioned "many more works of merit," and "all new works on the dark and mysterious subject of Freemasonry." He advertised a weekly newspaper, the *Anti-Masonic Boston Free Press*. In addition to being a publisher and book seller, he was a stationer and manufacturer of account books, operating at both the wholesale and retail level.

In addition to being involved in the sale of literature and related products, Marsh was the sole agent in the United States for a German product, "Gordak's Genuine Physical Drops." The root and herb derivative was advertised as a sure cure for colds, coughs, jaundice, bile, stomach weakness, headaches, and worms in children. The genuine concern of earlier almanac-makers for the health of the readers seems to have transgressed to a desire to profit from the sale of "snake oil" products.

The New England Anti-Masonic Almanac for 1831

The 1831 edition of the New England almanac does not differ greatly from the previous issue. The title page is the

---

[14] Morgan's exposure was, in fact, titled *Illustrations of Masonry*, not *Light on Masonry* which was the work of Bernard.

same with the exception of the date. On the second page, following the statement to the reader, there is a cartoon under which there is a Masonic dialogue. The two Masons in the drawing are named Jachin and Boaz. One represented Masonry "as it was (1826)," and the other represented Masonry "as it is (1831)." The former was shown to be fat and prosperous while the latter was drawn to appear weak and lean. The dialogue was an exchange of remarks bemoaning the demise of Freemasonry and the two characters bid each other farewell. The caricatures replacing the signs of the Zodiac are exactly the same as in the facsimile edition.

The section containing the anti-Masonic prattle begins with a sketch of William Morgan's life in which he is presented as a hero. Next appears "A Statement of Facts," a continuation of the harangue by Edward Giddins which began in the inaugural edition. There are denunciations of Freemasonry by European malcontents. Several pages contain the cartoons designed to reveal Masonic "secrets," those of the Knight's Templar added in this issue. Revealed in this section is what was titled the "Secret Monitor or Trader's Degree," presented as a degree for the purpose of assisting the membership in business dealings. There is a scattering of affidavits damning Freemasonry, several renunciations by turncoat Masons, and some letters attributed to George Washington which attempt to prove he had no regard for Masonry. Under the heading "Masonic Kings," there is listed some of the Masonic hierarchy, mainly in New England, and mention is made of a "number of subordinate kings." The balance of the almanac is made up of information on the courts of New England, mileage distances on the roads out of Boston, agricultural advice, poetry, anecdotes, and advertising.

The advertising shows Marsh to continue in the book and stationery business. He had expanded his line of home remedies to include Rheumatic Balsam, Eye Water, Balsam of Do, and a newcomer on the market, the Balsam of Colomba. In addition to the products offered by Marsh, there was advertising for other firms dealing in leather goods, boots and shoes, glassware, brushes, and live goose feathers. The last page lists the anti-Masonic publications for sale by Marsh.

IV

REFLECTIONS

Masonic almanacs, both for and against Freemasonry, have faded from the scene in recent years. However, at one time, Masonic almanacs (and/or calendars), as with almanacs in general, were timely, significant, and prevalent.

Under direction of the Masonic hierarchy in England, the original purpose of Masonic almanacs was to establish official records of the founding, location, and officers of the Masonic organizations. The same was true in American Freemasonry. As previously pointed out, the Grand Lodge of the Republic of Texas published an almanac as early as 1838, and this was probably the first official printed publication of the Grand Lodge. There was a resolution to print a similar publication for the following year. The resolution appeared in the reconstructed minutes of a Grand Lodge session which took place on December 30, 1838. It reads as follows,

> RESOLVED, That the Grand Secretary be, and he is hereby authorized and required to call forthwith on all the Lodges subordinate to this Grand Lodge, for a return of their officers elect, and, upon receipt thereof, to form a 'Masonic Almanac' for the year 1839, commencing with the Officers of this Grand Lodge, and enumerating the subordinate Lodges in numerical order, and cause two hundred and fifty copies thereof to be printed on a large sheet, and distribute the same among the Lodges subordinate to this Grand Lodge; also, among the Foreign Grand Lodges.
>
> RESOLVED, That the Committee on Printing be, and they are hereby, authorized to defray the expense of printing the said Masonic Almanac.

Of course, there were other Grand Lodges that employed the

Masonic almanac. In the same reconstructed minutes, there was another resolution:

> That the Grand Secretary be authorized to subscribe for the first volume of the Albany Masonic Register.

As Freemasonry grew, Masonic writers kept pace, and Masonic almanacs came to include, in addition to organizational records, items of general interest to the membership. In this manner, the almanac became a line of communication for the Fraternity. The Masonic almanac assumed the role of record, roster, guide, bulletin, compendium, and calendar of events.

The authors of Masonic almanacs, eventually used the publication as a forum for the ideals, goals, and accomplishments of the Fraternity. In this manner, the almanac became a voice of Freemasonry.

Considering the success of the almanac within the Fraternity, it is no surprise that the antagonists of Freemasonry employed the device to ridicule, expose, and attack. Thus, the anti-Masonic almanac was born. Depending on one's perspective, anti-Masonic almanacs could have been considered irritating and damaging. On the other hand, they might be considered ridiculous or ineffective. Some might even view them as humorous. The anti-Masonic forces probably were sincere in their belief that Freemasonry was dangerous to society. Equally probable is the fact that publishers, aware of anti-Masonic sentiment in society, recognized the profit potential in a market for anti-Masonic literature.

However popular anti-Masonic almanacs were to some and however sincere may have been the dedication of the compilers, they failed, as have all forms of exposures, to seriously damage the Fraternity. Actually, the Fraternity should be grateful to the makers of anti-Masonic almanacs, because they have provided documentary evidence of the difficulties of Freemasonry during specific periods of time. The same gratitude is due those who compiled Masonic almanacs, providing insight into the direction, progress, and achievements of the Fraternity. The Masonic almanac is history itself.

The Facsimile

ROB MORRIS'
FREEMASON'S ALMANAC, 1860

ROB MORRIS'

Freemason's Almanac

1860

Morris & Monsarrat.

ROB MORRIS'
FREEMASON'S ALMANAC

FOR THE YEAR OF OUR LORD

1860.

THE MASONIC ERA 5860; THE ROYAL ARCH ERA 2390; THE ERA OF CRYPTIC MASONRY 2860; THE ERA OF KNIGHT TEMPLARY, 742,

IT BEING BISSEXTILE OR LEAP YEAR.

CONTAINING, IN ADDITION TO AN

ACCURATE CALENDAR AND EPHEMERA,

A COMPLETE STATEMENT OF THE

ORIGIN, PROGRESS AND PRESENT CONDITION OF FREEMASONRY IN NORTH AMERICA, AS DISPLAYED IN LODGES, CHAPTERS, COUNCILS, ENCAMPMENTS AND CONSISTORIES,

TOGETHER WITH

TABULAR SYNOPSES, CHRONOLOGICAL TABLES, LITERARY ANNOUNCEMENTS, AND A THESAURUS OF MASONIC PRECEPTS, MAXIMS AND HISTORICAL ITEMS OF INCALCULABLE VALUE.

LOUISVILLE, KY.

PUBLISHED BY MORRIS & MONSARRAT,
472 MAIN STREET.
1860.

FRATERNAL READER,

It is now thirty-one years since the publication of the Masonic Almanacs of Isaiah Thomas, at Worcester, Mass., the last work of the kind, it is believed, in this country, was discontinued. The storm of antimasonry, which then raged through the land, so chilled the zeal, and discouraged the pens of the craft, that the statistics of their drooping and waning forces were little sought after or valued. Through all this period of thirty-one years, no one has come forward to cast into a cheap and popular form the everyday facts of Freemasonry. Is it not time then that a new series of Masonic Almanacs should be commenced, and this vast engine of popular usefulness again set in motion?

It is unnecessary to enlarge upon the fact, that the Masonic Institution at the present day, and especially in the United States and British Provinces, is riding upon the highest wave of prosperity. Its lodges number 4750; its membership, 200,000. Its gavels ring, its jewels gleam, its good deeds fructify in every town, village, and hamlet, in the land. Eclectic in the selection of its materials, (soundness in body, mind, and heart being the ancient prerequisites of its membership,) rigid in the exercise of its discipline, tender in the nurture of its faithful, it stands forward in the eyes of the community, venerable for age, respectable for members, admirable for the perfection of its doctrines, beautiful in its ritualistic ceremonies. The voice of such an association, in any shape, commands attention. It has spoken from the mouths of lecturers; it has had utterance in books and periodicals—shall not the million-tongued ALMANAC, that whispers in every family, and hangs by every fireside, and in every workshop, give an echo to its voice?

There is a special reason why the influence of Almanacs should be courted in the diffusion of Masonic knowledge, viz.: that of all the engines employed by our enemies against us in the cruel warfare of 1826 to 1836, none accomplished so much evil as the antimasonic almanacs of Giddins, and others, which were distributed by wagon-loads through the length and breadth of the country. They were a blight upon the Masonic Order not yet wholly healed; and as the best counteracting influence to the peculiar evils they disseminated, the same class of instrumentalities is now employed, of which the present Almanac is the exponent. Should it prove successful, it will be continued from year to year, with whatever emendations and additions may add to its value.

Louisville, Ky.   ROB MORRIS.

CONTENTS OF THIS WORK.

THE Freemason's Almanac gives all the Chronological Data of a Masonic character that is reliable and worthy of preservation. The meetings of Grand Lodges, Grand Chapters, Grand Councils, Grand Encampments, and Grand Consistories, are laid down from information furnished us by their respective Grand Secretaries, Grand Recorders, and Grand Chancellors. All Masonic publications, periodical and standard, have been searched to glean matter for this little volume, and at an expenditure of intellectual labor appreciable only by those who are familiar with such toil.

An immense amount of the purest and richest sentiment, bearing directly upon the law and philosophy of Freemasonry, has been compressed in the paragraphs, long and short, and the poetical selections, which make up the body of the work. In this the author has found his relief from the dryer task of preparing statistical matter, and to this he points with an honest pride. What influences these masses of masonic truth will exert when placed in the hands of the vast army of the workmen—what good cheer to weary craftsmen—what comfort to the sad —what light to the blind—who but the Omniscient can rightly tell!!!

☞ The astronomical calculations in this work are the labor of PROF. G. W. HOUGH, A. M., and for skill and accuracy are equal to any thing ever offered in this line. The statistical matter, elaborate paragraphs, and miscellany, are original with Mr. ROB MORRIS, except where credit is otherwise given.

ECLIPSES IN THE YEAR 1860.

This year there will be two Eclipses of the Sun, and two of the Moon, as follows:

1st. An Annular Eclipse of the Sun, Jan. 22d, invisible in the United States, but visible in the regions of the South Pole.

2d. A Partial Eclipse of the Moon, Feb. 6th, visible at Washington, in mean time, as follows:

		D.	H.	M.
First contact with the Penumbra,	Feb. 6	6	54.2
First contact with the shadow,	" 6	7	55.1
Middle of the Eclipse,	" 6	9	21.3
Last contact with the shadow,	" 6	10	48.5
Last contact with the Penumbra,	" 6	11	48.5

First contact of shadow with Moon's limb, 79° from North point toward the East.
Last contact of shadow with Moon's limb, 32° from North toward the West.
Magnitude of Eclipse, 0.812 of Moon's diameter.

3d.   A Total Eclipse of the Sun, July 18th, visible (as a partial one) at Washington.   It will be total in the northern part of Africa, Spain, British America, and at the mouth of the Columbia river, in the United States.

This Eclipse begins at Washington, mean time,

	D.	H.	M.
	July 18	6	55.9 morning.
Ends,	July 18	8	50.5 morning.

Quantity of the Eclipse, 7 digits on the northern limb.

4th. A Partial Eclipse of the Moon, Aug. 1st, invisible in the United States.

MERCURY.

This planet will be visible in the West, about March 16th, July 12th, and Nov. 7th, and in the East, just before sunrise, Jan. 3d, April 30th, Aug. 27th, and Dec. 16th.

EQUINOXES AND SOLSTICES FOR 1860.

	D.	H.	M.		D.	H.	M.
Vernal Equinox,	March 20	3	58 mor.	Autumnal Equinox,	Sept. 22	2	45 eve.
Summer Solstice,	June 21	0	23 mor.	Winter Solstice,	Dec. 21	8	41 mor.

Note.—The Sun's Declination and Meridian Passage are given for *Washington mean noon.*

LEAP-YEAR.

Every year the number of which is divisible by 4 without a remainder, is a leap-year, except the last year of the century, which is a leap-year only when divisible by 400 without a remainder.   Thus the year 1900 will not be leap-year.

CHARACTERS.

☾☉ Sun ; ☽ Moon ; ☿ Mercury ; ♀ Venus ; ⊕ Earth ; ♂ Mars ; ♃ Jupiter ; ♄ Saturn ; ♅ Uranus ; ☌ same longitude, or near each other ; □ 90° apart ; ☍ opposition, or 180° apart.

Signs of the Zodiac.—♈ Aries ; ♉ Taurus ; □ Gemini ; ♋ Cancer ; ♌ Leo ; ♍ Virgo ; ♎ Libra ; ♏ Scorpio ; ♐ Sagittarius ; ♑ Capricorn ; ♒ Aquarius ; ♓ Pisces.

Aspects and Nodes.—☌ Conjunction ; ✳ Sextile, 60 degrees ; □ Quartile, 90 degrees ; △ Trine, 120 degrees ; ☍ Opposition, 180 degrees ; ☊ Ascending Node ; ☋ Descending Node.

MORNING AND EVENING STARS.

Venus will be Evening Star until July 18th, then Morning Star the rest of the year. Mars will be Morning Star until July 18th, then Evening Star the rest of the year. Jupiter will be Morning Star until January 10th, then Evening Star until July 29th, then Morning Star the rest of the year. Saturn will be Morning Star until Feb. 11th, then Evening Star until August 22d, then Morning Star the rest of the year.

CHRONOLOGICAL CYCLES.

Dominical Letters, A and G ; Golden Number, 18 ; Epact (Moon's age, Jan. 1st,) 7 ; Solar Cycle, 21 ; Julian Period, 6573 ; Ago of the World, 5863.

DURATION OF THE SEASONS, ETC.

	D.	H.	M.		D.	H.	M.
Sun in Winter signs,	89	1	6	Tropical Year,	365	5	49
Sun in Spring signs,	92	20	35	Sun North of the Equator,	186	10	47
Sun in Summer signs,	93	14	12	Sun South of the Equator,	178	19	2
Sun in Autumn signs,	89	17	56	Difference,	7	15	45

TABLE OF MASONIC STATISTICS.

STATES.	Date of Organization of Grand Lodge.	Present No. of Lodges.	No. of Chapters.	No. of Councils.	No. of Encampm'ts.	No. of Masons in the Lodges.	Square Miles	Ratio of Square Miles to a Lodge.	Revenue of 1858-9.	Time of Meetings of Grand Lodges.	Place of Meeting of Grand Lodges.
Alabama,	Dec. 11, 1821,	285	53	29	2	7000	50722	215	$3500	1st Monday Dec.	Montgomery.
Arkansas,	Nov. 25, 1838,	128	22	8	1	6000	52198	408	2500	1st Monday Nov.	Little Rock.
California,	April 19, 1850.	122	23	0	6	4727	155980	1278	8000	2d Tuesday May,	Sacramento.
Canada,	Nov. 2, 1855,	110	6	0	3	3200				2d Wednesday July,	Itinerant.
Connecticut,	July 8, 1789,	57	21	13	6	5060	4674	82	600	2d Wednesday May,	Itinerant.
Delaware,	June 7, 1806,	12	0	0	0	600	2120	176	150	June 27,	Wilmington.
District of Columbia,	Feb. 19, 1811,	11	8	0	1	850	60	5	700	1st Tuesday Nov.	Washington.
Florida,	July 5, 1830,	40	15	4	1	1234	59268	1481	1500	2d Monday January,	Tallahassee.
Georgia,	Dec. 16, 1786,	226	44	17	1	12500	58000	256	9500	Last Tuesday October,	Macon.
Illinois,	——, 1823,	290	49	9	9	11000	55405	191	6500	1st Tuesday October,	Springfield.
Indiana,	Jan. 13, 1818,	250	40	12	6	8636	33809	155	10000	4th Monday May,	Indianapolis.
Iowa,	Jan. 8, 1844,	188	23	5	3	3950	50914	368	3100	1st Tuesday June,	Itinerant,
Kansas,	March 17, 1856,	23	1	0	0	500	114798	499	100	3d Tuesday October,	Lawrence,
Kentucky,	Oct. 16, 1800,	811	68	26	9	11500	37680	121	14000	3d Monday October,	Louisville.
Louisiana,	July 11, 1812,	112	20	4	2	4000	41255	868	14000	2d Monday February,	New Orleans.
Maine,	June 24, 1820,	93	11	7	4	3391	31766	341	1600	1st Tuesday May,	Portland.
Maryland,	July 31, 1783,	37	5	0	2	1779	11124	300	2600	3d Monday November,	Baltimore.
Massachusetts,	March 8, 1777,	99	19	0	11	3960	7800	78		2d Wednesday Dec.	Boston.
Michigan,	July 31, 1826,	104	21	4	5	4160	56243	540	2600	2d Wednesday Jan.	Itinerant,
Minnesota,	Feb. 23, 1853,	85	3	0	1	1600	166025	4743	1200	4th Tuesday October,	St. Paul.

STATES.	Date of Organisation of Grand Lodge.	Present No. of Lodges.	No. of Chapters.	No. of Councils.	No. of Encampm'ts.	No. of Masons in the Lodges.	Square Miles	Ratio of Square Miles to a Lodge.	Revenue of 1858-9.	Time of Meetings of Grand Lodges.	Place of Meeting of Grand Lodges.
Mississippi,	Aug. 25, 1818,	239	48	23	5	9537	47156	197	$8100	3d Monday January,	Itinerant.
Missouri,	May 4, 1821,	180	27	5	2	6000	67380	374	7900	4th Monday May,	Itinerant.
Nebraska,	Sept. 23, 1857,	6	0	0	0	140	335882	55980	600	2d Tuesday June,	Itinerant.
New Brunswick,	Sept. 24, 1856,	22	5	0	2	825	26000	1181		Tuesday after 1st Wednesday June,	St. Johns.
New Hampshire,	July 16, 1789,	39	7	0	8	1800	9280	237	600		Concord.
New Jersey,	Dec. 18, 1786,	52	5	0	2	2204	8320	160	1300	3d Tuesday January,	Trenton.
New York,	——, 1787,	413	88	5	24	32817	47000	113	16000	1st Tuesday June,	New York.
North Carolina,	Dec. 16, 1787,	127	—	—	1	5800	50704	399	1700		Raleigh.
Ohio,	Jan. 2, 1809,	298	76	33	15	13000	39964	134	8000	8d Tuesday October,	Itinerant.
Oregon,	Sept. 15, 1851,	26	3	0	0	728	185030	7116	650	2d Monday June,	Itinerant.
Pennsylvania,	Sept. 25, 1786,	159	28	9	18	6360	46000	289	32000	1st Monday Dec.	Philadelphia.
Rhode Island,	June 25, 1791,	16	5	0	2	1048	1306	81	500	Last Monday May,	Itinerant.
South Carolina,	March 24, 1787,	70	23	0	1	8500	29385	419	6600	2d Tuesday Nov.	Charleston.
Tennessee,	Dec. 27, 1813,	218	20	10	2	12000	45600	214	4400	1st Monday October,	Nashville.
Texas,	April 16, 1838,	210	60	12	6	8400	237504	1130	6000	2d Monday June,	Itinerant.
Vermont,	Oct. 19, 1794,	44	11	10	4	2063	10200	231	400	2d Wednesday Jan.	Burlington.
Virginia,	Oct. 30, 1778,	162	34	0	10	6480	61352	378	1400	2d Monday December,	Richmond.
Wisconsin,	Dec. 18, 1843,	106	17	5	3	3818	53924	508	2317	2d Tuesday June,	Milwaukee.
Washington Territory,	Dec. —, 1858,	7	0	0	0	180	123022	17574	150	1st Monday Sept.	Olympia.
		4802	904	245	173	212347					

THESE Tables have been prepared with great labor and care, and although many of the data are approximative, yet it is by far the most accurate summary of Masonic Statistics ever published. According to this table the five Grand Lodges governing the largest number of lodges, are, 1. New York. 2. Kentucky. 3. Ohio. 4. Illinois. 5. Indiana.

THE ANCIENT CHARGES AND CONSTITUTIONS.
ARTICLE FIRST.

The exhibit of Masonic doctrines, styled *The Masonic Charges*, and first published in 1723, under the auspices of Payne, Desaguliers and Anderson, constitutes the only code of Masonic law deserving the name *universal*. They can not be too carefully studied, or too implicitly obeyed. By how much the various Lodges, Grand and Subordinate around the globe have been guided by their dictates, by so much they have performed work which will stand the ravages of time. For comprehensiveness of detail, purity of language, and earnestness of purpose, these Charges are a model worthy the attention of the most learned.

The Ancient Charges are divided methodically into Six General Heads or Chapters. The first which treats of "God and Religion," establishes the Masonic duty of morality, and shows why an atheist or irreligious libertine can not be a Mason. The religion of the Institution is defined as "goodness and truth," a code in which it is said "all men agree, leaving their particular opinions to themselves." This religion is declared to be the center of union, and the means of conciliating true friendship among persons that must otherwise have remained at a perpetual distance.

The Second Chapter comprises the subject of "the Civil Magistrate, Supreme and Subordinate," and as the first treated of the religion, so this describes the politics of Masonry. In it the Mason is enjoined to be a peaceable subject to the Civil Powers wherever he resides or works, to avoid plots and conspiracies against the peace and welfare of the nation, and to be subservient to inferior magistrates. It declares that Masonry has always been injured by war, bloodshed and confusion, and that its nature is so essentially peaceable that ancient kings and princes were known to encourage the craftsmen, and promote the honor of the Fraternity. Such freedom of political opinion is accorded, that brethren engaged in rebellion must not be expelled from the lodge on that account.

The Third Chapter defines the subject "Of Lodges." Here we learn that the term lodge refers both to the *place* and the *assembly*, that every Brother ought to belong to one, and submit to its By-laws, as well as the Regulations of the Grand Lodge; and that a correct knowledge of a lodge is best acquired through attendance. Reference is made to an ancient rule which inflicted a severe censure upon any member who absented himself from its meetings without good cause. The members of a lodge are described as "good and true men, free born, of mature and discreet age, no bondmen, no women, no immoral or scandalous men, but of good report."

The Fourth Chapter establishes the relationship between the various grades of Masonry, official and affiliated, from the Grand Master to the Apprentice. All official preferment, it is enjoined, must be based upon real worth and personal merit only. Apprentices should only be received in a lodge where there is sufficient employment for them, and they must be men without maim or physical defect, and born of honest parentage, so that in their turns they may pass through the various degrees and official grades, even to that of Grand Master. Only Fellow-crafts, it is ordered, can be Wardens, only Wardens can be elected Masters, and only Masters be made Grand Masters, who in addition to the qualification of grade must be Noblemen, or Gentlemen of high degree, or eminent Scholars, Architects or Artists of singular great merit in the estimation of the lodges. A Deputy is allowed the Grand Master, to be the subject of his own choice, who like himself, must be a Past Master, and who may act as Grand Master in his absence. Obedience to these officers, each in his own degree, is strictly enjoined, and this to be manifested "with all humility, reverence, love and alacrity."

1st MONTH.   JANUARY, 1860.   31 DAYS.

MOON'S PHASES.

	D.	H.	M.
Full Moon,	8	10	15 mor.
Last Quarter,	15	1	50 mor.
New Moon,	22	7	8 eve.
First Quarter,	31	0	3 mor.

Sun on Merid.

	D.	H.	M.	S.
	1	12	3	42.88
	9	12	7	17.35
	17	12	10	17.56
	25	12	12	33.69

D. M.	D. W.	Sun's decl. S. ° ′ ″	Sun Rises. H. M.	Sun Sets. H. M.	Moon Sets. H. M.
1	Sun.	— 2 11	7 19	4 49	morn.
2	Mon.	22 57 6	7 19	4 50	0 55
3	Tue.	22 51 33	7 19	4 51	1 58
4	Wed.	22 45 33	7 19	4 52	3 4
5	Thu.	22 39 6	7 19	4 52	4 17
6	Fri.	22 32 13	7 19	4 53	5 27
7	Sat.	22 24 52	7 19	4 54	rises.
8	Sun.	22 17 5	7 19	4 55	5 1
9	Mon.	22 8 52	7 18	4 56	6 19
10	Tue.	22 0 13	7 18	4 57	7 35
11	Wed.	21 51 8	7 18	4 58	8 49
12	Thu.	21 41 38	7 18	4 59	10 0
13	Fri.	21 31 42	7 18	5 0	11 10
14	Sat.	21 21 22	7 17	5 1	morn.
15	Sun.	21 10 36	7 17	5 2	0 19
16	Mon.	20 59 26	7 17	5 3	1 28
17	Tue.	20 47 52	7 17	5 4	2 37
18	Wed.	20 35 55	7 16	5 5	3 46
19	Thu.	20 23 34	7 16	5 7	4 49
20	Fri.	20 10 49	7 15	5 8	5 47
21	Sat.	19 57 42	7 14	5 9	6 36
22	Sun.	19 44 13	7 13	5 10	sets.
23	Mon.	19 30 22	7 12	5 11	5 54
24	Tue.	19 16 9	7 12	5 12	6 53
25	Wed.	19 1 34	7 11	5 13	7 50
26	Thu.	18 46 39	7 10	5 14	8 48
27	Fri.	18 31 24	7 9	5 15	9 47
28	Sat.	18 15 48	7 9	5 16	10 45
29	Sun.	17 59 53	7 8	5 17	11 46
30	Mon.	17 43 39	7 8	5 19	morn.
31	Tue.	17 27 6	7 7	5 20	0 50

MASONIC EVENTS.

EXPLANATION OF SYMBOLS.—◻ Lodge; ⌒ Chapter; △ Council; † Encampment.

9th. Grand ⌒, Miss., Jackson; Grand ◻, Fla., Tallahassee; Grand ⌒, Mich., Detroit.

10th. Grand †, Vt.

11th. Grand ◻, Mich., Detroit; Grand ◻, Vt., Burlington; Grand ⌒, Florida, Tallahassee; Grand △, Florida, Tallahassee.

13th. Grand △, Miss., Vicksburg.

16th. Grand ◻, Mississippi, Jackson.

17th. Grand ◻, New Jersey, Trenton.

20th. Grand †, Mississippi, Vicksburg.

Whatever may be our situation or rank in life, we shall find, on examination, those in similar situations, who have dignified the Masonic Order, and rendered themselves useful to the craft.

Masons have increased faster, much faster than Masonry. The means of instruction are in a very low ratio with the demand and necessity for it.

The materials proper for the mystic walls on which the craftsmen labor, are *the good and sound*, and none other.

The nearer our brethren assimilate to the Scriptural standard of right and wrong, the less need will they find for written laws and regulations.

Of all Masonic decisions and systems of work that conflict wholly or partly with each other, the oldest is the best.

EARS OF CORN NEAR THE WATER FORD.

The practical argument against the reception of maimed and mutilated persons into Masonry, is that such persons can only be learners, and never teachers. Masons are required to be *both*, and to be teachers of Masonry requires the *mens sana in sano corpore*. The blind, the one-armed, the one-legged, the deaf, the dumb, can never travel as Masons, for no lodge having a proper understanding of the principles of the Order, would take a single step toward their examination.

JANUARY.

CHRONOLOGICAL EVENTS OF THIS MONTH.

FIRST.—1787. Conv. Charleston to est. G. L. of S. C. 1840. Prov. G. Ch., Brazil, est. 1851. Ancient Landmark, Mt. Clemens, Mich., est. 1855. Acacia, Natchez, Miss., est. 1855. Signet and Journal, Marietta, Geo., est. 1859. Voice of Masonry, Louisville, Ky., est.

SECOND.—1809. G. L., Ohio, est. 1844. Conv. Iowa City, to est. G. L., Io. 1844. Rich. Ellis, G. Treas. N. Y., d.

THIRD.—1844. Prince Joseph Bonaparte, G. M. France, d. 1855. Nat. Mas. Conv., Washington, D. C.

FOURTH.—1787. G. Ch. Harodim, London, Eng., est. 1808. Conv. Chillicothe, to est. G. L., Ohio. 1845. Benj. Russell, P. G. M., Mass., d. J. S. Reeves init.

FIFTH.—1841. Emperor Austria reëst. Knights Malta.

SIXTH.—

SEVENTH.—1718. Israel Putnam b. 1798. Joseph Bonaparte b. 1847. Joseph Norvell, P. G. M., Tenn., d. 1852. Mas. Mirror, Philadelphia, Pa., est.

EIGHTH.—1844. G. L., Iowa, est.

NINTH.—1806. 2d Conv. G. G. R. A. C. of U. S., Middletown, Ct.

TENTH.—1740. First Lodge, Barbadoes, W. I., est. 1821. Conv. Canandaigua, N. Y. 1822. Simon Greenleaf, G. M., Maine. 1842. John Chadwick d.

ELEVENTH.—1800. Philip C. Tucker b.

TWELFTH.—1818. G. L., Ind., est. 1828. Cor. stone Charleston College, S. C., pl. 1835. John H. Eaton, Hon. Member, G. L., Fla.

THIRTEENTH.—1780. Washington proposed G. G. M., by G. L., Pa. 1858. G. C., Mich., est. 1858. G. C., Fla., est.

FOURTEENTH.—

FIFTEENTH.—1817. Theo. S. Parvin b.

SIXTEENTH.—1825. J. Adams Allen b. 1859. Hall, Batesville, Ark., burnt

SEVENTEENTH.—1706. Franklin b. 1722. Duke Wharton, G. M. England. 1822. Hall, Lexington, Ky., ded.

EIGHTEENTH.—1836. Dallas, Chandler and others at the Bar of Pa. Legislature. 1855. Conv. San Antonio to est. G. Encpt., Texas.

NINETEENTH.—1855. G. Encpt., Texas, est. 1855. Henry Brush, P. G. M., Ohio, d. 1857. Conv. Hamilton, C. W., to est. G. Ch., Canada.

TWENTIETH.—1786. Nathan B. Haswell b. 1813. Wieland d.

TWENTY-FIRST.—1831. Robt. P. Dunlap, G. M., Maine.

TWENTY-SECOND.—1813. John Allen and John Simpson killed at River Raisin. 1857. Grand Encpt., Miss., est.

TWENTY-THIRD.—1833. Andrew Jackson, Hon. Mem. G. L., Fla.

TWENTY-FOURTH.—1712. Frederick the Great b. 1778. Fun. Obs. to Wm. St. Clair, G. M., Scotland. 1798. G. G. Ch. of U. S., est. 1846. R. D. Putford init. 1852. Honorarium to Henry Wingate, P. G. M., Ky.

TWENTY-FIFTH.—1759. Robert Burns b. 1820. Cor. stone Mon. to Burns at Alloway, Scotland, pl. 1856. Cor. stone Hall, Galveston, Texas, pl. 1859. Centennial Burns' birth largely celebrated.

TWENTY-SIXTH.—

TWENTY-SEVENTH.—1773. Duke of Sussex b. 1813. Great Fest., London, Eng., to Earl of Moira.

TWENTY-EIGHTH.—1857. Amand P. Pfister, G. Sec., Ala., d.

TWENTY-NINTH.—

THIRTIETH.—

THIRTY-FIRST.—1744. St. John's Lodge, Altenburg, Germany, est.

Each event above named has a strictly Masonic allusion.

THE TRUE TEACHER.

Do you desire to see an humble learner in Masonry? go then to the closet of the man best known among you as a teacher, a lecturer, a writer; and if he is what fame reports him, *an enlightened Mason*, see him devoting more days to Masonic study than you, who know so little, give minutes! See him drawing from every source the light, and spreading his hands upward for more light, for divine light. See him at every expense of money, time and trouble, securing books and literary appliances. Then, believe me, the man who has acquired the most knowedge, is he who is greediest for more.

MISCELLANEOUS READING.

Our institution asserts in language not to be misunderstood, the natural equality of mankind. It declares that all brethren are upon a level, and it throws open its hospitable doors to all men, of all nations. It admits of no rank, except the priority of merit, and its only aristocracy is the nobility of virtue.......As Christian Masons we have introduced the Bible into our lodges, to manifest our belief in the doctrines which it inculcates. In like manner, the followers of Moses, Mahomet and Burmah, may introduce into their Masonic assemblies their Pentateuch, their Koran and their Vedas, and yet the unity of Masonry would remain; the essential principles on which she moves would be the same.......In tracing the history of Masonry, the tear of sensibility involuntarily flows at the view of the persecutions and indignities it has suffered from the united efforts of priests and tyrants.

HISTORICAL AND STATISTICAL ITEMS.

American periodicals devoted to Freemasonry, in whole or part, are the following, given in alphabetical order: *Ashlar*, Chicago, Ill., Weston and Co., Monthly, $2.00; *Chronicle*, New York, D. Sickels, Monthly, $0.50; *Freemason*, (American) New York, J. F. Brennan, Monthly, $3.00; *Freemason*, (Indiana) Ft. Wayne, Ind., S. D. Bayless, Monthly, $2.00; *Freemason*, (Texas) Rusk, Texas, Yeomans and Jackson, Monthly, $2.00; *Freemason*, (Western) Iowa City, Iowa, J. R. Hartsock, Monthly, $1.00; *Journal*, Haverhill, Mass., Geo. W. Chase, Monthly, $1.00; *Magazine*, Boston, Mass., C. W. Moore, Monthly, $2.00; *Messenger*, New York, M. J. Drummond, Monthly, $0.50; *Mirror*, Philadelphia, Pa., L. Hyneman, Weekly, $2.00; *Review*, Cincinnati, O. C. Moore, Monthly, $2.00; *Signet*, Marietta, Ga., S. Lawrence, Monthly, $2.00; *Voice*, Louisville, Ky., Rob Morris, Semi-monthly, $1.00.......Brother Stephen Girard at his decease donated, in trust to the Grand Lodge of Pennsylvania, for charitable purposes, the sum of $20,000, which was to lie at interest until it should amount to $30,000, after which the interest was to be applied from time to time to the relief of poor and respectable brethren. This is now done.

THE MASONS' HOME.

Where hearts are warm with kindred fire,
  And love beams free from answering eyes,
Bright spirits hover always there,
  And *that's* the home the Masons prize.
    The Masons' Home! Ah, peaceful home,
      The home of love and light and joy:—
    How gladly does the Mason come
      To share his tender, sweet employ.

A weary task, a dreary round,
  Is all benighted man may know,
But here a brighter scene is found,
  The brightest scene that's found below.
    The Masons' Home! Ah, blissful home,
      Glad center of unmingled joy:—
    Long as I live I'll gladly come
      And share this tender, sweet employ.

All round the world, by land, by sea,
  Where Summers burn or Winters chill,
The exiled Mason turns to thee,
  And yearns to share the joys we feel.
    The Masons' Home! Ah, happy home,
      The home of light and love and joy:—
    There's not an hour but I would come
      And share this tender, sweet employ.

And when the hour of death shall come,
  And darkness seal my closing eye,
May hands fraternal bear me home,
  The home where weary Masons lie.
    The Masons' Home! Ah, heavenly home,
      To faithful hearts eternal joy:—
    How blest to find beyond the tomb
      The end of all our sweet employ.

ALABAMA.—ARKANSAS.—CALIFORNIA.

ALABAMA.—*Grand Lodge*, established 1821; has now 235 lodges, 7000 members. *Grand Chapter*, 1827; has 53 chapters, 1600 members. *Grand Council*, 1838; has 29 councils, 870 members.

ARKANSAS.—*Grand Lodge*, established 1838; has now 128 lodges, 6000 members. *Grand Chapter*, 1851; has 22 chapters, 600 members.

CALIFORNIA.—*Grand Lodge*, established 1850; has now 122 lodges, 4727 members. *Grand Chapter*, 1854; has 23 chapters, 784 members. *Grand Council*, ; has councils, members. *Grand Encampment*, 1858; has 6 encampments, 319 members.

UNIVERSAL MASONIC LIBRARY, Vol. I.

The first volume of the series embraces two works: I. The Dictionary of Symbolical Masonry, by GEORGE OLIVER, D. D., 301 pages. II. The Book of the Lodge, by the same, 119 pages; in all 420 pages.

THE ANCIENT CHARGES AND CONSTITUTIONS.
ARTICLE SECOND.

The Fifth Chapter defines the term *work*, and describes the manner of it. National Sabbaths and holidays must be observed, and all other time given to labor. The overseer of the work must be selected for his expertness, and be entitled *Master*. All ill language and discourtesy, both within and without the lodge, are forbidden, and the workmen enjoined to style each other *Brother* or *Fellow*. The work shall be undertaken by the Master, at reasonable prices, and he shall pay reasonable, yet not exorbitant wages, to the rest. All alike shall be faithful to the employer, and carefully distinguish, according to the

rules of the trade, between *task work* and *journey work*. None shall envy the prosperity of another, or attempt to supplant him in his work. The Wardens, as the medium between the Master and workmen, shall be true to both, and carefully oversee the work, and the brethren shall obey them. Wages shall be received meekly and without murmuring, nor shall the workmen desert their work before it is finished. Younger brethren shall be instructed in the trade, equally to preserve the materials from being spoiled, and for their proper advantage and improvement. The tools shall be approved by the Grand Lodge. No uninitiated laborer shall be employed or instructed as their own brethren, "nor shall Freemasons work with those who are not free, without an urgent necessity."

Chapter Sixth and last descants at considerable length upon the important subject of *behavior*. In open lodge, private conferences and conversations are prohibited, and interrupting a Brother while speaking. All jests and levity during serious labor are rebuked. Respect to the officers and brethren is commanded. In the decision of trials, the award of the lodge or the Grand Lodge upon appeal shall be final, and the brethren are forbidden to go to law "without an absolute necessity apparent to the Lodge."

After the Lodge is closed the members may remain and enjoy themselves with innocent mirth, but must avoid all excess or saying or doing any thing offensive to others. No private piques or quarrels may be alluded to, and no denominational or political quarrels broached.

Brethren when meeting in private are to dispense Masonic knowledge freely to each other, yet with great caution, and the relations of society must be regarded by the brethren, " who must give honor to whom it is due and avoid ill manners."

In the presence of strangers, Masons must be cautious in word and carriage, "that the most penetrating stranger " may not find out what it is not proper for them to know, and arguments upon Masonry with such are not to be encouraged.

At home each Brother must act " as becomes a moral and wise man," reserving from his neighbors, friends, and even his family, the concerns of the lodge. He must not remain overlate at the lodge, or neglect or injure his family by gluttony or drunkenness.

Toward strange brethren the utmost caution must be used. They must be examined with prudence, and if found impostors, rejected with contempt and derision. But if discovered to be true and genuine Masons, they must be respected and relieved, and employment tendered to them, if not incompatible with the duty of self-preservation.

The summary of the whole code is alike eloquent and forcible. Brotherly Love is declared to be the foundation and cap-stone, the cement and glory of Masonry, therefore, all quarreling, backbiting and slander, must be avoided, the character of honest brethren defended, and good offices extended, the one to the other. For injuries received, the Lodge is declared to be the proper tribunal, and lawsuits are forbidden, except in those extremities where the case can not be otherwise decided. In difficulties which arise, the Master and brethren are directed kindly to offer their mediation, and such efforts made by all for the perpetuation of Brotherly Love, "that all may see the benign influences of Masonry, as all true Masons have done from the beginning of the world, and will do to the end of time."

UNIVERSAL MASONIC LIBRARY, VOL. II.

The second volume of the series embraces two works: I. The Symbol of Glory, by GEORGE OLIVER, D. D, 310 pages. The Spirit of Masonry, by WILLIAM HUTCHINSON, 245 pages. In all 555 pages.

2d Month.   FEBRUARY, 1860.   29 Days.

MOON'S PHASES.

	D.	H.	M.
Full Moon,	6	9	27 eve.
Last Quarter,	13	1	43 eve.
New Moon,	21	2	30 eve.
First Quarter,	29	2	47 eve.

Sun on Merid.

D.	H.	M.	S.
1	12	13	50.73
9	12	14	28.82
17	12	14	17.21
25	12	13	21.29

MASONIC EVENTS.

EXPLANATION OF SYMBOLS.—□ Lodge; ⌒ Chapter; △ Council; † Encampment.

1st. Grand ⌒, Wis.

7th. Grand ⌒, New York, Albany.

13th. Grand □, La., New Orleans.

14th. Grand ⌒, La., New Orleans.

15th. Grand ⌒, Canada.

16th. Grand △, La., New Orleans.

20th. Grand ⌒, Pa., Q. C., Philadelphia.

21st. Grand ⌒, South Carolina, Charleston.

D. M.	D. W.	Sun's dec. S. °	′	″	Sun rises H.	M.	Sun sets H.	M.	Moon sets H.	M.
1	Wed.	—	10	14	7	6	5	21	1	54
2	Thu.	16	53	5	7	5	5	22	3	2
3	Fri.	16	35	38	7	4	5	23	4	17
4	Sat.	16	17	53	7	3	5	24	5	11
5	Sun.	15	59	52	7	2	5	26	rises.	
6	Mon.	15	41	35	7	1	5	27	5	10
7	Tue.	15	23	1	7	0	5	28	6	25
8	Wed.	15	4	12	6	59	5	29	7	41
9	Thu.	14	45	7	6	58	5	30	8	52
10	Fri.	14	25	48	6	57	5	31	10	5
11	Sat.	14	6	14	6	56	5	33	11	17
12	Sun.	13	46	26	6	55	5	34	morn.	
13	Mon.	13	26	24	6	54	5	35	0	28
14	Tue.	13	6	9	6	53	5	36	1	37
15	Wed.	12	45	42	6	52	5	38	2	44
16	Thu.	12	25	2	6	51	5	39	3	43
17	Fri.	12	4	9	6	50	5	40	4	34
18	Sat.	11	43	6	6	48	5	41	5	17
19	Sun.	11	21	51	6	47	5	42	5	52
20	Mon.	11	0	25	6	46	5	43	sets.	
21	Tue.	10	38	49	6	45	5	44	5	46
22	Wed.	10	17	4	6	44	5	45	6	44
23	Thu.	9	55	8	6	43	5	46	7	41
24	Fri.	9	33	4	6	42	5	47	8	40
25	Sat.	9	10	52	6	41	5	48	9	40
26	Sun.	8	48	31	6	40	5	49	10	42
27	Mon.	8	26	3	6	39	5	50	11	44
28	Tue.	8	3	27	6	38	5	51	morn.	
29	Wed.	7	40	45	6	37	5	52	0	52

The Bible may well be prized among Masons and Masons' wives, for it has banished idol worship, abolished infanticide, put down polygamy and divorce, exalted the condition of woman, raised the standard of public morality, created for families a home, and caused benevolent institutions to spring up as with the wand of enchantment. Oh let the Bible be in the center of your lodge, honored, opened, accessible to all!

The class of men from which Masons are selected, is that which is sound in mind and body, and unrebukable in morals, having at least average attainments in education, and sustaining more than an average character for sobriety and virtue. Much in behalf of social and moral reform is justly expected of such men.

No change in any part or point of Masonry can ever be tolerated.

EARS OF CORN NEAR THE WATER FORD.

No solicitation of any sort can be lawfully used in inducing men to become Masons. The only allurement proper is so to act toward all men, so to reverence God, so to obey the laws of the country and the divine injunctions, and so to honor Masonry, that outsiders may admire the Institution which contains such men, and the bond that unites such men, and become earnestly desirous of connecting themselves with such men.......The Seven Wonders of the World, sometimes referred to in Masonic illustrations, were the following: 1st. The Colossus of Rhodes. 2d. The Pyramids of Egypt. 3d. The Aqueducts of Rome. 4th. The Labyrinth of Psalmetticus. 5th. The Pharos of Alexandria. 6th. The Walls of Babylon. 7th. The Temple of Diana at Ephesus.

FEBRUARY.

CHRONOLOGICAL EVENTS OF THIS MONTH.

FIRST.—

SECOND.—1834. Lorenzo Dow d.

THIRD.—1728. Cor. stone Parliament House, Dublin, Ireland, pl. 1822. E. K. Kane b. 1827. Mas. Record, Albany, N. Y., est.

FOURTH.—1819. Honorarium from G. C., N. Y., to Salem Town.

FIFTH.—

SIXTH.—1775. G. L., Brunswick, Ger., est. 1787. Prince of Wales init. 1826. Benjamin Parke init.

SEVENTH.—1778. Voltaire init. 1821. G. Ch., Maine, est. 1827. Mas. Intelligencer, Batavia, N. Y., est.

EIGHTH.—

NINTH.—

TENTH.—

ELEVENTH.—1800. Obsequies of Washington, by G. L., Mass. 1828. DeWitt Clinton, P. G. M., N. Y., d. 1847. Freem. Hall, Dublin, Ireland, ded. 1851. Mas. Mission, Panama, O. A., est.

TWELFTH.—1744. Lodge "Charles of 3 Crowned Pillars," Germany, est. 1777. Henry Brush b. 1812. Duke of Sussex, D. G. M., England. 1857. Union of Knights Templar of Pa.

THIRTEENTH.—1858. G. Ch., N. J., re-established.

FOURTEENTH.—1809. John Snow init.

FIFTEENTH.—1818. Charles 13th of Sweden, d.

SIXTEENTH.—1830. Craftsman, Rochester, N. Y., est. 1856. G. C., La., est. 1857. E. K. Kane d.

SEVENTEENTH.—1842. Alex. V. Griswold d. 1859. Honorarium to W. M. Perkins, P. G. M., La.

EIGHTEENTH.—1843. Mas. Mirror, Columbia, Tenn., est.

NINETEENTH.—1811. G. L., D. C., est.

TWENTIETH.—1776. Am. Union Lodge, Rev. Army, est. 1788. G. C., Princes Jerusalem, Charleston, S. C., est. 1856. Woodlawn Mas. Institute, Camden, Ark., burnt.

TWENTY-FIRST.—Duke of York init.

TWENTY-SECOND.—1732. Washington b. 1850. Cor. stone Washington Mon., Richmond, Va., pl. 1854. Mas. Temple, Wheeling, Va., ded. 1858. Washington Mon., Richmond, Va., ded. 1859. Hall, Newark, N. J., ded.

TWENTY-THIRD.—1853. G. L., Min., est.

TWENTY-FOURTH.—

TWENTY-FIFTH.—1723. Sir Christ. Wren d. 1780. John Snow b.

TWENTY-SIXTH.—1809. S. C. Coffinbury b.

TWENTY-SEVENTH.—1764. G. L., Italy, est. 1813. Mas. Festival to Earl Moira, London, Eng.

TWENTY-EIGHTH.—

TWENTY-NINTH.—

Each event above named has a strictly Masonic allusion.

THE HAILING SIGN OF DISTRESS.

The force of the Masonic Grand Hailing Sign of Distress, has been illustrated by a modern writer in this manner: "A Brother in the whirl of life, in the embarrassments of business, may become negligent concerning many important duties enjoined by his covenant. He may do many things forbidden by the Masonic code, and, through his evils of omission and commission, scandal and reproach may befall our institution. But he can not resist, for never did Mason resist that mute gesture, that movable expression of pressing want, styled the grand hailing sign of distress! He can never neglect that while a spark of virtue exists in his bosom."

MISCELLANEOUS READING.

The cement of Masonry is composed of truth and justice, put up in true hearts, and sealed with Faith, Hope and Charity. It is warranted not to be affected by climate or time.......But few forms of prayer express so much, and suggest so much as this: Oh Eternal, have mercy upon me, because I am passing away! Oh Infinite, because I am weak! Oh Sovereign of Life, because I draw near to the grave! Oh Omniscient, because I am in darkness! Oh All-Sufficient, because I am nothing!........It is the practice in many lodges to provide places for the wives, daughters and female relatives of the brethren, in all their processions and festivities, and thus to pay a marked respect to their sex. The result is that Freemasonry is honored in the affection and esteem of these favored guests, and the cause of Masonry itself immensely strengthened. ......The real secrets of Masonry are those which bind heart to heart, and the members to their lodges. These have never been exposed, and never could be, though professed "Expositions" were thicker than "the leaves of Alhambrosa." Can a trained thief read and discover the moral principle that makes good men good? Can a harlot learn the secret of female purity? No more can a base heart learn the secrets of Freemasonry.

HISTORICAL AND STATISTICAL ITEMS.

When Brother E. K. Kane, the renowned Arctic navigator, sailed upon his last voyage, he was complimented by the Grand Lodge of New York with an introduction to an emergent session called in his honor. In reply to their greeting he said: "Our Brother, Franklin, was one who ruled his conduct by the compass and the square, and to him the accents of woe never fell on an unpitying ear.———The Mason, the true man, wherever is the Grand Lodge that the Most Worshipful has built up for our habitation, wherever it is that the cry of affliction is heard, hastens to the rescue of the widow's son."......The power of restoring an expelled or suspended Brother, is in the Lodge that exercised the discipline. Some Grand Lodges, however, have assumed this power to themselves.......A devotee to Masonry in Texas, a carpenter by profession, is an "Old Mortality" in his habit of seeking out the graves of deceased Masons, and enclosing them, at his own cost, with substantial fences.

ONE HOUR WITH YOU.

One hour with you, one hour with you,
  No doubt, nor care, nor strife,
Is worth a weary year of woe,
  In all that lightens life.
One hour with you, and you, and you,
  Bright links in mystic chain—
Oh may we oft these joys renew,
  And often meet again.

Your eyes with love's own language free,
  Your hand-grips, strong and true,
Your voice, your heart, do welcome me
  To spend an hour with you.

I come when morning skies are bright,
  To work my Mason's due—
To labor is my chief delight,
  And spend an hour with you.

I go when evening gilds the west,
  I breathe the fond adieu,
But hope again, by fortune blest,
  To spend an hour with you.
One hour with you, and you, and you,
  Bright links in mystic chain—
Oh may we oft these joys renew,
  And often meet again.

CANADA.—CONNECTICUT.—DELAWARE.—DISTRICT COLUMBIA.

CANADA.—*Grand Lodge*, established 1855; has now 110 lodges, 3200 members. *Grand Chapter*, 1856; has 6 chapters, 190 members. *Provincial Grand Conclave*, 1855; has 4 encampments, 140 members.

CONNECTICUT.—*Grand Lodge*, established 1789; has now 55 lodges, 4784 members. *Grand Chapter*, 1798; has 21 chapters, 837 members. *Grand Council*, 1819; has 13 councils, 377 members. *Grand Encampment*, has 6 encampments, 261 members.

DELAWARE.—*Grand Lodge*, established 1806; has now 11 lodges, 600 members.

DISTRICT COLUMBIA.—*Grand Lodge*, established 1811; has 11 lodges, 850 members. The *Grand Chapter* is united with Maryland, which see.

UNIVERSAL MASONIC LIBRARY, Vol. III.

The third volume of the series comprises Illustrations of Masonry, by William Preston; 405 pages.

THE ANCIENT CHARGES AND CONSTITUTIONS.
ARTICLE THIRD.

<table>
<tr>
<td>♎ LANDMARK III.

The Law of God is the rule and limit of Masonry.</td>
<td>The General Regulations attached to the Ancient Charges are not unchangeable in their character, like the former, but are like those Constitutions which the various Grand Lodges adopt, amend and reform at pleasure. Many of the principles embraced in them, however, are land-marks. They were compiled in 1720, by Payne, and published at the same time with the Charges. There are thirty-nine in all, many of them being purely local to the lodges of London and Westminster. The first is declaratory of the power of the Grand Master, who it is said, has the right to preside in every lodge, and place the Master</td>
<td>♎ LANDMARK IV.

The Civil Law, so far as it accords with the Divine, is obligatory upon Masons.</td>
</tr>
</table>

of that lodge on his left. The Master of a lodge (Reg. 2) may congregate his lodge at pleasure. In his absence his powers devolve upon the Wardens, according to seniority. No lodge can make more than five new members at a time (Reg. 4), nor any, without giving a month's previous notice to the lodge (Reg. 5). The unanimous consent of all the members of the lodge present, is essential to the choice of a candidate (Reg. 6). The candidate must solemnly promise to submit to the Constitutions, Charges and Regulations (Reg. 7). No members may withdraw from their affiliation, except to unite themselves with another lodge. Clandestine lodges must be treated as rebellious (Reg. 8).

Brethren whose conduct produces apprehension in the lodge, shall be twice admonished by the Master or Wardens, and on failure to reform, be punished according to the By-laws (Reg. 9). The majority of a lodge may instruct their Master and Wardens, who are their representatives in Grand Lodge (Reg. 10). All lodges are to observe the same usages as nearly as possible, and deputations between lodges for this end are to be encouraged (Reg. 11). The Grand Lodge is composed of the Master and Wardens of all the Lodges upon the Register, with the Grand Master at their head, the Deputy on his left, and the Grand Wardens in their places. All matters in Grand Lodge are determined by a majority of votes, of which the Grand Master has two, and each member one. Quarterly communications of the Grand Lodge are enjoined (Reg. 12). Business is to be quietly, sedately and maturely discoursed of, and transacted in Grand Lodge. Matters of appeal are disposed of, lists of members and other reports from lodges are examined, means for raising charity funds devised, and Apprentices made Crafts, and Crafts, Masters (Reg. 13). All business shall come to the hands of the Grand Master, through the Deputy (Reg. 16). The Grand Master, Deputy and Wardens, shall not during their continuance in office, act as Masters or Wardens of subordinate lodges (Reg. 18). No regulation is provided for an abuse of power on the part of the Grand Master, all former Grand Masters having behaved themselves worthy of that honorable office (Reg. 19). Upon the death, absence or incapacity of the Grand Master, the Grand Lodge may be called to an emergent meeting by the Deputy, the Wardens, or any three present Masters of lodges (Reg. 21). It is declared that every Grand Lodge has an inherent right and power to make new regulations, or to alter these for the real benefit of Masonry, provided the old landmarks be carefully observed (Reg. 39).

MEMORABILIA.

George M. Dallas was J. G. W. of the G. L. of Pa., in 1829.......In 1833 the Grand Lodge of Ms. appropriated $100 to the Bunker Hill Monument.......In 1821 the Masons of Providence, R. I., used to hold weekly meetings for the sole purpose of instruction.

UNIVERSAL MASONIC LIBRARY, Vol. IV.

The fourth volume of the series embraces two works: I. The Antiquities of Freemasonry, by GEORGE OLIVER D. D., 260 pages. II. Masonic Discourses, by THADDEUS MASON HARRIS, D. D., 176 pages. In all 436 pages.

3d MONTH.　　MARCH, 1860.　　31 DAYS.

MOON'S PHASES.

	D.	H.	M.
Full Moon,	7	7	36 mor.
Last Quarter,	14	4	0 mor.
New Moon,	22	8	47 mor.
First Quarter,	30	1	45 mor.

Sun on Merid.

D.	H.	M.	S.
1	12	12	26.61
9	12	10	33.53
17	12	8	19.11
25	12	5	53.99

MASONIC EVENTS.

EXPLANATION OF SYMBOLS.—□ Lodge; ⌒ Chapter; △ Council; † Encampment.

7th. Grand □, N. B., Q. C., St. John.

13th. Grand ⌒, Mass., Q. C., Boston.

14th. Grand □, Mass., Q. C., Boston.

D. M.	D. W.	Sun's decl. S. ° ′ ″	Sun Rises. H. M.	Sun Sets. H. M.	Moon Sets. H. M.
1	Thu.	— 17 55	6 33	5 54	1 53
2	Fri.	6 55 1	6 32	5 55	2 59
3	Sat.	6 31 59	6 31	5 56	3 55
4	Sun.	6 8 54	6 29	5 57	4 42
5	Mon.	5 45 42	6 28	5 58	5 23
6	Tue.	5 22 27	6 27	5 58	rises.
7	Wed.	4 59 7	6 25	5 59	6 28
8	Thu.	4 35 43	6 23	6 0	7 42
9	Fri.	4 12 15	6 22	6 1	8 55
10	Sat.	3 48 45	6 20	6 2	10 10
11	Sun.	3 25 11	6 19	6 3	11 23
12	Mon.	3 1 35	6 18	6 4	morn.
13	Tue.	2 37 57	6 17	6 5	0 32
14	Wed.	2 14 17	6 15	6 6	1 35
15	Thu.	1 50 36	6 13	6 7	2 31
16	Fri.	1 26 53	6 12	6 8	3 14
17	Sat.	1 3 10	6 10	6 9	3 51
18	Sun.	0 39 27	6 8	6 10	4 22
19	Mon.	0 15 44	6 6	6 11	4 48
20	Tue.	+ 7 58	6 5	6 12	5 12
21	Wed.	0 31 40	6 4	6 13	sets.
22	Thu.	0 55 21	6 2	6 14	6 34
23	Fri.	1 18 59	6 0	6 15	7 34
24	Sat.	1 42 36	5 58	6 16	8 35
25	Sun.	2 6 10	5 56	6 17	9 40
26	Mon.	2 29 41	5 54	6 18	10 44
27	Tue.	2 53 9	5 53	6 19	11 48
28	Wed.	3 16 34	5 51	6 20	morn.
29	Thu.	3 39 55	5 50	6 20	0 49
30	Fri.	4 3 11	5 48	6 21	1 45
31	Sat.	4 26 23	5 47	6 22	2 34

The Master of a lodge should be a well-read man, very familiar with the Constitution, Rules and usages of his Grand Lodge, understand thoroughly the By-laws of his own lodge, be skillful in the rules that govern ordinary deliberative assemblies, be well read in the Masonic literature of the day, and be personally and intimately acquainted with each member of his own lodge.

The chief difficulty under which a Masonic juris-consult labors in teaching the correct law and usage in controverted matters, lies in this, that heretofore, in this country, every Grand Lodge and almost every lodge and brother has been a law to itself in such things. The laborer in this field must therefore look for opposition in the pride and prejudice, as well as the ignorance of those he would instruct.

Any intelligent man who enters the Masonic Order, after reading its Monitor, and learning the reverence with which the Holy Scriptures are regarded in Masonry, stands committed to a belief in the Divine authenticity of that volume. Should he afterward declare that he *never* believed it, he must be ranked as ignorant, treacherous, or mendacious.

In Florida the lodges are required by their constitutional regulations to keep a Visiters' Book, in which the names of all Visiters, with their respective affiliations shall be duly recorded.

If you see a Brother bending under the *cross* of adversity and disappointment, look not idly on, neither pass by on the other side, but fly to his relief.

EARS OF CORN NEAR THE WATER FORD.

Brethren anxious to work the work of Masonry to the honor of our common Lord, should beware of inventing or perpetuating local tests. Nothing weakens the Masonic tie so effectually as for one lodge to practice customs not known to the rest. There are many of these unphilosophic and dangerous tests in vogue.......A Masonic editor should be a gentleman (a *gentle man*); his pen should be charged with fraternal sentiments. There should be no gall in his inkstand; he should have no quarrels with anybody.

MARCH.

CHRONOLOGICAL EVENTS OF THIS MONTH.

FIRST.—1848. Finlay M. King init.

SECOND.—1769. DeWitt Clinton b. 1770. Tyrian Lodge, Boston, Mass., est. 1790. Antiquity Lodge, London, Eng., re-inst.

THIRD.—1753. Washington passed. 1840. Cor. stone St. Thomas' Church, Lancaster, England, pl.

FOURTH.—1774. Jo. H. Daviess b.

FIFTH.—1779. Salem Town b. 1855. Hall, Altoona, Pa., burnt.

SIXTH.—1844. Earl of Zetland, G. M., England.

SEVENTH.—1792. Prov. G. L., Upper Canada, est. 1842. Nat. Mas. Conv., Washington, D. C.

EIGHTH.—1777. G. L., Mass., est. 1855. Hall, Weston, Mo., burnt.

NINTH.—1786. Duke of Clarence init. 1787. William IV init. 1819. Grand Hall, Philadelphia, Pa., burnt. 1822. Mas. Conv., Washington, D. C. 1852. Thomas M. Vinson d.

TENTH.—1841. Earl of Rothus, G. M., Scotland, d. 1854. G. C., Ill., est.

ELEVENTH.—1313. Jacques de Molay, burnt at Paris, France.

TWELFTH.—

THIRTEENTH.—1798. G. Ch., R. I., est.

FOURTEENTH.—1798. G. Ch., N. Y., est. 1838. Th. S. Parvin init.

FIFTEENTH.—1767. Andrew Jackson b.

SIXTEENTH.—1857. Sam'l Zimmerman killed.

SEVENTEENTH.—1822. Israel Israel, P. G. M., Pa., d. 1849. King of Holland d. 1856. G. L., Kansas, est.

EIGHTEENTH.—

NINETEENTH.—1788. N. G. Chesebro b.

TWENTIETH.—

TWENTY-FIRST.—1797. Daniel Balch b. 1825. Cor. stone Monuments Greene and Pulaski, Savannah, Ga., pl.

TWENTY-SECOND.—1312. Order Knights Templar in France extinguished.

TWENTY-THIRD.—1858. Cor. stone Library Build., Cape Good Hope pl.

TWENTY-FOURTH.—1787. G. L., S. C., est.

TWENTY-FIFTH.—1722. Ancient Charges ordered to be printed.

TWENTY-SIXTH.—1776. Lodge, Naples, Italy, surprised by police. 1854. Samuel Harrington d. 1857. Mas. Cemetery, Lodgeton, Ky., ded.

TWENTY-SEVENTH.—

TWENTY-EIGHTH.—1797. Moses Paul b. 1842. John Davenport d. 1842. Honorarium to Michael Furnell, Limerick, Ireland.

TWENTY-NINTH.—1721. Cor. stone St. Martin's Church, London, Eng., pl. 1801. Charles W. Moore b.

THIRTIETH.—

THIRTY-FIRST.—1772. Joseph Warren, Prov. G. M. of North America.

Each event above named has a strictly Masonic allusion.

A MASONIC PERIODICAL.

A periodical worthy to be styled *Masonic*, should be one deserving to be read, filed, and bound in volumes; deserving to lie on the pedestals of the lodge E. W. and S.; deserving to be studied by all men who aspire to know Freemasonry, whether without or within the pale of the Order; deserving of the fair hands of woman, intent to know the principles and practices of the craft; deserving a permanent place in Historical collections, that are to lighten up the current history of the day. How few of all nominally Masonic journals, answer in any rational degree to this definition!

MISCELLANEOUS READING.

There are at least four good reasons why a Brother, having taken one or two degrees, may be rejected on his application for advancement: 1st. He lacks original qualifications, and the fact has just come to light. 2d. He lacks proficiency. 3d. He lacks character; he has proved himself unworthy of advancement. 4th. He is not yet sufficiently known to the members; his standing and antecedents are not clear.......A Masonic editor should be a man of sound judgment, extensive knowledge, incorruptible integrity, bold, yet prudent, firm, without obstinacy, spurning dictation, yet open to advice, and above all, glowing with brotherly love.......Thousands of widows and orphans are proving every day that the tie of Masonry is indissoluble, since the power of death can not sunder it.

HISTORICAL AND STATISTICAL ITEMS.

Confucius, whose writings are said, like Mahomet's, to contain all the Moral Code of the Ancient Scriptures, taught the original purity, sinlessness and happiness of man, his fall, his punishment, the disappearance of good from the earth, the diminution of man's greatness, strength and longevity, the curse of sterility to the earth, and other traditions easily recognized by the readers of Holy Writ.......A settler in early days in the West, marked his cattle with a brand representing the Square and Compass. It was noticed by his neighbors, that while the Indians made the most serious depredations upon the stock of others, his were never harmed, nor was hide or hoof ever missing. After the war ended, the Indians admitted that their chiefs had instructed them *to respect that emblem as holy*, wherever they found it.......During the prevalence of Yellow Fever in New Orleans in 1853, the Masonic Fraternity of Cincinnati forwarded $1200 to the relief of the sufferers there. New York, at the same time, sent $1000 to New Orleans, and $500 to Mobile.......The four sacred signs of olden day were the crescent, the star, the trident, and the cross. Others, such as the winged globe, the bident, the horned cap, the sun, the moon, the seven stars, the sacred tree, the wedge, etc., etc., were much used.

KNIGHTS TEMPLAR DIRGE.

Precious in the sight of heaven
  Is the place where Christians die;
Souls with all their sins forgiven,
  To the courts of glory fly.
Every sorrow, every burden,
  Every CROSS they lay it down;
Jesus gives them richest guerdon
  In his own immortal CROWN.

Here, above our Brother weeping,
  Through our tears we seize this hope—
He in Jesus sweetly sleeping,
  Shall awake in glory up!

He has borne his CROSS in sorrow,
  Weary pilgrim, all forlorn,
When the sun shines bright to-morrow,
  'T will reveal his sparkling CROWN.

Knights of Christ, your ranks are broken!
  Close your front! the foe is nigh!
Shield to Shield behold the token
  As he saw it in the SKY!
By that Sign so bright, so glorious,
  Ye shall conquer if ye strive,
And like him, though dead, victorious
  In the courts of Jesus live.

FLORIDA.—GEORGIA.—ILLINOIS.

FLORIDA.—*Grand Lodge*, established 1830; has now 40 lodges, 1234 members. *Grand Chapter*, 1847; has 15 chapters, 375 members. *Grand Council*, 1858; has 4 councils, 121 members.

GEORGIA.—*Grand Lodge*, established 1786; has now 226 lodges, 12,500 members. *Grand Chapter*, 1822; has 44 chapters, 1630 members. *Grand Council*, ; has 17 councils, 435 members.

ILLINOIS.—*Grand Lodge*, established 1823; has now 290 lodges, 11,000 members. *Grand Chapter*, 1850; has 49 chapters, 1864 members. *Grand Council*, 1853; has 9 councils, 313 members. *Grand Encampment*, 1857; has 9 encampments, 378 members. *Grand Consistory*, has 0 subordinates, 35 members.

UNIVERSAL MASONIC LIBRARY, Vol. V.

The fifth volume of the series embraces three works: I. The History of Freemasonry, 1829 to 1841, by George Oliver, D.D., 137 pages. II. The Mirror for the Johannite Mason, by the same, 110 pages. III. The Star in the East, by the same, 91 pages. In all 338 pages.

Ⱥ LANDMARK V.

The Masonic Lodge and the Masonic Institution are one and inseparable.

DR. E. K. KANE.

This gentleman evinced an ardent attachment to Masonic principles, displayed on various interesting occasions. When he was preparing to sail on his last expedition to the Arctic Regions, the Grand Lodge of New York was called in emergent meeting to bid him God speed and farewell. He was addressed in the most eulogistic terms by the Grand Master, and replied in words chaste and appropriate. He sailed out of port with the square and compass conspicuously displayed on his foresail. At Newfoundland he met the lodge at that place, and accepted a brotherly token at their hands. In the most trying seasons of the expedition, the Masonic flag

Ⱥ LANDMARK VI.

Masonic qualifications regard the Mental, Moral and Physical nature of man.

was unfurled: once by the side of the National Banner at the farthest point northward ever obtained by civilized man, once by a lost group from the top of their snow-covered tent, when the boldest had well-nigh resigned all hope of life.

When the brethren in the United States heard of Bro. Kane's death, one general burst of sympathy expressed the sentiment that actuated them. The journey of his corpse from New Orleans by the way of the Mississippi and Ohio rivers, was a mark of triumph. Everywhere, at every stopping place on that long journey, the Freemasons met it, accompanied it, guarded it, and honored it. Every Grand Lodge, and hundreds of subordinate lodges inscribed his name in their proceedings, and already more than one "Kane Lodge" has sprung into being, to pass down to the future, the name of one who has elevated the standard of his country, his order and mankind.

GENERAL MASONIC CONVENTIONS.

Meetings of delegates of lodges, etc., for the purpose of securing uniformity in work and legislation have been frequent, but the following are the only ones of a National character:

March 9th, 1822, a mass meeting was held of Masons then present in Washington, D. C., who elected Henry Clay for chairman, and proposed by circular that the Grand Lodges should authorize a General Grand Lodge of the United States. Among the most noted Masons present were Clay, Thaddeus M. Harris, Jno. H. Eaton, Wm. W. Seaton, H. G. Burton, etc. The results of this Convention, like the most of those that followed it, were barren.

March 7th, 1842, a second Convention assembled at the same place; Charles Gilman was elected to the chair. Twelve delegates were in attendance, representing with more or less authority, the States of Ala., Ct., D. C., Md., Mass., N. H., N. Y., R. I., S. C. and Va. The only resolution of importance adopted, was to recommend a convention of Grand Lecturers at Baltimore, Md., the subsequent year.

May 8th, 1843, the third Gen'l Convention occurred. This was at Baltimore, Md., and was composed of twenty-five delegates, representing the States of Ala., D. C., Flo., Ga., La., Md., Mass., Miss., Mo., N. H., N. C., O., R. I., S. C., Tenn. and Va. John Dove was made chairman. Many eminent Masons were in attendance, among them Dove, John Barney, Chas. W. Moore, etc. A Monitor was ordered to be prepared, and a system of Work and Lectures approved. Adjourned to meet in 1846, at Winchester, Va.

The fourth attempt at General Conventions, was the adjourned session at Winchester, Va., as above. Eight delegates only appeared, representing the States of N. C., Va., Iowa, Mich., D. C., and Mo., and the Convention consequently failed to organize.

The fifth was a Mass Convention, opened at Lexington, Ky., Sept. 11th, 1853, during the Triennial Convocation. Its recommendations of a National Grand Lodge met with little favor.

The sixth and last was held Jan. 3d, 1855, at Washington, D. C. Representatives appeared from D. C., Md., Ala., N. Y., Min., Mich. and Cal. David Clopton of Alabama was elected chairman. The results were as futile as those of the Conventions that had preceded it.

UNIVERSAL MASONIC LIBRARY, Vol. VI.

The sixth volume of the series embraces two works: I. Disquisitions of Masonry, by Wellins Calcott, 176 pages. II. Masonic Manual, by Jonathan Ashe, D. D., 231 pages. In all 407 pages.

4th MONTH. APRIL, 1860. 30 DAYS.

MOON'S PHASES.

	D.	H.	M.
Full Moon,	5	4	52 eve.
Last Quarter,	12	8	26 eve.
New Moon,	21	0	37 mor.
First Quarter,	28	9	28 mor.

Sun on Merid.

D.	H.	M.	S.
1	12	3	45.25
9	12	1	25.21
17	11	59	22.71
25	11	57	45.79

D. M.	D. W.	Sun's decl. N. °	′	″	Sun Rises. H.	M.	Sun Sets. H.	M.	Moon Sets. H.	M.
1	Sun.	+ 49	30		5	46	6	24	3	16
2	Mon.	5	12	32	5	45	6	24	3	48
3	Tue.	5	35	28	5	43	6	25	4	21
4	Wed.	5	58	18	5	41	6	26	4	50
5	Thu.	6	21	2	5	40	6	27	5	21
6	Fri.	6	43	39	5	38	6	28	rises.	
7	Sat.	7	6	10	5	37	6	29	8	51
8	Sun.	7	28	34	5	35	6	30	10	13
9	Mon.	7	50	50	5	33	6	31	11	20
10	Tue.	8	12	58	5	32	6	32	morn.	
11	Wed.	8	34	58	5	30	6	33	0	19
12	Thu.	8	56	50	5	28	6	34	1	9
13	Fri.	9	18	33	5	27	6	35	1	50
14	Sat.	9	40	7	5	25	6	36	2	23
15	Sun.	10	1	31	5	23	6	37	2	50
16	Mon.	10	22	46	5	22	6	38	3	13
17	Tue.	10	43	50	5	21	6	39	3	38
18	Wed.	11	4	44	5	20	6	40	3	58
19	Thu.	11	25	27	5	19	6	41	4	20
20	Fri.	11	45	58	5	17	6	42	4	44
21	Sat.	12	6	18	5	16	6	43	sets.	
22	Sun.	12	26	26	5	15	6	44	8	37
23	Mon.	12	46	22	5	13	6	44	9	43
24	Tue.	13	6	5	5	12	6	45	10	45
25	Wed.	13	25	35	5	11	6	46	11	41
26	Thu.	13	44	52	5	10	6	47	morn.	
27	Fri.	14	3	55	5	8	6	48	0	29
28	Sat.	14	22	44	5	7	6	49	1	12
29	Sun.	14	41	19	5	5	6	50	1	46
30	Mon.	14	59	39	5	4	6	51	2	19

MASONIC EVENTS.

EXPLANATION OF SYMBOLS.—□ Lodge; ⌒ Chapter; △ Council; † Encampment.

25th. Grand ⌒, Geo., Augusta; Grand △, Geo.. Augusta.

30th. Grand ⌒, Me., Portland.

Steadiness of purpose is the helm of each man who would accomplish any thing useful in Masonry. A purpose rightly conceived, a plan rightly laid, a design rightly drawn, a beginning divinely blessed, then a persevering effort that acknowledges no obstacle, and submits to no difficulty. This is what is understood by the Masonic expression, "time, patience and perseverance accomplish all things."

A Masonic use of the Scriptural history of King Solomon's Temple, forms one of the finest themes upon which the Orator can expatiate. The subject is almost inexhaustible in its analogies and practical applications. The best division of it is thus: 1st. The purpose; 2d. The time; 3d. The place; 4th. The preparation; 5th. The plan; 6th. The furniture. Each of these divisions affords an hour's lecture.

It is all-important to Masonic usefulness that there should be *peace in the lodge.* And this is not so difficult as some think. Any Brother can be courteous, patient and forbearing in another lodge; what is so natural and easy abroad, is equally so at home.

No neighborhood would long be antimasonic, if the one or two or half dozen Masons who live in it, would but display the practical virtues of the Institution. "Let your light shine before men that they may see your *good* works!" Your *evil* works will be evident enough.

Nothing merits the name of *work* or *lectures* in Masonry, but such as admits of a rational explanation.

EARS OF CORN NEAR THE WATER FORD.

We look into the records of the Antimasonic period not for the purpose of exhuming buried hatreds and enmities long since forgotten; not to separate those whom a truce of twenty years has endeared to each other, but to afford to patient Masons these golden truths, alike the truths of prosperity and affliction, that God is with the right, and that the right is with Masons, so long as they work their science by its ancient and admitted principles. To awaken sympathies for sufferings endured, and congratulations for victories won through exceeding patience and fidelity.

APRIL.

CHRONOLOGICAL EVENTS OF THIS MONTH.

First.—1809. Wieland init. 1811. Fr. Monthly Mag., Philadelphia, Pa., est. 1828. Amaranth, Boston, Mass., est. 1834. Fr. Quart. Rev., London, Eng., est. 1855. Mas. Messenger, New York, est. 1857. Western Freemason, Iowa City, Iowa, est.

Second.—

Third.—1842. Thaddeus M. Harris d. 1846. C. K. K. Tynte, G. M., G. Conclave, England and Wales.

Fourth.—

Fifth.—

Sixth.—1840. G. L., Ill., re-estab.

Seventh.—1813. Duke Sussex, G. M., England. 1814. Wm. Hutchinson d. 1844. Morgan Lewis, G. M., N. Y., d. 1853. Cor. stone Univers., Nashville, Tenn., pl. 1857. G. Encpt., Mich., est.

Eighth.—

Ninth.—

Tenth.—

Eleventh.—1841. Maj. R. C. McDonald d.

Twelfth.—1777. Henry Clay b. 1792. Lord Durham b. 1854. G. Encpt., Pa., re-est. 1856. Cor. stone Mon. to Clay, New Orleans, La., pl. 1857. E. Smith Lee, P. G. M., Mich., d.

Thirteenth.—1853. Cor. stone Epis. Church, Austin, Texas, pl.

Fourteenth.—1859. Geo. M. Bibb, P. G. M., Ky., d.

Fifteenth.—1858. Wm. R. Cannon, P. G. M., Miss., d.

Sixteenth.—1821. Cor. stone St. John's Chapel, Lexington, Ky., pl. 1841. Cor. stone Hall, Lincoln, Eng., pl.

Seventeenth.—1787. G. L., Md. re-est. 1790. Franklin d. 1809. Cor. stone Mas. Hall, Philadelphia, Pa., pl.

Eighteenth.—

Nineteenth.—1850. G. L., Cal., est. 1854. Cor. stone Mech. Hall, Toronto, C. W., pl.

Twentieth.—1842. Samuel Thaxter d. 1843. Duke of Sussex d.

Twenty-first.—A. L. 2992. Cor. stone Temple, Jerusalem, pl. 1821. G. L., Mo., est. 1843. Duke of Sussex, G. M., England, d. 1848. Bela Latham, P. G. C., Ohio, d.

Twenty-second.—

Twenty-third.—1350. Order of Garter inst. 1825. Lafayette visited G. L., La.

Twenty-fourth.—

Twenty-fifth.—1748. First Temperance Soc. Italy, est.

Twenty-sixth.—1838. Cor. stone Europa Light House, Gibraltar, pl. 1841. Cor. stone Literary Institute, Gravesend, England, pl.

Twenty-seventh.—1785. Prince Julian Maximilian, Brunswick, Ger., d.

Twenty-eighth.—1738. First Papal Bull against Fr. pub. 1783. Charter to Alexandria Lodge, Va. 1842. Cor. stone Rutherford Monument, Glasgow, Scotland, pl. 1852. Masonic Charity Ball, Dublin, Ireland. 1855. Hall, Clinton, Ky., ded.

Twenty-ninth.—1856. Hall, Benton, Ark., destroyed.

Thirtieth.—1733. Charter for Prov. G. L., Mass.

Each event above named has a strictly Masonic allusion.

MASONIC TALES.

Masonic tales and sketches, properly written, are not merely food for the passing appetite. They are the very corn of Nourishment, the wine of Refreshment, and the oil of Joy, to an informed Mason. They present under a vail, too dense for the blinded cowan, but transparent to the instructed eye, mighty truths. They convey fundamental principles, solemn and thrilling references to death, the resurrection and the judgment day. Like the inimitable parables of Scripture, they are vehicles for bearing to the mind the grandest ideas comprised in the Masonic philosophy. No other means, so elegant and sure, are given us for these purposes, as what is sometimes styled, *Masonic fiction.*

MISCELLANEOUS READING.

There are at least two good reasons for rejecting an applicant for Masonic privileges. 1st. A known want of qualifications, mental, moral and physical, on the part of the applicant. 2d. A want of information on the part of the brethren, as to his standing and antecedents. In the one case, *you know too much* to admit him; in the other, *you know too little.*.......A Committee is only the representative of the lodge, detailed for the performance of certain specified acts, and entrusted with sufficient power to perform them. They have no *rights* as a Committee, and are bound to make report at the next stated meeting after their appointment.......Five good precepts to write upon the memory are these : 1st. Pay your first homage to Deity. 2d. Our mother country is the *world.* 3d. Pity the erring. 4th. Be pious without bigotry or fanaticism. 5th. Love all men.

HISTORICAL AND STATISTICAL ITEMS.

The ancient craft of six hundred years "lang syne," were straitly enjoined in eight regulations, viz.: 1st. To be true to the King. 2d. To their Master. 3d. To one another. 4th. To use no foul or unfraternal epithets to one another. 5th. To do their work faithfully, and earn their wages honorably. 6th. To make their wisest man, Master. 7th. To allow reasonable wages to their employees. 8th. To assemble annually in Grand Communication.......In the Pennsylvania Chronicle for June 1st, 1767, published at Philadelphia, we observe " that Mr. Wall having been so unfortunate as to lose his chest, which contained near a thousand tickets, has been obliged to have a new set printed, on which are engraved the emblems of Masonry." ....Mahomet in his directions for the burial of the dead, followed the Masonic usage, in requiring that they be laid E. and W., but with the face turned to the N.......Eleven questions embracing a very extensive range of subjects, were adopted by the Anti-masonic Committee of investigation, appointed by the Legislature of Pennsylvania in 1836; of these the first six were substantially as follows : 1st. Are you a Mason? 2d. Did you take oaths or obligations? 3d. Can you repeat them? 4th. Did you ever know an affirmation substituted for an oath? 5th. Are all the Masonic obligations contained in Allyn's Ritual? 6th. Is Masonry the same everywhere ?

THE QUARRY OF LIFE.

Darkly hid beneath the quarry,
  Masons, many a true block lies;
Hands must shape and hands must carry,
  Ere the stone the Master prize.
    Seek for it—measure it—
    Fashion it—polish it—
  Then the Master will it prize.

What though shapeless, rough and heavy,
  Think ye God his works will lose?
Raise the block with strength he gave ye,
  Fit it for the Master's use !

Seek for it—measure it—
Fashion it—polish it—
Then the Master will it use.

'T was for this our Fathers banded—
  Through life's quarries they did roam,
Faithful-hearted, skillful-handed,
  Bearing many a true block home.
    Noticing—measuring—
    Fashioning—polishing—
  For their glorious Temple home.

INDIANA.—IOWA.—KANSAS.

INDIANA.—*Grand Lodge,* established 1818; has now 250 lodges, 8636 members. *Grand Chapter,* 1845; has 40 chapters, 1331 members. *Grand Council,* 1855; has 12 councils, 353 members. *Grand Encampment,* 1854; has 6 encampments, 260 members.

IOWA.—*Grand Lodge,* established 1844; has now 138 lodges, 3950 members. *Grand Chapter,* 1854; has 23 chapters, 643 members. *Grand Council,* 1857; has 5 councils, 154 members. *Grand Encampment,*   ; has 3 encampments, 145 members.

KANSAS.—*Grand Lodge,* established 1856; has now 23 lodges, 500 members.

UNIVERSAL MASONIC LIBRARY, Vol. VII.

The seventh volume of the series embraces two works: I. The Revelations of a Square, by GEORGE OLIVER, D. D., 328 pages. II. Introduction to Freemasonry, Anonymous, 87 pages. In all 415 pages.

THE AMERICAN LIBRARY AND MUSEUM.

A complete collection of the literature and publications of Masonry, enriched by copies of medals, seals and rarities, has never been undertaken in the United States, until within the last ten years. The projector is Mr. Rob Morris, of Louisville, Ky. Mr. Enoch T. Carson, of Cincinnati, Ohio, made the initiative in the matter, but on a smaller scale, and to him Mr. Morris is indebted for the original conception, which has resulted in his vast collections; but Mr. Carson's gatherings are comparatively few, though highly valuable, and his search is confined mainly to printed matter.

Mr. Morris began his collections in the winter of 1849, by securing a large number of the proceedings of the Grand Lodge and Grand Chapter of Mississippi, of which bodies he was then an officer. These were increased from time to time until 1853, when a conference with Mr. Carson set him upon the more extensive idea to which he has since been devoted. Since that period, in conjunction with such collectors as Mr. Carson, Dr. R. Barthelmess, Brooklyn, N. Y., Dr. A. G. Mackey, Charleston, S. C., Dr. Geo. D. Norris, New Market, Ala., Sidney Hayden, Athens, Pa., Rev. Salem Town, Aurora, N. Y., Joseph Covell, Jay Bridge, Me., Major W. J. B. McL. Moore, Ottawa, C. W., Dr. Alfred Creigh, Washington, Pa., William H. White, London, Eng., A. T. C. Pierson, St. Paul, Min., Michael Furnell, Limerick, Ireland, Geo. W. Chace, Haverhill, Mass., Dr. J. S. Reeves, McConnellsville, O., N. N. Barrett, Collinsville, Ct., A. W. Wilson, Pine Bluff, Ark., Wm. P. Preble, Portland, Me., L. S. Bancroft, Pepperill, Mass., J. B. Borden, Providence, R. I., together with the Grand Secretaries of the one hundred and twenty Grand Masonic Bodies of the United States and British Provinces, and other zealous friends, he has increased his accumulations to more than *forty thousand* articles of Masonic interest, large and small, and made a collection several times larger than any other, of a similar character, in the world. This, too, is daily increasing by gifts, purchases and exchanges, from every quarter.

The plan upon which this admirable effort is conducted, is so comprehensive and vast, that every lover of Masonic intelligence can take an honored part in it. Mr. Morris desires a copy of every edition of every Masonic work published; also a copy of the Constitutions, By-laws and Proceedings of every Grand Lodge, Grand Chapter, Grand Council, Grand Encampment, Grand Consistory, etc., at each of their meetings (whether stated or emergent) respectively; also of every Address, Sermon and Oration upon any department of Masonic science; also descriptions of all celebrations, festivals and obsequies of a Masonic character, or in which Masons took a part as such, whether published in pamphlet form, in newspapers, or remaining in manuscript; also the By-laws of every Lodge, Chapter, Council, Encampment. Consistory, etc., each edition published; also the printed forms of summons, diplomas, demits, etc., etc., as used by any Masonic body; also the proceedings and by-laws of Masonic Boards of Relief, Masonic Building Associations, and Masonic combinations of every sort. Also impressions of seals, medals, old and new, ancient diplomas and certificates, Masonic letters of early date, ancient regalia, engravings, portraits, and whatever else is hallowed by Masonic associations.

Beside this vast fund of books and relics now scattered through the world and esteemed of little value by their possessors, Mr. Morris seeks for everything upon the adverse side of the subject, as Anti-masonic books and journals, proceedings of Anti-masonic conventions, and the like.

For all donations, Mr. Rob Morris gives due credit to the donors in the *Voice of Masonry,* and will, if desired, exchange objects of similar rarity and value, or pay reasonable prices in money. As every intelligent Mason in the world is interested in an effort of this sort, it is hoped that the one hundred thousand readers of this *Almanac* will each contribute something of Masonic value, from a bound volume to a newspaper paragraph, and thus aid in the formation of a collection, which will be a monument of Masonic intelligence.

Address,   ROB MORRIS, LOUISVILLE, KY.

UNIVERSAL MASONIC LIBRARY, Vol. VIII.

The eighth volume of the series embraces two works: I. History of Initiation, by GEO. OLIVER, D. D., 234 pages. II. History and Illustration of Freemasonry, Anonymous, 91 pages. In all 325 pages.

5th Month. MAY, 1860. 31 Days.

MOON'S PHASES.

	D.	H.	M.
Full Moon,	5	1	54 mor.
Last Quarter,	12	2	8 eve.
New Moon,	20	1	38 eve.
First Quarter,	27	2	56 eve.

Sun on Merid.

D.	H.	M.	S.
1	11	56	52.85
9	11	56	12.20
17	11	56	8.84
25	11	56	41.52

MASONIC EVENTS.

EXPLANATION OF SYMBOLS.—□ Lodge; ⌒ Chapter; △ Council; † Encampment.

D. M.	D. W.	Sun's dec. N. ° ′ ″	Sun rises. H. M.	Sun sets. H. M.	Moon sets. H. M.
1	Tue.	+ 17 45	5 2	6 52	2 48
2	Wed.	15 35 35	5 1	6 53	3 17
3	Thu.	15 53 10	5 0	6 54	3 48
4	Fri.	16 10 29	4 59	6 55	4 22
5	Sat.	16 27 32	4 58	6 56	4 55
6	Sun.	16 44 18	4 57	6 57	rises.
7	Mon.	17 0 49	4 55	6 58	10 5
8	Tue.	17 17 2	4 54	6 59	10 59
9	Wed.	17 32 58	4 53	7 0	11 44
10	Thu.	17 48 37	4 52	7 1	morn.
11	Fri.	18 3 58	4 51	7 2	0 17
12	Sat.	18 19 1	4 50	7 3	0 48
13	Sun.	18 33 45	4 49	7 4	1 15
14	Mon.	18 48 11	4 48	7 5	1 38
15	Tue.	19 2 17	4 48	7 6	2 0
16	Wed.	19 16 5	4 47	7 6	2 22
17	Thu.	19 29 32	4 46	7 7	2 47
18	Fri.	19 42 41	4 45	7 8	3 12
19	Sat.	19 55 29	4 44	7 9	3 42
20	Sun.	20 7 56	4 43	7 10	4 20
21	Mon.	20 20 4	4 42	7 10	sets.
22	Tue.	20 31 49	4 41	7 11	9 35
23	Wed.	20 43 15	4 41	7 12	10 26
24	Thu.	20 54 18	4 40	7 13	11 10
25	Fri.	21 5 0	4 40	7 14	11 45
26	Sat.	21 15 20	4 39	7 15	morn.
27	Sun.	21 25 18	4 38	7 16	0 18
28	Mon.	21 34 54	4 37	7 17	0 49
29	Tue.	21 44 8	4 37	7 18	1 17
30	Wed.	21 52 59	4 36	7 18	1 45
31	Thu.	22 1 27	4 36	7 18	2 15

1st. Grand □, Me., Portland; Grand †, Me., Portland.

2d. Grand △, Me., Portland.

3d. Grand ⌒, Cal., Sacramento.

8th. Grand □, Cal., Sacramento; Grand ⌒, Ct., New Haven; Grand △, Ct., New Haven.

8th. Grand □, Ct., New Haven.

10th. Grand †, Ct., New Haven.

14th. Grand □, Md., Sem. An., Baltimore.

15th. Sup. Council △, North Juris., Boston, Mass.

21st. Grand ⌒, Pa., Q. C., Philadelphia.

22d. Grand ⌒, Ind., Indianapolis; Grand △, Ind., Indianapolis.

24th. Grand ⌒, Mo., St. Louis.

28th. Grand □, R. I.; Grand □, Ind., Indianapolis; Grand □, Mo., St. Louis.

Lodges should hold meetings for purposes of instruction, and at least as frequently as four or five times a year.

EARS OF CORN NEAR THE WATER FORD.

"The statue which enchants the world" lies within the block. The statuary's part is but to remove the superfluities. So within many a mass incrusted with warts and knobs and unsightly excrescences, lies a noble soul, fit for the highest place of Masonic honor and usefulness. It is but to apply vigorously, but skillfully, first the common gavel, after that the chisel.......Nothing will induce a favorable estimate of Freemasonry among a community, like the dissemination of good, sound Masonic literature. 

MAY.

CHRONOLOGICAL EVENTS OF THIS MONTH.

FIRST.—1769. Wellington b. 1775. Cor. stone Fr. Hall, London, Eng., pl. 1782. Duke Cumberland, G. M., England. 1808. G. Ch., Va., est. 1847. Cor. stone Smithsonian Ins., Washington, D. C., pl. 1848. Mas. Signet, St. Louis, Mo., est. 1854. Hall, Bristol, Pa., ded.

SECOND.—1775. Duchess Bourbon, Grand Mistress Ad. Rite, France. 1777. Daniel Wooster, G. M., Ct., killed. 1859. First Ses. Mas. School Instruction, Louisville, Ky.

THIRD.—1806. Conv. Norfolk to est. G. Ch., Va. 1855. G. C., Me., est.

FOURTH.—1813. J. S. Reeves b. 1825. Lafayette vis. G. L., Tenn.

FIFTH.—1758. Pope Benedict 14th d. 1821. Napoleon d. 1841. Cor. stone New Museum, Perth, Scotland, pl. 1852. Cor. stone Scotch Presb. Church, Ceylon, pl. 1856. G. Encpt., Me., est.

SIXTH.—1776. Conv. Williamsburg to est. G. L., Va.

SEVENTH.—1835. James Hogg, the Ettrick Shepherd, init. 1856. Wm. C. Dawson, G. M., Ga., d.

EIGHTH.—1843. Conv. Baltimore, Md., to est. unif. work.

NINTH.—1822. First Nat. Mas. Conv., Washington, D. C.

TENTH.—

ELEVENTH.—1838. G. L., Texas, est. 1846. Conv. Winchester, Va., to est. unif. work. 1851. Wm. Page, D. G. M., D. C., d. 1853. Grand Mas. Dem., Tippecanoe, Ind.

TWELFTH.—1310. Fifty-four Knights Templar burnt at Paris, France. 1797. Conv. at Philadelphia to est. G. Encpt., Penn. 1822. James L. Orr b.

THIRTEENTH.—

FOURTEENTH.—1801. Cor. stone Wet Docks, Leith, Scotland, pl.

FIFTEENTH.—1854. G. Encpt., Ind., est.

SIXTEENTH.—1843. Cor. stone New Colonial Buildings, Pr. Edwd's Is., pl. 1852. John Snow, P. G. M., Ohio, d. 1854. G. Encpt., Ind., est.

SEVENTEENTH.—1798. G. Ch., Ct., est.

EIGHTEENTH.—1846. G. Ch., Miss., est. 1850. Cor. stone New Church, Heptonstall, Eng., pl. 1858. Cor. stone Custom House, Detroit, Mich., pl.

NINETEENTH.—1797. G. Encpt., Penn., est. 1823. Conv. Mobile to est. G. Ch., Ala. 1857. Wm. H. Earl, P. G. M., N. J., d.

TWENTIETH.—1780. Henry Price, P. Prov. G. M., Mass., d. 1829. Eli Bruce incarcerated. 1834. Lafayette d. 1850. Winslow Lewis, Sen., d. 1852. Cor. stone Hall, Little Rock, Ark., pl. 1858. Cor. stone Arsenal, Dunkirk, N. Y., pl.

TWENTY-FIRST.—1838. Earl of Dalhousie, P. G. M., Scotland, d.

TWENTY-SECOND.—1853. American Freemason, Louisville, Ky., est.

TWENTY-THIRD.—1776. Fr. Hall, London, Eng., ded. 1844. Benj. B. Appleton d. 1859. Geo. Breckenridge, P. G. M., Ky., d.

TWENTY-FOURTH.—1530. Malta occupied by Knights of Rhodes. 1854. Cor. stone Hall, Gordonsville, Ky., pl. 1857. Chas. S. Frailey, P. G. M., D. C., d.

TWENTY-FIFTH.—

TWENTY-SIXTH.—1790. Israel Putnam d. 1858. Cor. stone Custom H., N. H., pl.

TWENTY-SEVENTH.—

TWENTY-EIGHTH.—1850. J. Newland Maffit d.

TWENTY-NINTH.—1812. G. Ch., S. C., est. 1851. Grand Hall, Indianapolis, Ind., ded.

THIRTIETH.—1810. Wm. Ball, P. G. M., Pa. d. 1832. Temple, Boston, Mass., ded.

THIRTY-FIRST.—1801. Sup. Council, 33° South. Juris., est. at Charleston, S. C.

Each event above named has a strictly Masonic allusion.

DUTIES OF A MASON TO HIS BROTHER.

None have stated the duties of Masonry more clearly and succinctly than DeWitt Clinton. In 1793, he said, " A Mason is bound to consult the happiness and to promote the interests of his Brother; to avoid everything offensive to his feelings; to abstain from reproach, censure, and unjust suspicions; to warn him of the machinations of his enemies; to advise him of his errors; to advance the reputation and welfare of his family; to protect the chastity of his house; to defend his life, his property, and what is dearer to a man of honor, his character against unjust attacks; to relieve his wants and his distress; to instil into his mind proper ideas of conduct in the department of life which he is called to fill; and let me add, to foster his schemes of interest and promotion, if compatible with the paramount duties a man owes to the community."

MISCELLANEOUS READING.

The cable tow of a Mason is the three-twist cord of Brotherly Love, Relief, and Truth. Each strand represents a class of duties essentially sacred in its character.......Every Mason has a perfect right, in which he is not in the least restricted by the action of Grand or Subordinate Lodges, to receive and impart whatever side or honorary degrees he may think proper.......The most politic and sensible method of work is to confer the degrees of Masonry upon only one candidate at a time. This is the usage in nine-tenths of the lodges in this country, and is founded in the philosophy of the institution.

HISTORICAL AND STATISTICAL ITEMS.

A lodge in Germany, famed for its devotion to charity, sustained the charge of educating, during five years, eleven hundred children.......The records of the Provincial Grand Lodge, of which Gen. Warren was for six years Grand Master, prove that in all that period, though much engaged in professional and much in political pursuits, he was never once absent from its assemblages.......January 10, 1740, seven Masons united in the island of Barbadoes, and organized a lodge, the first in that region of the earth.......The records of Cannongate Kilwinning lodge, Edinburgh, Scotland, in allusion to the election of Robert Burns as an honorary member, describes him as " A great poetic writer, and well known from a late publication of his works, which have been universally commended.".......The first masonic work ever published in America was printed by Bro. Benjamin Franklin, in 1734. It was the Masonic Book of Constitutions, and published by that zealous brother on his own account.

ASK! SEEK!! KNOCK!!!

Ask, and ye shall receive! Seek, and ye shall find!! Knock, and it shall be opened unto you!!!

Ask, and ye shall receive:
 Seek, ye shall surely find:
Knock, ye shall no resistance meet,
 If come with ready mind.
For all that ask, and ask aright,
Are welcome to our lodge to-night.

Lay down the bow and spear:
 Resign the sword and shield:
Forget the arts of warfare here,
 The arms of peace to wield.
For all that seek, and seek aright,
Are welcome to our lodge to-night.

Bring hither thoughts of peace:
 Bring hither words of love:
Diffuse the pure and holy joy
 That cometh from above.
For all that knock, and knock aright,
Are welcome to our lodge to-night.

Ask help of Him that's high:
 Seek grace of Him that's true:
Knock patiently, the hand is nigh,
 Will open unto you.
For all that ask, seek, knock, aright,
Are welcome to our lodge to-night.

KENTUCKY.–LOUISIANA.–MAINE.

Kentucky.—*Grand Lodge*, established 1800; has now 307 lodges, 11,500 members. *Grand Chapter*, 1817; has now 68 chapters, 1661 members. *Grand Council*, 1827; has now 26 councils, 781 members. *Grand Encampment*, 1847; has now 9 encampments, 365 members. *Grand Consistory*, 1852; has now 25 members; no subordinate bodies.

Louisiana.—*Grand Lodge*, established 1812; has now 112 lodges, 4000 members. *Grand Chapter*, 1848; has now 20 chapters, 700 members. *Grand Council*, 1856; has now 4 councils, 165 members. *Grand Consistory*, ; has now members, subordinate bodies.

Maine.—*Grand Lodge*, established 1820; has now 93 lodges, 3391 members. *Grand Chapter*, 1821; has now 11 chapters, 550 members. *Grand Council*, 1855; has 7 councils, 155 members. *Grand Encampment*, 1852; has 4 encampments, 148 members.

UNIVERSAL MASONIC LIBRARY, Vol. IX.

The ninth volume of the series embraces three works: I. The Constitutions of the Grand Lodge of England, 92 pages. II. The Constitutions of the Grand Lodge of Ireland, 91 pages. III. The Constitutions of the Grand Lodge of Scotland, 117 pages. In all 300 pages.

THE ANCIENT AND ACCEPTED RITE, S. J.

The names of the Thirty-Three Degrees of this Rite, as worked in the Southern Jurisdiction of the United States, are thus given: 1st. Entered Apprentice. 2d. Fellow Craft. 3d. Master Mason. 4th. Secret Master. 5th. Perfect Master. 6th. Confidential Secretary. 7th. Provost and Judge. 8th. Intendant of the Buildings. 9th. Knight Elu of Nine. 10th. Illustrious Elu of Fifteen. 11th. Prince Ameth, or Sublime Elu of Twelve. 12th. Grand Master Architect. 13th. Royal Arch. 14th. Grand Elect, Perfect and Sublime Mason. 15th. Knights of the Sword, of the East or of the Eagle. 16th. Prince of Jerusalem. 17th. Knight of the East and West. 18th. Knight, or Sovereign Prince of Rose Croix of Heredon. 19th. Grand Pontiff, or Sublime Scotch Mason. 20th. Venerable Grand Master of all Symbolical Lodges, or Master *ad vitam*. 21st. Noachite, or Prussian Knight. 22d. Knight of the Royal Axe, or Prince of Libanus. 23d. Chief of the Tabernacle. 24th. Prince of the Tabernacle. 25th. Knight of the Brazen Serpent. 26th. Prince of Mercy, or Scotch Trinitarian. 27th. Knight Commander of the Temple, or Teutonic Knight of the House of St. Mary of Jerusalem. 28th. Knight of the Sun, or Knight Adept. 29th. Grand Ecossais of St. Andrew, or Patriarch of the Crusades. 30th. Knight Kadosh. 31st. Grand Enquiring Commander. 32d. Sublime Prince of the Royal Secret. 33d. Grand Inspectors General.

This Order, which was first introduced into the United States at Charleston, S. C., has recently revived, and is rapidly diffusing itself through the South. The gentlemen who have received the 33d and last Degree, and who form the Supreme Council, S. J., are Albert Pike, Ark.; Albert G. Mackey, S. C.; Chas. M. Furman, S. C.; Achille Le Prince, S. C.; Jno. H. Honour, S. C.; Wm. S. Rockwell, Ga.; Jno. R. McDaniel, Va.; C. Samory, Va.; C. Laffon, La.; Fred. Webber, Ky.; B. R. Campbell, S. C.; A. Ramsay, S. C.; Henry Buist, S. C.; Charles Scott, Tenn.: James Penn, Tenn.

MEMORABILIA.

There are still three Mark Lodges in Penn., and these are all that are left of the great number at work in the early part of this century.......The whole expense of building the Temple of Solomon is estimated by Prideaux at the almost incomprehensible figures of $4,000,000,000. .....The Grand Convocation at York, under Prince Edwin, of which so much is said in the Masonic records, was held in the year 930, A. D.......The Koran of Mahomet contains 114 chapters. It is well worthy the perusal of every Mason.......The first Mormon lodge at Nauvoo, was established in 1842.

MASONIC RULINGS.

Degree of P. M. is conferred with equal propriety by a Royal Arch Chapter, or a Convocation of three or more Past Masters.......Reception of petitions and ballotings can only be done at stated meetings.......Lodges can only discipline their own members or non-affiliated Masons within their own jurisdiction.......The veto of a member upon a petition is absolute; no process can introduce the petitioner against the will of a member. That veto may be expressed orally, (privately to a member,) or by the ballot.......Masons can not be members of two or more chartered lodges at a time, but lodges U. D. do not rank as chartered lodges.......A lodge may refuse to grant demits at discretion, being only amenable to the G. L. for refusal.......Public exhibitions of the craft should relate to business purely Masonic.......No lodge can be opened in the absence of the Holy Scriptures, and the other lights; the Charter and the By-laws.......The Master should have the By-laws of his lodge perfectly committed to memory.......The loss of a Charter, whether by accident or theft, renders the lodge incapable of work. Should it proceed with further labor it would be clandestine.

UNIVERSAL MASONIC LIBRARY, VOL. X.

The tenth volume of the series embraces two works: I. Theocratic Philosophy of Masonry, by GEORGE OLIVER, D. D., 205 pages. II. Signs and Symbols of Masonry, by GEO. OLIVER, D. D., 184 pages. In all 389 pages.

6th MONTH.   JUNE, 1860.   30 DAYS.

MOON'S PHASES.

	D.	H.	M.
Full Moon,	3	11	38 mor.
Last Quarter,	11	7	56 mor.
New Moon,	19	0	15 mor.
First Quarter,	25	7	28 eve.

Sun on Merid.

D.	H.	M.	S.
1	11	57	35.18
9	11	58	59.11
17	12	0	39.07
25	12	2	22.91

MASONIC EVENTS.

EXPLANATION OF SYMBOLS.—□ Lodge; ⌒ Chapter; △ Council; † Encampment.

4th. Grand ⌒, N. C.

5th. Grand †, Mich., Detroit; Grand □, Iowa, Burlington; Grand □, N. Y., New York.

6th. Grand □, N. B., Q. C., St. John.

7th. Grand †, Ky., Lexington.

11th. Grand ⌒, N. H., Concord; Grand □, Texas; Grand □, Oregon.

12th. Grand □, Nebraska; Grand □, N. H., Concord; Grand □, Wis., Milwaukee.

13th. Grand □, Mass., Q.C., Boston.

27th. Grand □, Del., Wilmington.

D. M.	D. W.	Sun's decl. N. ° ′ ″	Sun Rises. H. M.	Sun Sets. H. M.	Moon Sets. H. M.
1	Fri.	+ 9 32	4 36	7 19	2 51
2	Sat.	22 17 14	4 36	7 19	3 28
3	Sun.	22 24 33	4 36	7 20	4 13
4	Mon.	22 31 28	4 35	7 21	rises.
5	Tue.	22 38 0	4 35	7 21	9 35
6	Wed.	22 44 8	4 35	7 22	10 15
7	Thu.	22 49 52	4 34	7 22	10 51
8	Fri.	22 55 13	4 34	7 23	11 15
9	Sat.	23 0 9	4 34	7 23	11 38
10	Sun.	23 4 41	4 34	7 24	morn.
11	Mon.	23 8 48	4 34	7 24	0 1
12	Tue.	23 12 31	4 34	7 25	0 23
13	Wed.	23 15 50	4 34	7 25	0 45
14	Thu.	23 18 44	4 34	7 26	1 10
15	Fri.	23 21 13	4 34	7 26	1 38
16	Sat.	23 23 18	4 34	7 26	2 11
17	Sun.	23 24 58	4 34	7 27	2 53
18	Mon.	23 26 12	4 34	7 27	3 41
19	Tue.	23 27 3	4 34	7 28	sets.
20	Wed.	23 27 27	4 34	7 28	9 7
21	Thu.	23 27 28	4 34	7 28	9 46
22	Fri.	23 27 4	4 35	7 28	10 20
23	Sat.	23 26 15	4 35	7 29	10 51
24	Sun.	23 25 1	4 35	7 29	11 18
25	Mon.	23 23 22	4 35	7 29	11 47
26	Tue.	23 21 19	4 35	7 29	morn.
27	Wed.	23 18 51	4 36	7 29	0 16
28	Thu.	23 15 59	4 36	7 29	0 49
29	Fri.	23 12 42	4 37	7 29	1 25
30	Sat.	23 9 1	4 37	7 29	2 6

As a Mason is a person who both *knows* the right and *performs* it, it follows that, in strictness there can not be such a thing as a seceding or renouncing Mason. But no man with a soul and conscience in him ever did renounce Masonry.

Anti-masonry in blowing its blast, actually benefited the cause it assailed, for it blew away the chaff and thus purified the Order.

The more disinterestedly and tenderly we love another, the more unworthy we feel of that other's love.

EARS OF CORN NEAR THE WATER FORD.

The politics of Masonry are simple, easily defined, and yet of great importance. They consist in submitting patiently to legal authority, and conforming with cheerfulness to the laws and constitutions of the government set over you....... Among the writers who have given their pens to the exhibition of Masonic things, but one lady has made herself conspicuous, Miss C. M. Barber of Georgia, whose contributions to the Masonic press in the shape of Tales and Sketches form a most graceful and pleasing collection.

JUNE

CHRONOLOGICAL EVENTS OF THIS MONTH.

FIRST.—1793. Freemason's Magazine, London, Eng., commenced. 1820. G. L., Maine, est. 1842. Cor. stone Royal Lunatic Asylum, Glasgow, Scot., pl. 1850. Mas. Union, (periodical,) Pt. Byron, N. Y., est. 1851. Mas. Temple, (periodical,) Carlisle, Pa., est.

SECOND.—1796. Columbian Hall, Boston, Mass., ded. 1827. G. Ch., Al., est. 1856. Mas. Pioneer, (periodical,) Montreal, C. E., est. 1858. Wilkins Tannehill, P. G. M., Tenn., d.

THIRD.—1816. Third Conv. G. G. Ch., U. S., New York.

FOURTH.—1846. Cor. stone Hall, Cincinnati, O., pl. 1852. Honorarium from G. L., N. Y., to Salem Town.

FIFTH.—1249. Battle Damietta, Egypt. 1820. Hall, Newcastle, Ky., ded. 1857. G. L., N. Y., cel. Obsequies E. K. Kane.

SIXTH.—1813. Capt. James Lawrence killed. 1855. N. B. Haswell, G. M., Vt., d. 1858. Wm. R. Lackey, G. Lect., Miss., killed.

SEVENTH.—1566. Cor. stone Royal Exchange, London, Eng., pl. 1856. Lodge No. 1, Washington, Del., cel. its 50th Anniv.

EIGHTH.—1825. Lafayette elected Hon. Mem. G. L., N. H. 1845. Andrew Jackson d. 1857. Mas. Congress, Paris, France.

NINTH.—1859. Daniel L. Potter d.

TENTH.—1819. G. Ch., N. H., est.

ELEVENTH.—1818. Conv. Hopkinton to est. G. Ch., N. H. 1821. Conv. Cahawba to est. G. L., Ala. 1840. Wm. Mercer Wilson init. 1844. Cor. stone C. H., Shelbyville, Ky., pl. 1856. Cor. stone Hall, Napanee. Canada, pl.

TWELFTH.—1798. Malta surrendered to the French. 1798. G. Ch., Mass., est. 1851. Cor. stone Church, Charlestown, Va., pl.

THIRTEENTH.—1855. Gov. James T. Moorhead interred, Frankfort, Ky.

FOURTEENTH.—1821. Conv. to est. G. L., Ala.

FIFTEENTH.—1849. James K. Polk d. 1859. Hall, Adams Fork, Ky., burnt.

SIXTEENTH.—1795. St. John's Lodge, No. 1, Newark, N. J., est. 1817. G. L., Mass., incorp. 1851. Cor. stone Temple, Louisville, Ky., pl. 1858. Cor. stone C. H., Vicksburg, Miss., pl.

SEVENTEENTH.—1775. Joseph Warren, Prov. G. M, North America, killed. 1783. Conv. Talbot C. H. to est. G. L, Md. 1825. Cor. stone Mon. Bunker Hill pl. 1843. Cor. stone Hall, Pulaski, Ky., pl. 1857. Statue of Warren, Bunker Hill, ded.

EIGHTEENTH.—1819. Moses Paul init.

NINETEENTH.—1740. Frederick the Great held his 1st Lodge, Berlin. 1792. Union of Masons in Mass.

TWENTIETH.—1764. Charter to est. Prov. G. L., Pa. 1816. G. G. En., U. S., est. 1823. Edict against Freemasonry, by King John of Portugal. 1837. William IV d. 1843. George Craghead d. 1851. Austin W. Morris, G. Sec., Ind., d.

TWENTY-FIRST.—

TWENTY-SECOND.—1850. Dabney Lipscomb d.

TWENTY-THIRD.—

TWENTY-FOURTH.—1502. Henry VII, G. M. England. 1719. Dr. Desaguliers, G. M. England. 1721. First Mas. work ordered printed. 1734. Charter to open First Lodge in Philadelphia, Pa. 1738. Duke de Antin, G. M. France, d. 1744. G. L., Berlin, Prussia, est. 1769. Joseph Warren, Prov. G. M., Mass. 1791. G. Conclave, England and Wales, est. 1811. Temple, Philadelphia, Pa., ded. 1816. Cor. stone, St. Paul's Ch., Providence, R. I., pl. 1841. Cor. stone Penitentiary, Halifax, N. B., pl. 1844. First Mas. Fest., Wisconsin. 1852. Cor. stone Capitol, Austin, Texas, pl. 1854. Cor. stone Hall, Brandenburgh, Ky., pl. 1854. Mas. Fest., Honolulu, S. I. 1856. G. Mas. Rally, Lodgeton, Ky. 1856. Temple, Chicago, Ill., ded. 1857. Cent. Cel. St. John's Lodge, No. 2, Providence, R. I. 1858. Richmond Encpt., Va., visited Bunker Hill. 1858. Cor. stone, Widows and Orphans Home, Pine Bluff, Ark., pl. 1859. 2d Sess. Mas. School Instruction, Harrodsburg, Ky. 1859. Cor. stone City Hall, Covington, Ky., pl.

TWENTY-FIFTH.—1791. G. L., R. I., est. 1819. Cor. stone, Asylum, Coasters Harbor, R. I., pl. 1827. Cor. stone G. Hall, Natchez, Miss., pl.

TWENTY-SIXTH.—1827. Hall, Pawtucket, R. I., ded. 1852. Cor. stone Institute Hall, Natchez, Miss., pl.

TWENTY-SEVENTH.—1098. Antioch captured. 1825. Lafayette elected Hon. Mem. by G. L., Del.

TWENTY-EIGHTH.—1822. Cor. stone City Hospital, Louisville, Ky., pl. 1826. G. L., Mich., est. 1845. Obsequies Andrew Jackson, by G. L., Mo.

TWENTY-NINTH.—1801. Cor. stone Bridge over Spey, Scotland, pl. 1852. Clay d. 1859. Obsequies Geo. Breckenridge, P. G. M., Ky.

THIRTIETH.—1842. Earl of Leicester d.

Each event above named has a strictly Masonic allusion.

WHY BELIEVE THE WORD?

Does any one ask, Why need a Brother pin his faith to Scripture? We answer: 1. Because without Scripture, Masonic traditions have no basis; Masonic morals no sanction. 2. Our profession of trust in God is scriptural. 3. Our means of recognition are scriptural. 4. Our prayers are scriptural. 5. Our chief light is the Scriptures. 6. The center of our gatherings and of our circuits is the Scriptures. 7. The most honored objects in our public displays is the Scriptures. 8. Our Master is bound to make the Scriptures the chief source of his instruction. Other reasons may be given, but surely these are enough.

MISCELLANEOUS READING.

A Journal devoted to Masonic intelligence should be entirely independent of local influences, yielding no deference to mere opinion, and none to precedent, only when sustained by fundamental reasoning, neither dictating, nor suffering dictation, and offering and receiving no crude theories.......It is the duty of Masons to throw the broad mantle of charity over the imperfections and frailties of their brethren, yet not to permit themselves to extend its ample folds for the purpose of screening those who have disgraced themselves, and disturbed the peace of society by their crimes.

HISTORICAL AND STATISTICAL ITEMS.

We are members of an association, consisting of 5000 lodges, and 200,000 members. These are select men, endowed with mental, moral and physical merits of a high order. They have come in "of their own free will and accord," having been subjected, upon their application, to the most rigid scrutiny. They are bound in ties of an indissoluble character, with millions like them, who have gone to the celestial lodge above, where the Supreme Architect of the Universe presides. Is there not room for honest self-congratulation in the reflection "I too am a member of the Masonic Order!".......A lodge should never resolve itself into a "Committee of the Whole." Such an act virtually dissolves the lodge, and turns it, for the time being, into an unofficial convention of Masons.......The Ancient Charges of Masonry are above all Grand Lodges, and Grand Masters' edicts or control. They constitute the unchangeable and indisputable chart of Masonic government.

THE OLD-TIME FREEMASON.

Ho! Brothers of the mystic Tie,
  Come round me if you please;
Lay down the gavel and the square,
  And let the trowel cease;
The work may stop a little while,
  The Master will not blame,
While I from memory sing of one
  Right worthy of the name,—
    A true old-time Freemason
    They called him Washington.

When bloody war at foreign hands,
  His country threatened sore,
He thought it *right* to take the sword,
  And guard his native shore;
He stood where bravest hearts are found—
  He struck for liberty.
But when the conquered foeman sued,
  A man of mercy he!
    This true old-time Freemason
    The glorious Washington.

Of every superfluity
  His mind he did divest;
He would not set a timber up
  Unless it was the best:
He plumbed, and squared, and leveled well
  The blocks, and set them true,
Then turned his apron Master-wise
  And spread the mortar due!
    This true old-time Freemason
    His name was Washington.

Upon his girdle was no stain,
  His work had no defect;
The overseer accepted all,
  And nothing to reject.
He lived in peace with God and man,
  He died in glorious hope,
That Christ, the Lion, Judah's pride,
  Would raise his body up!
    This true old-time Freemason
    Our Brother Washington.

MARYLAND.—MASSACHUSETTS.—MICHIGAN.

MARYLAND.—*Grand Lodge*, established 1783; has now 37 lodges, 1779 members. *Grand Chapter*, (with District Columbia,)   ; has 5 chapters, 212 members.

MASSACHUSETTS.—*Grand Lodge*, established 1777; has now 99 lodges, 3960 members. *Grand Chapter*, 1798; has 19 chapters, 760 members. *Grand Encampment*, (with Rhode Island,) 1805; has 11 encampments, 560 members. *Grand Consistory*,   ; has 0 subordinates,   members.

MICHIGAN.—*Grand Lodge*, established 1826; has now 104 lodges, 4160 members. *Grand Chapter*, 1848; has 21 chapters, 800 members. *Grand Council*, 1858; has 4 councils, 130 members. *Grand Encampment*,   ; has 5 encampments, 217 members.

UNIVERSAL MASONIC LIBRARY, Vol. XI.

The eleventh volume of the series comprises the first volume of The Historical Landmarks of Freemasonry, by GEORGE OLIVER, D. D. 426 pages.

THE ANCIENT AND ACCEPTED RITE, N. J.

The names of the Thirty-Three Degrees of this Rite, as practiced in the Northern Jurisdiction of the United States, are thus given: 1st. Entered Apprentice. 2d. Fellow Craft. 3d. Master Mason. 4th. Secret Master. 5th. Perfect Master. 6th. Intimate Secretary. 7th. Provost and Judge. 8th. Intendant of the Building. 9th. Elect of Nine. 10th. Master Elect of Fifteen. 11th. Sublime Knight Elected. 12th. Grand Master Architect. 13th. Knight of the Ninth, or Royal Arch. 14th. Perfection; or Grand, Elect, Perfect and Sublime Master. These fourteen are conferred in Sublime Grand Lodges of Perfection.

15th. Knight of the East or Sword. 16th. Prince of Jerusalem. 17th. Knight of the East and West. 18th. Prince of Rose Croix of H. R. D. M. These three are conferred in Chapters of Rose Croix.

19th. Grand Pontiff. 20th. Grand Master *ad vitam.* 21st. Patriarch Noachite, or Chevalier of Prussia (Prussian Knight.) 22d. Prince of Libanus, Knight of the Ax. 23d. Chief of the Tabernacle. 24th. Prince of the Tabernacle. 25th. Prince of Mercy. 26th. Knight of the Brazen Serpent. 27th. Commander of the Temple. 28th. Knight of the Sun. 29th. Knight of St. Andrew. 30th. Knight Kadosch. 31st. Grand Inquisitor Commander. 32d. Sublime Prince of the Royal Secret. These fourteen are conferred in Grand Consistory of S. P. R. S.

33d. Grand Inspector-General. This is conferred in the council of G. I. G., 33°.

The Order in the Northern States is extending rapidly. There are Grand Consistories, 32° in Mass., N. Y., Ohio and Illinois The gentlemen who possess the 33° and last degree and form the Supreme Council, are Wm. B. Hubbard, Ohio; K. H. Van Rensellaer, Ohio; Giles F. Yates, New York; C. R. Stack weather, Ill.; Chas. W. Moore, Mass.; Edward A. Raymond, Mass.; Albert Case, Mass.; Simon W. Robinson, Mass.; Paul Dean, Mass.; Robt. P. Dunlap, Me.; A. B. Young, D. C.; Charles Gilman, Md.; John Christie, N. H.; J. J. J. Gourgas, N. Y.; Arch. Bull, N. Y.; Francis Turner, Ct.

SPECIFIC DUTIES OF LODGE OFFICERS.

On another page we give the specific duties of the Master of a Lodge, and here follow up the subject by presenting those of the other officers.

The *Senior Warden* is looked to, to exercise all the powers of the Master in his (the Master's) absence. To represent the Lodge in conjunction with the Master and Junior Warden in the Grand Lodge. To act on the standing Committee of Charity. To appoint the Junior Deacon, and to take charge of the brethren during hours of labor.

The *Junior Warden* is required to exercise all the powers of the Master, in the absence of the Master and Senior Warden. To represent the Lodge in conjunction with the Master and Senior Warden. To act on the standing Committee of Charity, and to take charge of the brethren during hours of refreshment.

The *Treasurer* must receive all moneys from the hands of the Secretary, keep just and regular accounts of the same, and pay them out by order of the Master with the consent of the Lodge. At the close of his official year, he must prepare full statements of his accounts and deliver them to the Lodge.

The *Secretary* must observe the Master's will and pleasure, record the proceedings of the Lodge, receive all moneys, and pay them to the Treasurer. Also attend trials and keep the proceedings thereof, furnish demits, etc., by order of the Lodge, prepare annual reports to Grand Lodge, act as librarian, etc., etc.

The *Senior Deacon* is to act as the Master's proxy in the floor work, give courteous reception to visitors, and wait on candidates.

The *Junior Deacon* must act as the Senior Warden's proxy in the floor work, and secure the Lodge.

The *Stewards* have charge of the property of the Lodge, furnish its lights and fuel, and attend to its cleanliness.

The *Tyler* tyles the door, serves notices, summonses, and the like, by Order of the Master.

The Lodge at its discretion may appoint supernumerary officers, such as *Chaplain, Marshal, Physician, Organist, Director of Ceremonies,* and the like, whose duties may be inferred from their titles.

In every Grand Lodge jurisdiction, the duties of the various officers of lodges receive shape and form from local legislation, therefore the sketch given upon this page must be construed subordinate to such regulations as may be made by competent authority.

UNIVERSAL MASONIC LIBRARY, Vol. XII.

The twelfth volume of the series comprises the second volume of Historical Landmarks of Masonry, by GEO. OLIVER, D. D., 450 pages.

7th Month.   JULY, 1860.   31 Days.

MOON'S PHASES.

	D.	H.	M.
Full Moon,	2	10	59 eve.
Last Quarter,	11	0	50 mor.
New Moon,	19	9	12 mor.
First Quarter,	25	0	32 mor.

Sun on Merid.

D.	H.	M.	S.
1	12	3	35.28
9	12	4	55.99
17	12	5	51.08
25	12	6	12.63

MASONIC EVENTS.

EXPLANATION OF SYMBOLS.— ☐ Lodge; ⌒ Chapter; △ Council; † Encampment.

11th. Grand ☐, Canada, Ottawa.

13th. Grand †, Canada, Ottawa.

D. M.	D. W.	Sun's dec. °	′	″ N.	Sun rises. H.	M.	Sun sets. H.	M.	Moon sets. H.	M.
1	Sun.	+	4	55	4	38	7	29	2	54
2	Mon.	23	0	26	4	38	7	29	3	48
3	Tue.	22	55	32	4	39	7	28	4	46
4	Wed.	22	50	15	4	39	7	28	5	46
5	Thu.	22	44	34	4	40	7	28	rises.	
6	Fri.	22	38	29	4	41	7	28	9	41
7	Sat.	22	32	0	4	41	7	27	10	3
8	Sun.	22	25	8	4	42	7	27	10	23
9	Mon.	22	17	53	4	43	7	27	10	46
10	Tue.	22	10	15	4	44	7	26	11	10
11	Wed.	22	2	13	4	44	7	26	11	38
12	Thu.	21	53	49	4	45	7	26	morn.	
13	Fri.	21	45	3	4	45	7	25	0	6
14	Sat.	21	35	54	4	46	7	25	0	42
15	Sun.	21	26	23	4	46	7	24	1	28
16	Mon.	21	16	29	4	47	7	24	2	21
17	Tue.	21	6	15	4	48	7	23	3	22
18	Wed.	20	55	38	4	49	7	23	sets.	
19	Thu.	20	44	41	4	49	7	23	8	18
20	Fri.	20	33	22	4	50	7	22	8	49
21	Sat.	20	21	43	4	51	7	21	9	19
22	Sun.	20	9	43	4	52	7	21	9	49
23	Mon.	19	57	23	4	53	7	20	10	25
24	Tue.	19	44	44	4	53	7	20	10	50
25	Wed.	19	31	44	4	54	7	19	11	24
26	Thu.	19	18	25	4	55	7	18	morn.	
27	Fri.	19	4	48	4	56	7	17	0	4
28	Sat.	18	50	51	4	57	7	16	0	50
29	Sun.	18	36	36	4	58	7	15	1	42
30	Mon.	18	22	2	4	59	7	14	2	38
31	Tue.	18	7	11	4	59	7	13	3	38

Try the tools to that unworthy applicant. Apply the twenty-four inch gauge; *he gives no part to God.* Lay the plumb-line; *he does not walk erect before God or man.* Put the square upon him; *there is no form that we should desire him.* Put the level; *would you share an equality with such a man!* Show him the ladder; *he has not mounted it. Faith itself, the lowest round, is too high for his strength.* Try the trowel; *does not the cement fail to adhere!* Cast him out among the rubbish.

The grand objects of **Masonry** are: to cause Jehovah's name to be honored, and his laws respected; to increase love and goodfellowship on earth; to cultivate the human intellect, and to lessen the hardships of the human lot.

"Masons never solicit any persons to become Masons."

"But I was solicited," said a drunken fellow present, "and after I had come among you, you turned me out!"

"Yours is the exception that proves the rule," was the ready answer, "and the trouble we had with you, proves the danger of varying from our principles!"

There are three prominent theories as to what Masonry is, and our best writers divide upon them. Some maintain it to be a system of morals, some a system of mutual relief, and some a system of esoteric knowledge. Better deem it *all three.*

The virtue of *Silence* was declared by Aristotle the most difficult thing to practice. St. Andrew placed it among the principal foundations of virtue.

The greatness of T. G. A. O. T. U. consists in his power and majesty, his authority and eternity, his omniscience, omnipresence and unchangeableness.

EARS OF CORN NEAR THE WATER FORD.

While engaged in watching the sea where the tide ebbs and flows twice in twenty-four hours, neither the mind nor the eye ever becomes weary. Each wave has some novelty, each waif cast at our feet is a wonder. Grandest symbol of immensity is that wide, wide sea!.......The best monument of the distinguished Mason DeWitt Clinton, was executed in bronze, by Henry K. Brown, of Brooklyn, N. Y. It is 10½ feet high. Its pedestal represents the great Erie Canal in different stages of construction.

JULY.

CHRONOLOGICAL EVENTS OF THIS MONTH.

FIRST.—1821. Mas. Miscellany, Lexington, Ky., est. 1847. Port Folio, Nashville, Tenn., est. 1857. Am. Quart. Review of Fmy., New York, est. 1858. Honararium to John Fitz Henry Townsend, Dublin, Ireland. 1859. Cor. stone German Lutheran Church, Augusta, Ga., pl.

SECOND.—

THIRD.—1840. Cor. stone G. Hall, Lexington, Ky., pl.

FOURTH.—1781. Robert Burns init. 1795. Cor. stone State House, Boston, Mass., pl. 1815. Cor. stone Washington Mon., Baltimore, Md., pl. 1825. Cor. stone C. H., Canandaigua, N. Y., pl. 1848. Cor. stone Nat. Washington Mon., Washington, D. C., pl. 1850. Cor. stone Hall, Pittsburg, Pa., pl. 1851. Cor. stone Capitol Extension, Washington, D. C., pl. 1856. Cor. stone Insane Hospital, Northampton, Mass., pl. 1857. Cor. stone Mon. Clay, Lexington, Ky., pl. 1857. Cor. stone new C. H., Canandaigua, N. Y., pl. 1859. Cor. stone Custom House, Dubuque, Iowa, pl.

FIFTH.—1829. Anti-masonic Conv., Montpelier, Vt. 1830. G. L., Fla., est. 1858. Cor. stone Academy for Blind, Macon, Ga., pl. 1858. Cor. stone new City Hall, Portland, Me., pl.

SIXTH.—1812. Conv. New Orleans to est. G. L., La. 1819. Thomas Smith Webb d. 1835. Chief Justice Marshal d.

SEVENTH.—1768. Thaddeus M. Harris b.

EIGHTH.—1789. G. L., Ct., est. 1789. Conv. Portsmouth to est. G. L., N. H. 1818. Cor. stone Mechanics' Relief Soc. Hall, Washington, D. C., pl.

NINTH.—1856. Hall, Nashville, Tenn., burnt.

TENTH.—

ELEVENTH.—1812. G. L., La., est.

TWELFTH.—1191. St. Jean D'Acre captured.

THIRTEENTH.—1846. Rob Morris passed and raised.

FOURTEENTH.—1846. Cor. stone University, Oxford, Miss., pl. 1858. Union Masons in Canada.

FIFTEENTH.—1099. Jerusalem captured by Crusaders.

SIXTEENTH.—1789. G. L., N. H., est. 1845. Cor. stone King Chapel, Brunswick, Me., pl.

SEVENTEENTH.—1841. Thomas Dibdin d. 1858. John A. Quitman, P. G. M., Miss., d.

EIGHTEENTH.—

NINETEENTH.—1810. Mas. Relief Board, Boston, Mass., est. 1855. Conv. at Niagara Falls, C. W., to est. G. L., Canada. 1859. Hall, Portsmouth, N. H., ded.

TWENTIETH.—1855. Michael Z. Kreider, P. G. M., Ohio, d.

TWENTY-FIRST.—1796. Robert Burns d.

TWENTY-SECOND.—1817. Mas. Hall in Exchange Coffee H., Boston, Mass., ded. 1827. Obsequies Samuel K. Woodson, P. G. M., Ky. 1858. Cor. stone Temple, Cincinnati, O., pl.

TWENTY-THIRD.—

TWENTY-FOURTH.—

TWENTY-FIFTH.—1314. Battle Bannockburn. 1842. Sir William Woods d. 1859. Third Sess. Mas. School Instruction, Maysville, Ky.

TWENTY-SIXTH.—

TWENTY-SEVENTH.—1818. Conv. Natchez to est. G. L., Miss.

TWENTY-EIGHTH.—1742. William Preston b. 1840. Lord Durham d. 1853. Hall, Leesburg, Ky., ded. 1854. G. Ch., Cal., est.

TWENTY-NINTH.—1820. Cor. stone 2d Presb. Ch., Washington, D. C., pl.

THIRTIETH.—1733. Prov. G. L., Mass., (St. John's,) est. 1841. Cor. stone, Meth. Church, Richmond, Ky., pl.

THIRTY-FIRST.—1783. G. L., Md , est.

Each event above named has a strictly Masonic allusion.

THE DEAD OF THE CRAFT.

The extrinsic interest given by Masonic associations to a corpse discovered floating in the river, is thus described in *The Life in the Triangle*—"that semblance of humanity, putrid and broken up as it is, and cast by its unknown murderer into the water-depths, as a useless thing, has become suddenly a thing of price. Suspended around its neck, and well-nigh hidden in the ruffles of the shirt, *a medal* is beheld, marked with divers emblems of great meaning to the initiate, while all other eyes only see the fatal wound through which life has leaked out."

MISCELLANEOUS READING.

An enraged Brother attacking a man in an ungovernable fit of passion, was stopped by two of the craft, who stepped between the parties. Both were men of low stature; he was tall; he was possessed of a cane and might easily have struck the object of his resentment; but the fear of inadvertently wounding a Brother restrained him, and he moved away.......In the current business of the lodge, in all ballotings, all elections, all appropriations of money, etc., every member is bound to vote, unless expressly excused by the lodge.......There are but three penalties known to Freemasonry, and all the allegations of its enemies further than these, are malicious falsehoods. They are reprimand, suspension, and expulsion.

HISTORICAL AND STATISTICAL ITEMS.

These thirteen traditions are common to the religious theories of nearly every nation in the world. They doubtless originated before the dispersion of Babel. 1st. The decimal system. 2d. Seven days to the week. 3d. The seventh part for the Sabbath. 4th. Sacrifices. 5th. Temples and altars. 6th. Places of refuge and sanctuaries. 7th. Tithes. 8th. Worshiping barefoot. 9th. Abstinence before sacrifice. 10th. A priesthood. 11th. Legal defilements. 12th. The deluge. 13th. The rainbow.......The sweet placid smile on the face of Brother ——, has become a feature there. It can never be effaced. It will remain when there is nothing above it but the coffin-lid, and the clods heaped over it. Is it any wonder that such a man controls his lodge with a power unknown to the wisest and strongest. What power has Masonic *law*, like the power of Masonic *love!*.......The larger part of the best Masonic literature is still concealed from the merely English reader, in the French and German tongues, especially the latter.

THE LOVING TIE.

The Loving Tie we feel,
No language can reveal,
'Tis seen in the sheen of a fond Brother's eye;
It trembles on the ear
When melting with a tear,
A Brother bids us cease to sigh.
Behold how good and how pleasant
For Brothers in unity to dwell!
As heaven's dews are shed
On Zion's sacred head—
The blessings of the Lord we feel.

'Twas at a sufferer's bed
Now moldering with the dead,
This *Bond*, ah, so fond, was discovered first to me!
I saw his dying eye,
Light up with speechless joy,
And I felt how fond that love can be.

I ever will proclaim
With gratitude the name
Of Him, the Divine, who has granted this to me,
That weary tho' I stray
O'er nature's rugged way,
I never, never, alone can be.

There 's some I know will smile
And others may revile;
'Tis so as we know with the evil heart alway—
But if I can but prove
Through life *a Mason's love,*
I little care what man may say.
Behold how good and how pleasant
For Brothers in unity to dwell!
As heaven's dews are shed
On Zion's sacred head—
The blessings of the Lord we feel!

MINNESOTA.—MISSISSIPPI.—MISSOURI.

MINNESOTA.—*Grand Lodge*, established 1853; has now 28 lodges, 1600 members.

MISSISSIPPI.—*Grand Lodge*, established 1818; has now 239 lodges, 9337 members. *Grand Chapter*, ; has 48 chapters, 1900 members. *Grand Council*, ; has 23 councils, 719 members. *Grand Encampment*, 1857; has 5 encampments, 218 members.

MISSOURI.—*Grand Lodge*, established 1821; has now 180 lodges, 6000 members. *Grand Chapter*, ; has 27 chapters, 1016 members.

UNIVERSAL MASONIC LIBRARY, Vol. XIII.

The thirteenth volume embraces five works: I. Stray Leaves from a Freemason's Note Book, Anonymous, 165 pages. II. Apology for the Order, Anonymous, 41 pages. III. The Masonic Schism, by GEORGE OLIVER, D. D., 46 pages. IV. Insignia of the Royal Arch, by GEORGE OLIVER, D. D., 35 pages. V. The Secret Discipline, Anonymous, 37 pages. In all 324 pages

TITULAR DIGNITIES.

The names of officers in the various Masonic bodies, although possibly, to the uninitiated, frivolous and ill-chosen, are selected with exact reference to the theory of their appointment, which has a reference equally exact to the general theory of the system upon which Masons work. There is nothing superfluous in our titular selections, if the general purpose of Masonry is admitted to be well chosen.

As considerable insight, of a lawful character, into the purpose of a Masonic Order may be obtained by examining its titles, we give them here in full, as used in the three Orders most common to this country:

SYMBOLICAL MASONRY (Lodges). 1st. Master; 2d. Senior Warden; 3d. Junior Warden; 4th. Treasurer; 5th. Secretary; 6th. Senior Deacon; 7th. Junior Deacon; 8th. Tyler.

CAPITULAR MASONRY (Mark Lodges). 1st, 2d and 3d, same as last; 4th. Master Overseer; 5th. Senior Overseer; 6th. Junior Overseer; 7th. Senior Deacon; 8th. Junior Deacon; 9th. Tyler. (Past Master Lodges.) 1st, 2d and 3d, same as last. (Most Excellent Master Lodge.) 1st and 2d, same as last. (Royal Arch Chapter.) 1st. High Priest; 2d. King; 3d. Scribe; 4th. Captain of Host; 5th. Principal Sojourner; 6th. Royal Arch Captain; 7th. Master 3d Veil; 8th. Master 2d Veil; 9th. Master 1st Veil; 10th. Tyler.

CHIVALRIC MASONRY (Knights of the Red Cross). 1st. Sovereign Master; 2d. Chancellor; 3d. Master of the Palace; 4th. Prelate; 5th. Master of Cavalry; 6th. Master of Infantry; 7th. Master of Finances; 8th. Master of Dispatches; 9th. Standard Bearer; 10th. Sword Bearer; 11th. Warden; 12th. Captain of Guards. (Knights Templar.) 1st. Commander; 2d. Generalissimo; 3d. Captain General; 4th. Prelate; 5th. Senior Warden; 6th. Junior Warden; 7th. Treasurer; 8th. Recorder; 9th. Standard Bearer; 10th. Sword Bearer; 11th. Warden.

THE EAVESDROPPERS.

A certain lodge had been excessively annoyed by a gang of loafers from a neighboring grogshop, who made it a practice to gather under the windows of the lodge so soon as the sound of the gavels was heard, and to remain there during the whole process of the meeting. This was annoying in the extreme, especially as the building was a low one, and in summer evenings it was necessary to leave the windows open. The interference with the work of the lodge was serious; raps became taps; lectures were delivered in whispers, and the whole ceremony was performed on tiptoe with signs and signals. Occasionally, in spite of every precaution, a word or sentence would escape above low breath, and be caught by the eavesdroppers, who would retail it as a gem of rare price.

All evils, however, submit to patient waiting. The Tyler, who was likewise Steward, who was likewise S. J. (Senior Joker) of the lodge, gathered up the spittoons one afternoon and emptied all their contents into a bucket: a frightful collection. This he set upon the window-sill behind the Master's chair, and waited. Some of the members, by strenuous rappings, called the loafers around, and when a considerable group was seen to be collected immediately underneath, the bucket was gently tilted over, to the inexpressible horror and disgust of those who received its contents. To the immense damage of eyes and clothing, the nauseous fluid found its way to its mother earth, but never more was the lodge annoyed with eavesdroppers.

MEMORABILIA.

In 1828 three mountebanks, who were strolling through the State of New York giving shows, which professed to be the Masonic ritual exposed, were imprisoned in Johnstown jail as vagabonds.......The Temple at Chicago, Ill., is 60 feet front, 80 feet deep, and 85 feet high.......The first instance on record of Expulsion for non-payment of dues, is that of the notorious Pritchard, in 1729. To revenge himself he published a professed exposition....... The oldest form of By-laws extant, offered as a model, is in Calcott's Disquisition, 1769.

UNIVERSAL MASONIC LIBRARY, Vol. XIV.

The fourteenth volume of the series comprises The Lights and Shadows of Freemasonry, by ROB MORRIS, 390 pages.

8th Month.   AUGUST, 1860.   31 Days.

MOON'S PHASES.

	D.	H.	M.
Full Moon,	1	0	25 eve.
Last Quarter,	9	4	15 eve.
New Moon,	16	5	12 eve.
First Quarter,	23	7	42 mor.
Full Moon,	31	3	49 mor.

Sun on Merid.

D.	H.	M.	S.
1	12	5	59.85
9	12	5	9.31
17	12	3	43.25
25	12	1	45.03

MASONIC EVENTS.

Explanation of Symbols.— □ Lodge; ⌒ Chapter; △ Council; † Encampment.

9th. Grand ⌒, Vt.
10th. Grand △, Vt.
15th. Grand ⌒, Iowa.
17th. Grand △, Iowa.
20th. Grand ⌒, Pa., Q. C., Philadelphia.

D. M.	D. W.	Sun's dec. ° ' "	Sun rises. H. M.	Sun sets. H. M.	Moon rises. H. M.
1	Wed.	+ 52 1	5 0	7 12	7 20
2	Thu.	17 36 35	5 1	7 11	7 43
3	Fri.	17 20 51	5 2	7 10	8 6
4	Sat.	17 4 50	5 3	7 9	8 27
5	Sun.	16 48 32	5 4	7 8	8 49
6	Mon.	16 31 53	5 5	7 7	9 11
7	Tue.	16 15 8	5 6	7 6	9 37
8	Wed.	15 58 2	5 6	7 4	10 4
9	Thu.	15 40 41	5 7	7 2	10 41
10	Fri.	15 23 4	5 8	7 1	11 18
11	Sat.	15 5 13	5 9	7 0	morn.
12	Sun.	14 47 7	5 10	6 59	0 10
13	Mon.	14 28 46	5 11	6 53	1 4
14	Tue.	14 10 12	5 12	6 57	2 9
15	Wed.	13 51 24	5 13	6 55	3 20
16	Thu.	13 32 23	5 14	6 53	sets.
17	Fri.	13.13 9	5 15	6 52	7 17
18	Sat.	12 53 42	5 16	6 51	7 47
19	Sun.	12 34 3	5 17	6 50	8 17
20	Mon.	12 14 12	5 17	6 48	8 48
21	Tue.	11 54 10	5 18	6 47	9 23
22	Wed.	11 33 56	5 19	6 46	10 3
23	Thu.	11 13 32	5 20	6 45	10 48
24	Fri.	10 52 57	5 21	6 43	11 37
25	Sat.	10 32 12	5 22	6 41	morn.
26	Sun.	10 11 16	5 23	6 40	0 32
27	Mon.	9 50 11	5 24	6 39	1 28
28	Tue.	9 28 57	5 25	6 37	2 33
29	Wed.	9 7 31	5 26	6 36	rises.
30	Thu.	8 46 2	5 26	6 34	6 9
31	Fri.	8 24 21	5 27	6 32	6 30

It may be looked upon as a requisition of common honesty, to say nothing of Masonic honesty, that when a man, who has long entertained a favorable opinion of Masonry, signs a petition, deposits a fee, and submits himself to the regulation of the Fraternity, he ought to receive all the light that belongs to him. Yet how many an initiate is dishonorably dealt with in this regard!

Nothing in modern politics is more likely than that the same dispute which kindled up the fire of the Crusades, the possession of the Holy Shrine, may be revived during the present generation, and result in a general war, in which Europe will meet Asia upon the plains of Esdraelon as so frequently before.

Freemasonry is a mystic science, wherein, under apt figures, select numbers, and choice emblems, solemn and important, naturally tending to improve the understanding, to mend the heart, and to bind us more closely to one another, are most expressly contained.

There is a providence directs our ends, and he "that will bring righteousness to the plummet," oftentimes has a use for men, bloodstained and abandoned as they are.

No obligation is binding upon a man who has not belief in Deity, and he who shows his disrespect to Deity by blasphemy, thereby proves his unbelief and his unworthiness to be made or retained a Mason.

It may be that a black ball is sometimes cast out of malice; but the white ball is oftener cast out of partiality, negligence or ignorance.

EARS OF CORN NEAR THE WATER FORD.

Genuine Masonry is loving, peaceable, unobtrusive. Its true spirit is pure as the dew of heaven, free and refreshing as its zephyrs. It is a divine manna for the clear-sighted to gather, every one according to his own eating, some more and some less.......Masonry has been termed the light that gleams in the dark places, that brings peace and joy to the disconsolate, that shines into the heart of the widow and fatherless. 

AUGUST.

CHRONOLOGICAL EVENTS OF THIS MONTH.

First.—1785. Cor. stone South Bridge, Edinburgh, Scotland, pl.

Second.—1858. G. Consistory, Ark., est.

Third.—

Fourth.—1753. Washington raised. 1804. James M. Howry b.

Fifth.—1813. Sup. Council, 33° North. Juris., est. at New York. 1820. Henry C. Lawrence b.

Sixth.—1812. Duke of Sussex, G. M. Grand Conclave, England and Wales. 1844. Grand Fete in honor of Burns, Ayr, Scotland.

Seventh.—1800. John B. Hammatt init. 1814. Twenty-five Freemasons incarcerated in Spain. 1845. Cor. stone Presbyterian Ch., Victoria, C. W., pl. 1850. G. Ch., Wis., est.

Eighth.—

Ninth.—

Tenth.—1854. G. C., Vt., est. 1858. G. En., Cal., est.

Eleventh.—

Twelfth.—1750. First Lodge in Mo. chartered. 1821. Freemasonry prohibited in Russia.

Thirteenth.—

Fourteenth.—

Fifteenth.—1738. Frederick the Great init. 1771. Walter Scott b. 1840. Cor. stone Monument to Walter Scott, Edinburgh, pl. 1842. D. S. Goodloe init.

Sixteenth.—1826. Cor. stone Temple, Wheeling, Va., pl. 1851. Conv. Oregon City to est. G. L., Oregon.

Seventeenth.—1786. Frederick the Great d.

Eighteenth.—

Nineteenth.—

Twentieth.—1737. The last Masonic meeting in Rome, Italy. 1835. Cor. stone St. Andrew's Chapel, Ashton, England, pl. 1852. G. Consist., Ky., 32° est. at Louisville.

Twenty-first.—1858. Francis J. Oliver, P. G. M., Mass., d.

Twenty-second.—1820. Cor. stone City Hall, Washington, D. C., pl.

Twenty-third.—1845. B. D. Crookshanks d.

Twenty-fourth.—1736. Wm. St. Clair resigned hereditary G. Mastership, Scotland. 1813. Wm. Mercer Wilson b. 1841. Theodore Edmund Hook d. 1842. Cor. stone St. James Church, Vandreuil, C. E., pl.

Twenty-fifth.—1818. G. L., Miss., est. 1845. Henry C. Lawrence init.

Twenty-sixth.—1848. Cor. stone Hall, Vicksburg, Miss., pl.

Twenty-seventh.—1797. Wm. C. Barker b. 1812. Obsequies Jos. H. Daviess, G. M., Ky. 1818. Prov. G. Ch., Upper Canada, est. 1855. Dempsey Carrell d.

Twenty-eighth.—1852. Hall, Alexandria, La., burnt.

Twenty-ninth.—1820. Henry Clay, G. M., Ky.

Thirtieth.—1835. William T. Barry d. 1842. Don Pedro Legayroy d. 1854. Code of By-laws (Morris) pub.

Thirty-first.—1818. Rob. Morris b. 1845. Mas. Congress at Steinbach, Ger.

Each event above named has a strictly Masonic allusion.

THE JURISPRUDENCE OF THE ORDER.

Masonic law has little of the republican or democratic spirit about it. All its greater principles, termed iu Masonic parlance, *landmarks*, and most of the minor details of its governmental polity, are provided to our hands, as they were provided to our fathers' hands ages since, in the traditions and publications of the Order. Of all the wrotched theories into which even some learned in the economy of Masonic government have been misled, none have been so pernicious in their results, as that assumption which places the original and sole authority of Masonic government *in the consent of the governed.* This error strikes a blow at the very base of the structure on which all government and order rests among men, *the inviolable sanctity of law.* It substitutes popular caprice for the authority of antiquity, and, perhaps, it is not too much to add, in view of the high and mighty purposes for which the Masonic institution was originally set up, *the authority of God.* It writes upon the sand of the wave-washed sea shore the laws which ought to be carved in the rock of eternal justice.

MISCELLANEOUS READING.

The Master of a lodge is responsible for his official acts to the Grand Lodge alone. He can not be subjected to discipline by the members of his own lodge, while he wields the gavel as their Master.......If a lodge seeks to swell its numbers, irrespective of mental and moral qualifications, W. being absent in the choice, there will be no B. W. and B. being absent, there can be no S., and thus the lodge will crumble and fall.

HISTORICAL AND STATISTICAL ITEMS.

Many pirates and freebooters among the Moors and Spaniards were Masons; that is, they had taken some of its covenants and learned some of its physical means of recognition. They were generally prompt to the signal of distress, and generous to a fault in dispensing charity to Brothers. But they were clandestine Masons, for they had never entered lawfully-constituted lodges, even as visiters, and only in a mutilated way understood and practiced the *art* of Masonry. Its *science* they never learned.

QUARRY, HILL AND TEMPLE.

Thine in the Quarry, whence the stone
For mystic workmanship is drawn :
    On Jordan's shore,
    By Zarthan's plain,
Tho' faint and weary, *thine alone.*
The gloomy mine knows not a ray—
The heavy toil exhausts the day—
    But love keeps bright
    The weary heart,
And sings, *I'm thine without decay.*

Thine on the Hill whose cedars rear
Their perfect forms and foliage fair :
    Each graceful shaft
    And deathless leaf,
Of Masons' love the symbols are.
Thine when a smile pervades the heaven—
Thine when the sky 's with thunder riven—
    Each echo swells
    Through answering hills,
My Mason prayer *for thee 't is given.*

Thine in the Temple, holy place—
Where silence reigns, the type of peace ;
    With grip and sign,
    And mystic line,
My Mason's love I do confess.
Each block I raise, my friendship grows ;
Cemented firmly ne'er to lose,
    And when complete,
    My work I greet,
Thine in the joy my bosom knows.

Thine at the midnight in the cave—
Thine on the floats upon the wave—
    By Joppa's hill,
    By Kedron's rill,
And *thine* when Sabbath rest we have.
Yes, yes, dear friend, my spirit saith—
I'm thine until and after death.
    No bounds control
    The Mason's soul
Cemented with a Mason's faith.

NEBRASKA.—NEW BRUNSWICK.—NEW HAMP-SHIRE.—NEW JERSEY.

NEBRASKA.—*Grand Lodge,* established 1857 ; has now 6 lodges, 140 members.

NEW BRUNSWICK.—*Provincial Grand Lodge,* established 1856 ; has now 22 lodges, 825 members.

NEW HAMPSHIRE.—*Grand Lodge,* established 1789 ; has now 39 lodges, 1800 members. *Grand Chapter,* 1819 ; has 6 chapters, 392 members.

NEW JERSEY.—*Grand Lodge,* established 1786 ; has now 52 lodges, 2204 members. *Grand Chapter,*   ; has 5 chapters, 178 members.

UNIVERSAL MASONIC LIBRARY, Vol. XV.

The fifteenth volume of the series embraces two works : I. The Ancient Charges and Constitutions, by WM. ANDERSON, 108 pages. II. History of Freemasonry up to 1829, by ALEX. LAWRIE, 203 pages. In all 311 pages.

THE SEALED CASKET.

An incorrigible joker, on his way to represent his lodge in Grand Lodge, in eccentric mood feigned deafness as he stepped into the stage, and great was the sport experienced thereby. At almost every town a new batch of passengers would be taken up, whom the Driver would notify that the old gentlemen was "deefer nor a post." The result was that they talked of the most confidential matters, as though none but themselves were present. A pair of lovers, a little on the other side of matrimony, gave him great amusement, especially when the female partner blushingly intimated, "'t would be necessary to borrow mammy's cradle at first!" A group of boarding school girls yielded a crowd of tender confidences.

But at last there entered a couple of delegates, bound like himself, to Grand Lodge, and one of them, regardless of the presence of the deaf old gentleman, asked the other to take advantage of the time, and give him some lectures. To this the elder made this striking reply : "I would n't utter the secrets of Masonry before him, if he were deaf, dumb, blind and drunk! I would n't lecture on the secrets of Masonry, in the presence of a corpse, though hermetically sealed in an air-tight coffin!"

RELIEF LODGES.

"To relieve the distressed is a duty incumbent on all men ; but particularly on Masons, who are linked together by an indissoluble chain of sincere affection. To soothe the unhappy, to sympathize with their misfortunes, to compassionate their miseries, and to restore peace to their troubled minds, is the grand aim we have in view. On this basis we form our friendships and establish our connections." This is the sublime lesson imparted to the Mason upon the first visit he pays the lodge. These precepts, expressed in the forcible language of Preston, are still further enforced in part, by a ceremonial admirably contrived to impress the duty of benevolence or almsgiving upon the young brother's mind. The whole leaves indelible traces of the Masonic chisel.

But how best, how most surely, how most systematically to do the work of charity,—how to avoid the impostors who swarm around us, while we neglect not the worthy poor who shrink modestly from our gaze—these are the problems which have exercised the minds of our wisest and most experienced, nor yet received a proper solution.

The most successful effort, however, yet set in motion, is the establishment of *Relief Lodges*, from which all the Masonic benefactions of a community may emanate, and whose experience in the examination of applicants will enable them to guard the Fraternity against unworthy objects. Of this sort are those now in existence in New Orleans, New York, San Francisco, St. Louis, Buffalo and Louisville, each established for the sole purpose of dispensing Masonic charity, in the most economical and systematic manner, and each having a history of its own, which affords encouragement for perseverance and imitation. The general plan involves a Committee of Examination, who look carefully into an applicant's antecedents and present condition ; a Financial Committee, who have an eye to judicious supplies of money for current demands, and stated reports to the lodges, etc., represented therein. The practical results are to lessen the number of impostors, draw larger sums from the purses of the Brotherhood, and suitably dispense them to the reduction of human misery, and the honor of the Masonic institution.

The millionaire, Stephen Girard, upon his death, (Dec. 26, 1831,) donated an amount which in a few years, by arrears of interest, made an aggregate of thirty thousand dollars, and which by his will he ordained as a perpetual fund, the interest upon which should be forever appropriated to the relief of distressed worthy Masons. This bequest yields an income of nearly three thousand dollars per annum, all of which is faithfully appropriated as designed by the giver.

MEMORABILIA.

The somewhat celebrated Mrs. Aldworth, "the female freemason," was born in 1731, died 1811.......Fannin who was butchered at Goliad, was Senior Deacon of Holland Lodge, No. 36, Houston, Texas.......In 1823 the Grand Lodge of Maine appointed a Committee to institute inquiries, whether any vestiges of Masonry were remaining in Palestine.

UNIVERSAL MASONIC LIBRARY, VOL. XVI.

The sixteenth volume of the series embraces two works: I. Masonic Sermons, by JETHRO INWOOD, B. A. 268 pages. II. Three Sermons, by WM. JOHN PERCY, M. A., 54 pages. In all 322 pages.

9th MONTH. SEPTEMBER, 1860. 30 DAYS.

MOON'S PHASES.

	D.	H.	M.
Last Quarter,	8	5	59 mor.
New Moon,	15	1	1 mor.
First Quarter,	21	6	17 eve.
Full Moon, ·	29	8	32 eve.

Sun on Merid.

D.	H.	M.	S.
1	11	59	39.92
9	11	57	0.49
17	11	54	13.05
25	11	51	26.36

D. M.	D. W.	Sun's decl. N. °	′	″	Sun Rises. H.	M.	Sun Sets. H.	M.	Moon Rises. H.	M.
1	Sat.	+ 2	33		5	28	6	31	6	53
2	Sun.	7	40	37	5	29	6	30	7	15
3	Mon.	7	18	33	5	30	6	29	7	39
4	Tue.	6	56	21	5	31	6	27	8	6
5	Wed.	6	34	3	5	32	6	25	8	36
6	Thu.	6	11	30	5	33	6	23	9	14
7	Fri.	5	49	8	5	34	6	21	9	57
8	Sat.	5	26	31	5	35	6	20	10	50
9	Sun.	5	3	43	5	35	6	18	11	51
10	Mon.	4	41	0	5	36	6	17	morn.	
11	Tue.	4	18	7	5	37	6	16	0	58
12	Wed.	3	55	10	5	38	6	14	2	10
13	Thu.	3	32	8	5	39	6	13	3	24
14	Fri.	3	9	2	5	40	6	12	sets.	
15	Sat.	2	45	58	5	41	6	10	6	13
16	Sun.	2	22	41	5	42	6	8	6	45
17	Mon.	1	59	25	5	43	6	6	7	20
18	Tue.	1	36	8	5	44	6	4	7	58
19	Wed.	1	12	48	5	45	6	5	8	42
20	Thu.	0	49	27	5	46	6	3	9	33
21	Fri.	0	26	4	5	46	6	1	10	27
22	Sat.	+ 2	40		5	47	5	59	11	25
23	Sun.	— 20	45		5	48	5	57	morn	
24	Mon.	0	44	9	5	49	5	55	0	26
25	Tue.	1	7	9	5	50	5	53	1	27
26	Wed.	1	30	59	5	51	5	52	2	26
27	Thu.	1	54	23	5	52	5	50	3	24
28	Fri.	2	17	46	5	53	5	48	rises.	
29	Sat.	2	41	8	5	54	5	47	5	20
30	Sun.	2	54	28	5	55	5	46	5	43

MASONIC EVENTS.

EXPLANATION OF SYMBOLS.—□ Lodge; ⌒ Chapter; △ Council; † Encampment.

4th. Grand ⌒, N. J., Trenton.

5th. Grand □, N. B., Q. C., St. John.

11th. Grand ⌒, Mass., Boston; Grand ⌒, R. I.

12th. Grand □, Mass., Boston.

25th. Grand †, N. Y.

Masonry does not undertake to follow a Brother beyond the boundaries of the grave. All that relates to his morals and behavior *here*, to his relations to God, his country and himself *here*, and to the disposition of his body both at its burial *here*, and at its certain resurrection hereafter, belongs to Masonry. But the flight of the soul, the future state—these are the themes of that higher, nobler branch, *Religion*.

There is an inexhaustible field for original research in our craft; every Mason who has given careful thought to the work and lectures, can communicate valuable deductions.

Take the Sabbath from the Calendar of a good Mason, and there is a long, dark, blank week. Religion decays; vice triumphs; the sense of duty vanishes; the acknowledgment, and even the remembrances of God fade away. Our ancient brethren consecrated this day, and there is no better evidence of the wisdom of King Solomon than the fact that they did so.

Nothing in the present aspect of Freemasonry appears more ridiculous to the discerning eye, than the wondrous diversity of costume worn in Masonic processions. What tastes are manifested! what want of all taste!

EARS OF CORN NEAR THE WATER FORD.

The symbolical adornment of a Lodge ceiling, is thus described: "The arched ceiling above the Master's chair is painted to represent *sunrise;* proceeding downward toward the center, *noon* is reached, and still further down it fades till *sunset* is represented, glowing with all its golden, crimson and purple splendor.......All instruction in Masonic matters should be based upon the antiquity and unchangeableness of the Institution; and this whether communicated by private lectures, public addresses, or by the aid of the pen. A thing is *right* in Masonry, because it is *ancient*.

SEPTEMBER.

CHRONOLOGICAL EVENTS OF THIS MONTH.

First.—1807. Cor. Stone North Pier, Frazersburg, Scotland, pl. 1819. Obsequies Thomas Smith Webb by G. L. and G. Ch., Ky. 1820. Am. Mas. Register, New York, est. 1836. Jacob Morton and Elisha W. King, P. G. Masters, N. Y., d. 1841. Grand Hall, Lexington, Ky., ded. 1855. Code Masonic Law (Morris) pub. 1855. Ashlar, Detroit, Mich., est.

Second.—1851. Cor. stone Hall, Detroit, Mich., pl. 1856. Grand Consistory, Ill., est.

Third.—1833. Cor. stone Jamaica St. Bridge, Glasgow, Scotland, pl.

Fourth.—1800. B. B. French b. 1809. Mas. Union, S. C. 1829. Fourth Con. G. G. En. and Sixth Con. G. G. Ch., U. S., New York.

Fifth.—1733. Wieland b. 1781. Prov. G. L., N. Y., est. 1789. Prov. G. L., N. Y., dissolved. 1850. Cent. Cel., Hiram Lodge, No. 1, New Haven, Ct.

Sixth.—1757. Lafayette b. 1826. Cor. stone Monument, Groton, Ct., pl.

Seventh.—1857. Univ. Masonic Library completed. 1858. G. Consistory, Ark., 32°, est.

Eighth.—1530. Turks retired from Malta. 1800. Conv. Lexington to est G. L., Ky.

Ninth.—1806. Luke E. Barber b. 1854. Edmund P. Hunter, G. M., Va., d. 1856. Thirteenth Con. G. G. En. and Fifteenth Con., G. G. Ch., U. S., Hartford, Ct. 1857. Honorarium to Wm. B. Hubbard, G. G. M. of G. G. En., U. S.

Tenth.—1761. Joseph Warren init. 1786. John J. Crittenden b. 1804. G. L., Mass., ceased numbering its lodges. 1814. D. T. Moussarrat b. 1844. Ninth Con. G. G. En. and Eleventh Con., G. G. Ch., U. S., New Haven, Ct. 1850. Eleventh Con. G. G. En. and Thirteenth Con. G. G. Ch., U. S., Boston, Mass.

Eleventh.—1826. William Morgan disappeared. 1848. First Lodge opened on Pacific coast. 1851. Cor. stone Court House, Chicago, Ill., pl. 1853. Conv. Lexington, Ky., to est. unif. work.

Twelfth.—

Thirteenth.—1753. Cor. stone New Ex., Edinburgh, pl. 1853. Twelfth Con. G. G. En. and Fourteenth Con. G. G. Ch., U. S., Lexington, Ky. 1858. Six hundredth Anniv. Ded. Salisbury Cath., England.

Fourteenth.—1815. Cor. stone Epis. Ch., Washington, D. C., pl. 1841. Eighth Con. G. G. En. and Tenth Con. G. G. Ch., U. S., New York.

Fifteenth.—1851. G. L., Oregon, est.

Sixteenth.—1819. Second Con. G. G. En., and Fourth Con. G. G. Ch., U. S., New York.

Seventeenth.—1677. Freemasons of England incorp. 1851. King of Sweden, Honorary Member G. L. Scotland. 1856. Cor. stone Custom House, Wheeling, Va., pl.

Eighteenth.—1793. Cor. stone Capitol, Washington, D. C., pl. 1826. Third Con. G. G. En. and Fifth Con. G. G. Ch., U. S., New York. 1852. Wellington d. 1855. Hall, Matagorda, Texas, destroyed by tornado. 1856. J. Worthington Smith, P. G. M., Va., d.

Nineteenth.—1826. Cor. stone Mas. Hall, Washington, D. C., pl.

Twentieth.—1854. Hall Preston Lodge, No. 281, Louisville, Ky., ded.

Twenty-first.—1832. Walter Scott d.

Twenty-second.—1841. Hall, Charleston, S. C., ded.

Twenty-third.—1847. Conv. Baltimore, Md. 1857. Conv. Omaha City to est. G. L., Neb.

Twenty-fourth.—1832. Eli Bruce d. 1858. Cor. state Ineb. Asylum, Binghampton, N. Y., pl.

Twenty-fifth.—1744. Fred. Wm. Second b. 1786. G. L., Penn., est. 1796. Geo. Craghead b.

Twenty-sixth.—1831. Ant. Mas. Conv., Baltimore, Md. 1842. Marquis Wellesley d. 1853. $1500 remitted to New Orleans and Mobile for charity, by G. L., N. Y. 1855. Temple, Philadelphia, Pa., ded.

Twenty-seventh.—

Twenty-eighth.—

Twenty-ninth.—1853. Mas. Cemetery, Santa Fe, N. M., ded. 1858. Stephen Lovell, P. G. H. P., Mass., d.

Thirtieth.—1826. Cor. stone Methodist Church, Pt. Gibson, Miss., pl. 1851. Remains Stephen Girard re-interred. 1856. Samuel Daviess, P. G. M., Ky, d.

Each event above named has a strictly Masonic allusion.

THE WORK OF THE APPRENTICE.

The Apprentice in moral Masonry has oftentimes much to accomplish. Many years may be required for the task. His means may be scattered as the cloud-waters are thunder-shaken upon the hills. Many a pang may selfishness and the remains of a corrupt nature give him, as he casts off, one by one, the vices and superfluities of life. Many a time will he be tempted to turn back, leaving the plow in the furrow. But the labor once accomplished, he shall be a glorious block, a shining ashlar, a living stone, fit for the MASTER'S use, fit for the MASTER'S honors. The reward is ample, even though the labor were doubly greater than it is.

MISCELLANEOUS READING.

In the social assemblages of the craft, what friendships are formed and sealed that defy the frosts of time! Nay more. If there be permitted within the precincts of the eternal world, remembrances of the happiest scenes in the world behind, something of it will be found even there, translated to heaven to bloom in perpetual green......The good have sought to imitate our society to do good; the evil its secresy to do evil; the persecuted have forged co-fraternal links which they hoped would be permanent—but all have been mistaken in the durability of their system. An *unknown ingredient* was wanting........The five-pointed star, as a Masonic emblem, is pregnant with all holy remembrances, all heavenly aspirations. No wonder it is so popular among Masons.

HISTORICAL AND STATISTICAL ITEMS.

The Eastern Star Degree, so popular in this country, is conferred upon the wives, widows, sisters and daughters of Master Masons. Any Master Mason, in good standing, has the power to confer it, but only to five or more ladies at a time. Its explanations are scriptural; its hues are blue, orange, white, green and red; its symbols a sword, sheaf, crown and scepter, broken column and clasped hands. The names of its several divisions are Jephthah's Daughter, Ruth, Esther, Martha and Electa. It is as pure and innocent in its principles as the blush of the new-blown rose........The Jews derived the punishment of the crucifixion from the Romans; Moses allowed no such barbarous lingering penalty in his criminal code. By it the victim died under the most frightful sufferings, often continued through twenty and thirty hours. It is natural that a Knight Templar should leave his Asylum with serious countenance, whose mind has been impressed with the story of tortures such as these.

WRITTEN IN HEAVEN.

Some years since, an English Brother, whose name is yet concealed, donated large sums to various Grand Lodges in the United States, to be by them distributed among the more needy lodges for purposes of charity.

Written in Heaven
What he has given!
Placed on the records in letters of gold ;—
Read by the spirits,
Judges of merits—
Some day the name to us all will be told.

Blest was the offering ;
Voices of suffering
Hushed under sympathy noble as that ;
Tear-drops were trailing—
Sighs and bewailing
And tear-drops and sorrow the orphans forgot.

Meantime let silence,
Free from all violence,
Drop its mute vail o'er the face of the man.
Seek not to show it—
Strive not to know it—
Go and do likewise, ye Brothers, who can.

England, our Mother,
Toward thee each Brother
Reverently turns at this noble emprise ;
" *This* makes the cable
Holy and stable,
Binding our lodges forever," he cries.

NEW YORK.—NORTH CAROLINA.—OHIO.

NEW YORK.—*Grand Lodge*, established 1787 ; has now 413 lodges, 32,817 members. *Grand Chapter*,   ; has 88 chapters, 2117 members. *Grand Council*, 1854 ; has 5 councils, 200 members. *Grand Encampment*, 1814 ; has 24 encampments, 1000 members. *Grand Consistory*, 0 ; subordinates,   members.

NORTH CAROLINA.—*Grand Lodge*, established 1787 ; has now 127 lodges, 5800 members. *Grand Chapter*,   ; has   chapters,   members.

OHIO.—*Grand Lodge*, established 1809 ; has now 284 lodges, 12,000 members. *Grand Chapter*,   ; has 76 chapters, 3000 members. *Grand Council*,   ; has 33 councils. 1107 members. *Grand Encampment*,   ; has 15 encampments, 722 members. *Grand Consistory*,   ; has 0 subordinates,   members.

UNIVERSAL MASONIC LIBRARY, Vol. XVII.

The seventeenth volume of this series embraces The Principles of Masonic Law, by A. G. MACKEY, M. D., 371 pages.

A VIGILANT POLICEMAN.

I had been to my lodge that night until a late hour, and was returning with some Masonic books in a small pasteboard box. Passing up the Bowery at a quick step, I was accosted nearly opposite the old theater by a wide-awake policeman, with a "Halloo! what you got there?" "Some books," said I, "that I brought from Bleecker street." "Ah! but this is not the right direction if you came from Bleecker street." "Yes, but I was taking them back again," responded I, as demurely as I could. "Well, set them down, and let me look at them."

I deposited the box on the railroad track, and with apparent unwillingness took off the lid. "What sort of a book is this?" asked watchy, picking up an elegantly embossed and gilt volume, and trying to make out the title by the gaslight. "It's a manual," said I. "A manual of what? What sort of a manual?" asked he. "A manual of Freemasonry," I returned; "a book to teach Masonry." "Oh! a Masonic book, is it?" said he, gyrating his fins as if something hurt him. "Just so," answered I, gyrating my own in kindred style. "And what's it worth?" asked the policeman, putting one in his pocket with one hand, and hauling out his purse with the other. "One dollar only," said I, shutting up my box, and putting it under my arm. "Here's your change," said the good fellow, turning away. And that's the last I ever saw of him.

GOVERNING BODIES.

There are at this time one hundred and fifteen Grand or Governing Bodies of Masons in the United States and British provinces, viz:

Grand Encampment of the United States	1
Grand Royal Arch Chapter of the United States	1
Supreme Council, 33° A. and A. R., South. Juris.	1
" " " North. "	1
Grand Consistories (N. Y., O., La., Ark., Ky., Ill.)	6
Grand Encampments (Cal., Can., Conn., Ill., Ind., Ky., Me., Mass., Mich., Miss., N. Y., O., Pa., Texas, Vt., Va.)	19
Grand Councils, Royal and Select Masters, (Ala., Cal., Conn., Fla., Ga., Ill., Ind., Iowa, Ky., La., Mo., Mich., Miss., N. H., N. Y., O., Pa., Tenn., Texas, Vt.)	16
Grand Chapters, (Ala., Ark., Cal., Can., Conn., Fla., Ga., Ill., Ind., Iowa, Ky., La., Me., Mass., Md., Mich., Miss., Mo., N. H., N. J., N. Y., N. C., O., Pa., R. I., S. C., Tenn., Texas, Vt., Va., Wis.)	31
Grand Lodges, (Ala., Ark., Cal., Can., Conn., Del., D. C., Fla., Ga., Ill., Ind., Iowa, Kansas, Ky., La., Me., Md., Mass., Mich., Minn., Miss., Mo., N. B., Neb., N. H., N. J., N. Y., N. C., O., Or., Pa., R. I., S. C., Tenn., Texas, Vt., Va., W. Ter., Wis.)	39
Total	115

Besides these, there are Grand Councils of High Priesthood in various States (as Ohio, Kentucky, etc.,) but as these have no subordinates, they are not ranked among the governing or supreme bodies.

The subordinate lodges, chapters, councils, etc., under the jurisdiction of these 116 powers, form an aggregate of 5,300.

MEMORABILIA.

Previous to 1854, the Masons of Sacramento City had given in charity more than $50,000.......Lewis Cass was D. G. M. of Ohio 1809; G. M. Ohio 1810, 1811, and 1812; G. M. Michigan 1827.......The Masonic Hall at Muscatine, Iowa, is four stories high, and thirty by eighty-five feet in dimensions.

UNIVERSAL MASONIC LIBRARY, Vol. XVIII.

The eighteenth volume of the series embraces two works: I. The History of Masonic Persecutions, by GEO. OLIVER, D. D., 233 pages. II. Masonic Institutes, by GEO. OLIVER, 196 pages. In all, 429 pages.

10th Month. OCTOBER, 1860. 31 Days.

MOON'S PHASES.

	D.	H.	M.
Last Quarter,	7	5	57 eve.
New Moon,	14	9	29 mor.
First Quarter,	21	9	2 mor.
Full Moon,	29	1	42 eve.

Sun on Merid.

D.	H.	M.	S.
1	11	49	27.86
9	11	47	7.90
17	11	45	18.27
25	11	44	6.89

D. M.	D. W.	Sun's dec. S. ° ′ ″	Sun rises. H. M.	Sun sets. H. M.	Moon rises. H. M.
1	Mon.	— 27 47	5 55	5 44	6 10
2	Tue.	3 51 3	5 56	5 42	6 39
3	Wed.	4 14 17	5 57	5 41	7 14
4	Thu.	4 37 27	5 58	5 40	7 56
5	Fri.	5 0 35	5 59	5 38	8 45
6	Sat.	5 23 38	6 0	5 37	9 41
7	Sun.	5 46 38	6 1	5 35	10 44
8	Mon.	6 9 34	6 2	5 33	11 51
9	Tue.	6 32 24	6 3	5 32	morn.
10	Wed.	6 55 10	6 4	5 30	1 2
11	Thu.	7 17 50	6 5	5 28	2 13
12	Fri.	7 40 24	6 6	5 27	3 26
13	Sat.	8 2 51	6 7	5 25	4 38
14	Sun.	8 25 12	6 8	5 24	sets.
15	Mon.	8 47 26	6 9	5 22	5 48
16	Tue.	9 9 32	6 10	5 21	6 33
17	Wed.	9 31 31	6 11	5 20	7 22
18	Thu.	9 53 21	6 12	5 18	8 18
19	Fri.	10 15 2	6 13	5 16	9 18
20	Sat.	10 36 34	6 14	5 15	10 19
21	Sun.	10 57 56	6 15	5 14	11 20
22	Mon.	11 19 9	6 16	5 12	morn.
23	Tue.	11 40 11	6 17	5 11	0 20
24	Wed.	12 1 2	6 18	5 10	1 19
25	Thu.	12 21 42	6 19	5 9	2 17
26	Fri.	12 42 11	6 21	5 8	3 14
27	Sat.	13 2 28	6 22	5 7	rises.
28	Sun.	13 22 33	6 23	5 5	4 12
29	Mon.	13 42 25	6 24	5 4	4 41
30	Tue.	14 2 4	6 25	5 2	5 15
31	Wed.	14 21 29	6 26	5 1	5 55

MASONIC EVENTS.

EXPLANATION OF SYMBOLS.—▢ Lodge; ⌒ Chapter; △ Council; † Encampment.

1st. Grand ▢, Tenn., Nashville.

2d. Grand ▢, Ill., Springfield.

4th. Grand △, Ill., Springfield.

5th. Grand ⌒, Ill., Springfield.

8th. Grand ⌒, Tenn., Nashville; Grand △, Tenn., Nashville.

15th. Grand ▢, Ky., Louisville.

16th. Grand ⌒, Ky., Louisville; Grand †, Illinois.

17th. Grand △, Ky., Louisville.

20th. Grand ▢, Kansas.

23d. Grand ▢, Minn., St. Paul.

30th. Grand ▢, Georgia, Macon.

However some of the affiliated privileges of Masonry may be borrowed and enjoyed in the ephemeral associations of the day, there are two things no imitative society can borrow, viz: 1st. Our history past; 2d. Our permanency future.

How many there are, lying in graveyards from Maine to Texas, from Florida to Minnesota, with whom we have interlocked the strong handgripe peculiar to the craft!

EARS OF CORN NEAR THE WATER FORD.

The most inexcusable offense that a Mason can commit is Blasphemy, or taking the name of Deity in vain. For this offense has no temptation to induce it; no pleasure however temporary is produced by it; nothing but evil of the grossest character results from it. Lodges should set blasphemy at the top of their criminal code, remembering that "the Lord is with you, while ye be with Him—but if ye forsake Him, he will forsake you."

OCTOBER.

CHRONOLOGICAL EVENTS OF THIS MONTH.

FIRST.—1755. Jeremy Gridley, Prov. G. M., Mass. 1791. James Salsbury b. 1801. Benjamin Parke b. 1845. Mas. Review, Cincinnati, O., est.

SECOND.—1806. Conv. Lexington, Ky., to est. Cons. Reg. G. L., Ky. 1824. Lafayette vis. G. L., La. 1850. Augustus Peabody, P. G. M., Ms., d.

THIRD.—1814. Ft. Hiram, Providence, R. I., built by G. L., R. I.

FOURTH.—

FIFTH.—1847. G. En., Ky., est.

SIXTH.—1842. Lord Frederick John Morrison d. 1845. Cor. stone Gas Works, Cape Town, Africa, pl. 1853. Simeon Greenleaf, P. G. M., Me., d. 1858. Cor. stone Temple, Nashville, Tenn., pl.

SEVENTH.—1748. Charles XIII of Sweden b. 1787. Lodge Perfect Unanimity, Madras, E. I., est. 1822. Andrew Jackson, G. M., Tenn.

EIGHTH.—1840. Cor. stone Market, Aberdeen, Scotland, pl.

NINTH.—1782. Lewis Cass b. 1857. Hall, Smithland, Ky., burnt.

TENTH.—1825. Lafayette elected Hon. Member, G. L., Tenn. 1830. G. Mas. and Pat. Feast to Lafayette, Paris, France.

ELEVENTH.—

TWELFTH.—

THIRTEENTH.—1307. French Knights Templar arrested. 1778. G. L., Va., est. 1789. Cor. stone University, Edinburgh, Scotland, pl. 1853. Hall, Hong Kong, China, ded.

FOURTEENTH.—1819. Conv. to est. G. L., Me. 1830. Cor. stone Temple, Boston, Mass., pl. 1842. Honorarium to Earl of Mexborough, England. 1858. Sword of Jos. H. Daviess presented to G. L., Ky.

FIFTEENTH.—

SIXTEENTH.—1646. Elias Ashmole init. 1754. Morgan Lewis b. 1800. G. L., Ky., est. 1824. Masons declared outlaws in Spain.

SEVENTEENTH.—

EIGHTEENTH.—1841. Cor. stone G. Hall, Lancaster, O., pl.

NINETEENTH.—1794. G. L., Vt., est.

TWENTIETH.—1853. Cor. stone R. R. Buildings, Chillicothe, O., pl.

TWENTY-FIRST.—

TWENTY-SECOND.—

TWENTY-THIRD.—1667. Cor. stone New Ex., London, Eng., pl. 1820. Conv. Batavia, N. Y.

TWENTY-FOURTH.—1735. First Lodge opened at Amsterdam, Holland. 1797. Conv. Boston, Mass., to est. G. G. Ch. of Northern States, U. S. 1855. Cor. stone Court House, Kingston, C. W., pl.

TWENTY-FIFTH.—1762. G. Masonic Cons., A. and A. R. adopted. 1799. Wm. Tracey Gould b. 1826. G. Hall, Lexington, Ky., ded. 1848. Cor. stone G. Hall, Indianapolis, Ind., pl.

TWENTY-SIXTH.—1789. Reuben N. Walworth b. 1842. Cor. stone Episcopal Church, Reading, England, pl. 1858. M. M. Tyler, P. G. M., Ky., d.

TWENTY-SEVENTH.—1842. Cor. stone Victoria Harbor, Dunbar, England, pl. 1854. Cor. stone Court House, Sacramento, Cal., pl. 1857. G. Encpt., Ill., est.

TWENTY-EIGHTH.—1813. Joseph R. Chandler init. 1846. Cor. stone Hall, Pawtucket, R. I., pl.

TWENTY-NINTH.—

THIRTIETH.—1825. Lafayette visited G. L., Va. 1857. Mon. to J. C. Ball, Ionia, Mich., ded. 1858. Nat. Mas. School Instruction, est. at Louisville, Ky.

THIRTY-FIRST.—

Each event above named has a strictly Masonic allusion.

MASONIC LABOR DELIGHTFUL.

An objection sometimes made by a Brother when urged to commit the Webb Lectures to memory, is that he would soon forget them. There is no danger of this. If he will do his duty, and be ever ready to communicate them when requested, he will be kept in such constant practice as to make the forgetting them an absolute impossibility. The celebrated Dr. Samuel Johnson, so remarkable for the vastness of his learning, and the richness of his resources, was much indebted for the latter to his great communicativeness. He was constantly talking, always talked well, and thus he retained what he acquired. Remember that, every zealous Brother, and if you would *keep* what has been given you, *communicate* it freely and frequently to others. "It is more blessed to give than to receive."

MISCELLANEOUS READING.

A demitted Mason is released from all the responsibilities strictly growing out of a membership relation. These are payment of dues, service on Committees, regular attendance on the lodge, etc. He is also deprived of all the privileges strictly growing out of a membership relation. These are visiting lodges, sharing in treasury benefactions, masonic burial, etc.......The best Masters now wielding the gavel in our lodges, have the Ancient Charges and the Constitutions of their own Grand Lodges, respectively, fairly committed to memory, and at their tongues' ends.

HISTORICAL AND STATISTICAL ITEMS.

After the emancipation of Hayti, lodges were established by the more intelligent mulattoes in the Island, which soon became the center of all the literature and learning there. They proved to be schools of mutual help, as well as social gatherings, at which each member endeavored to contribute his quota of entertainment in the form of dissertations, toasts, fables, dramatic essays, and funeral orations.......Washington, speaking of Masonic publications in 1792, said : "It is most fervently to be wished that those publications that discover the principles which actuate Masons, may tend to convince mankind that the grand object of Masonry is to promote the happiness of the human race."

NUNC DIMITTIS.

"Now dismiss me, while I linger,
    For one fond, one dear word more,
Have I done my labor fairly?
    Is there aught against my score?
Is there one in all our circle,
    Wronged by deed, or word, or blow?
Silence speaks my full acquittance—
    Nunc dimittis, let me go.

"Let me go, I crave my wages ;—
    Long I 've waited, long I 've toiled ;
Never once through work days idle—
    Never once my apron soiled—
In the chamber—where the Master
    Waits with smiling to bestow
Corn, and wine, and oil abundant,
    Nunc dimittis, let me go.

"Let me go, but *you* must tarry,
    Till the Sixth day's close has come.
Heat and burden patient bear ye
    While you 're absent from your home ;

But a little, and the summons
    Waits alike for each of you ;—
Mine is sounding, spirits wait me,
    Nunc dimittis, let me go.

"Oh, the Sabbath-day in Heaven !
    Oh, the joys reserved for them,
Faithful builders of the Temple,
    Type of blest Jerusalem !
Oh, the raptures of our meeting
    With the friends 't was bliss to know !
Strive no longer to detain me—
    Nunc dimittis, let me go."

    ❖   ❖   ❖   ❖   ❖

Hushed that voice its fond imploring:
    Faded is that eager eye ;
Gone the soul of labor wearied,
    To repose eternally ;—
But the memory of his service
    Oft shall lighten up our woe,
Till the hour *we too* petition,
    "*Nunc dimittis*, let me go !"

OREGON.—RHODE ISLAND.—PENNSYLVANIA.—SOUTH CAROLINA.

Oregon.—*Grand Lodge*, established 1851 ; has now 26 lodges, 728 members.

Pennsylvania.—*Grand Lodge*, established 1786 ; has now 150 lodges, 6300 members. *Grand Chapter*,   ; has 28 chapters, 739 members. *Grand Council*,   ; has 9 councils, 417 members. *Grand Encampment*,   ; has 18 encampments, 648 members.

Rhode Island.—*Grand Lodge*, established 1791 ; has now 16 lodges, 1048 members. *Grand Chapter*, 1798, has   chapters,   members. *Grand Encampment* is with Massachusetts, which see.

South Carolina.—*Grand Lodge*, established 1787 ; has now 70 lodges, 3500 members. *Grand Chapter*,   ; has 23 chapters, 865 members. *Grand Consistory*,   ; has   subordinates,   members.

UNIVERSAL MASONIC LIBRARY, Vol. XIX.

The nineteenth volume of the series, comprises the first volume of the History of the Knights Hospitallers, by De Vertot, 387 pages.

FAMILY COMPACT WELL KEPT.

During the course of the celebrated anti-masonic excitement, 1826 to 1836, a gentleman in Western New York received notice from his church, that he should be expelled unless he renounced his connection with Freemasonry. This he refused to do; but offered, as a compromise, to cease further visits to the meetings of the lodge; and this, for awhile, was accepted.

But as the anti-masonic feeling became more intense, a second summons like the first was sent him, and he had now to choose between the church and the lodge. He maintained his hold upon the latter, moved thereto by the following advice of his wife, to whom he had referred the whole question: "When I first married you, we were both sinners. After a few years, I became converted, and asked your permission to join the church. This you refused. A few years later, you requested my assent to your becoming a Mason. I agreed, on condition that I should unite with the church; and so we were both satisfied. The result was that ere long you began to attend church with me, and you know we have been members of it now for more than ten years. It has been a holy union, the church and the lodge, Don't break it!" He did not break it; and when men's reason began to return to them, he was reinstated in his church with higher honors than ever.

THE BURIAL OF THE DEAD.

A Masonic funeral, conducted with the order, solemnity and decorum proper to the occasion, exemplifies the proverb of the Royal Master, "It is better to go to the house of mourning than to go to the house of feasting." And there are no occasions in which the peculiarities of the Masonic Institution appear to so much advantage, in the eyes of the world, as the public burial of the dead.

When the brethren prepare for a solemnity of this character, the whole exorcises should be placed in charge of some well-skilled and experienced Past Master, who, under the title of *Marshal*, has the disposing the ranks, the order of march, the admission of newcomers, etc., in his exclusive charge, for the proper conduct of which he is only responsible to the acting Master. If several lodges are represented, the obsequies are in charge of that to which the deceased belonged, or if a stranger, to the oldest lodge in the procession. The Grand Master, or Deputy Grand Master, if present, has the command, as in all other Masonic exercises, and the Marshal is responsible to him.

None but Master Masons can enter the procession, or take any Masonic part in the exercises. It is lawful also for the Marshal, at his discretion, to forbid non-affiliated Masons from uniting in the obsequies. The most suitable badges are plain white aprons, and sprigs of evergreen inserted in button-holes in the left bosom of the coat. The files are formed in twos, touching elbows, and march six feet asunder. Music should be secured to regulate the step, and increase the solemnity of the march. Perfect silence must be maintained, the government while in public being of the same rigid character as that of the lodge. Assistant Marshals may be appointed at the rate of one for every twenty-five files in line. Marshals march upon the left of the procession.

The grave is approached, if practicable, *from the east*. The procession is halted at fifteen paces from the grave, when the lines open, and the brethren counter-march, the Marshal conducting them, followed in due order by the Master, the Bible-bearer, etc., etc., according to the stereotyped order of processions in the *Monitor*. A complete circuit of the grave is then made once and a half, leaving it *on the right*. This brings the Master at the west of the grave, and makes a closely-joined circle, within which none are permitted to enter, save the officers, the mourning friends, clergymen, and those who are specially invited by the Marshal.

The burial services should be performed strictly in accordance with the *Monitor*, no deviation being lawful. Upon their completion, all return to the lodge, or other place of meeting, in the same order as their approach; and the scene closes by an humble petition to the God of "the quick and the dead," that the solemnities of the occasion may be impressed upon surviving friends, and the living lay them to heart.

UNIVERSAL MASONIC LIBRARY VOL. XX.

The twentieth volume of the series comprises the second volume of the History of the Knights Hospitallers, by DE VERTOT, 391 pages.

11th MONTH. NOVEMBER, 1860. 30 DAYS.

MOON'S PHASES.

	D.	H.	M.
Last Quarter,	6	4	9 mor.
New Moon,	12	7	28 eve.
First Quarter,	20	3	44 mor.
Full Moon,	28	6	30 mor.

Sun on Merid.

D.	H.	M.	S.
1	11	43	41.59
9	11	44	1.64
17	11	45	16.37
25	11	47	23.04

D. M.	D. W.	Sun's decl. S. ° ′ ″	Sun Rises. H. M.	Sun Sets. H. M.	Moon Rises. H. M.
1	Thu.	— 40 41	6 27	5 0	6 45
2	Fri.	14 59 39	6 28	4 59	7 38
3	Sat.	15 18 22	6 29	4 58	8 38
4	Sun.	15 36 50	6 30	4 57	9 44
5	Mon.	15 55 3	6 32	4 56	10 52
6	Tue.	16 12 59	6 33	4 55	morn
7	Wed.	16 30 40	6 34	4 54	0 00
8	Thu.	16 48 4	6 35	4 53	1 9
9	Fri.	17 5 10	6 37	4 52	2 19
10	Sat.	17 21 59	6 38	4 51	3 30
11	Sun.	17 38 31	6 39	4 50	4 45
12	Mon.	17 54 44	6 40	4 49	sets.
13	Tue.	18 10 38	6 41	4 48	5 7
14	Wed.	18 26 13	6 42	4 47	6 1
15	Thu.	18 41 29	6 43	4 46	7 1
16	Fri.	18 56 24	6 44	4 46	8 5
17	Sat.	19 10 59	6 45	4 45	9 7
18	Sun.	19 25 14	6 46	4 44	10 10
19	Mon.	19 39 7	6 47	4 44	11 10
20	Tue.	19 52 39	6 48	4 43	morn.
21	Wed.	20 5 49	6 49	4 42	0 9
22	Thu.	20 18 37	6 50	4 42	1 6
23	Fri.	20 31 2	6 51	4 41	2 4
24	Sat.	20 43 4	6 52	4 40	3 1
25	Sun.	20 54 44	6 53	4 40	4 1
26	Mon.	21 6 0	6 55	4 40	rises.
27	Tue.	21 16 52	6 56	4 40	3 52
28	Wed.	21 27 20	6 57	4 39	4 37
29	Thu.	21 37 23	6 58	4 39	5 36
30	Fri.	21 47 2	6 59	4 38	6 32

MASONIC EVENTS.

EXPLANATION OF SYMBOLS.—□ Lodge; ⌒ Chapter; △ Council; † Encampment.

1st. Grand ⌒, Ark., Little Rock.

5th. Grand □, Ark., Little Rock.

6th. Grand □, D. C., Washington City.

12th. Grand ⌒, Md. and D. C.

19th. Grand ⌒, Pa., Philadelphia; Grand □, Md., Baltimore.

20th. Grand □, South Carolina, Charleston.

No brother can lawfully know how any other brother balloted, even though the secret may be communicated by the indiscretion of the brother himself, the matter remains a secret as though it had never been told, although the indiscretion may and ought to be punished.

The minutes of the meeting should always be read for confirmation and adoption, just prior to closing the lodge. At the opening of the next stated meeting they should be read the second time for signature and suggestion.

There never was a rupturing of Masonic ties by death, but what some tender heart of woman, or orphan child, claimed fraternal sympathy for the sorrow that grew therefrom.

To be susceptible to the impulses of passion is natural; to govern, subdue and control the passions, is the first lesson in Masonry.

Duty is the highest joy, when love is the inducement.

EARS OF CORN NEAR THE WATER FORD.

How few of our craft appreciate the advancements in Masonic knowledge to be made by reading and study. For the most part the brethren are Initiated, Passed and Raised, they live out their Masonic life more or less usefully, and lie down with their forefathers, without once dreaming what treasures lie hidden in the Golconda of Masonic truth......Nothing tends to produce true eloquence and sublimity of language so surely as a study of the Holy Writings. Brethren striving to acquire the one, must familiarize themselves with the other.

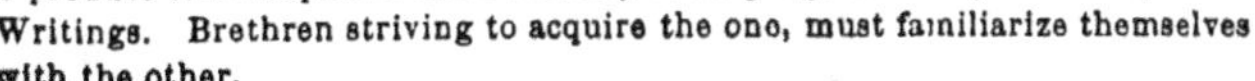

NOVEMBER.

CHRONOLOGICAL EVENTS OF THIS MONTH.

First.—1820. Temple, Philadelphia, Pa., ded. 1841. Fr. Monthly Mag., Boston, Mass., est. 1849. South. and West. Mas. Misc., Charleston, S. C., est. 1856. James Webb, P. G. M., Texas, d.

Second.—1841. Sir Alex. Burnes killed. 1855 G. L., Canada, est.

Third.—1811. D. S. Goodloe b. 1818. Ex. Coffee H., Boston, Mass., burnt. 1830. Winslow Lewis init.

Fourth.—1736. G. L., Scotland, est. 1752. Washington init. 1819. Thomas Smith Webb re-interred. 1852. Cent. Cel. Washington's Init. largely attended. 1854. Obsequies Edmund P. Hunter, G. M., Va. 1857. Cor. stone St. John's College, Little Rock, Ark., pl.

Fifth.—

Sixth.—

Seventh.—1811. Jos. H. Daviess slain. 1813. Robert R. Livingstone d.

Eighth.—1781. First Lodge in Vt. chartered. 1821. Philip C. Tucker init. 1855. Mas. Scientific Lectures, (Mackey,) New York.

Ninth.—

Tenth.—1857. Mas. Biog. Reminiscences, (Morris,) Louisville, **Ky.**

Eleventh.—

Twelfth.—1840. Cor. stone Athenæum, Sunderland, England, pl.

Thirteenth.—1756. St. Andrew's Lodge, Boston, Mass., chartered. **1856.** Willis Stewart, P. G. M., Ky., d.

Fourteenth.—1855. Conv. Leavenworth to est. G. L., **Kansas.**

Fifteenth.—

Sixteenth.—1789. Cor. stone New College, Edinburgh, Scotland, **pl.**

Seventeenth.—

Eighteenth.—1855. Joseph C. Harrison, G. H. P., **Texas, d.**

Nineteenth.—

Twentieth.—1827. Cor. stone Wolfe and Montcalm Mon., Quebec, C. **E., pl.**

Twenty-first.—1835. James Hogg, the Ettrick Shepherd d.

Twenty-second.—1815. Henry Wingate init.

Twenty-third.—

Twenty-fourth.—1790. Prince of Wales, G. M., England. 1798. Paul I., G. M. of Knights of Malta. 1836. Frederick Dalcho d. 1846. Hall, Worcester, Mass., ded. 1855. Office Signet, Marietta, Ga., burnt.

Twenty-fifth.—1838. G. L., Ark., est. 1851. John Posey d. 1857. Monument to General Worth, New York, ded. 1858. Masonic College, Uniontown, Ala., burnt.

Twenty-sixth.—

Twenty-seventh.—

Twenty-eighth.—1794. Baron Steuben d. 1849. John Q. A. Fellows init. 1849. Frederick Hall init.

Twenty-ninth.—1822. G. Hall, Baltimore, Md., ded. 1832. Fifth Con. G. G. En. and Seventh Con. G. G. Ch., U. S., Baltimore, Md.

Thirtieth.—1737. G. L., Scotland, adopted this day for its G. A. C. 1820. G. L., Espagnola, Cuba, est.

Each event above named has a strictly Masonic allusion.

KEY-NOTE TO MASONIC MUSIC.

There is an *anthem* of fraternal feeling, whose grand and heavenly notes have been pealing since the day the matchless Solomon arranged the deathless harmony. Myriads who are making their solemn march toward the boundary of time, *understand the music*, and join their voices to the accord. They seize the echo as it rolls back to them from the myriads who have gone beyond their straining sight into the shadows of the unknown world; they teach the key-note and the pitch to those who *are* to follow after them, and thus Friendship's music is never silent, its secret is never lost. The air will never cease to vibrate with it until time shall be no more.

MISCELLANEOUS READING.

Steadiness of purpose overcomes difficulties; gives the strength of a happy conscience; imparts dignity and honor to the character, and insures success. Many a Master, profoundly discouraged at the outset with the weight of ignorance and obstinacy opposing him, has found in steadiness of purpose, a victory as glorious to himself, as profitable to those upon whose minds he is at work.......The goodness of God consists in his justice, wisdom, truth and mercy. How proper then that whenever his adorable name is uttered in the performance of our mystic rites, we should all—from the youngest Entered Apprentice to the Worshipful Master—with reverence most humbly bow.......It was an ancient practice among Masons, while working the lectures, to close every section with a toast. This is still continued among many foreign Masons.

HISTORICAL AND STATISTICAL ITEMS.

More than one episode occurred on the fearful battle-field of Buena Vista, in which Masonry bore its wonted part. An American officer borne down in the fatal ravine by the press of foes, made the mystic sign. It was recognized by a Mexican officer, who rushed obediently forward to the rescue, but in vain. Before he could interpose his hand, the bayonet had done its work. ....The Masonic Apron belonging to Washington, is now the property of the Grand Lodge of Pennsylvania; a lock of his hair is in the possession, carefully enclosed in a golden casket, of the Grand Lodge of Massachusetts. Much of his Masonic regalia may be seen in the hall of the old lodge at Alexandria, Va.......The dissolution of a lodge by the loss, surrender or forfeiture of its charter, demits all its members and places them precisely as other non-affiliated Masons.......They wrong Freemasonry who deem the great architect of Solomon's Temple a mere abstraction, a personification of fidelity to duty. He is a real man, a finely conceived and subtly executed character.

THE CONTRAST.

How *sad to the Grave* are our feet slowly tending,
  The cold form of one whom we loved, on the bier!
What sighs swell our hearts while above him we 're bend
  And shudder to think we must part with him here!
Ah, gloomy is life when our friend has departed!
  Ah, weary the pathway to travel alone!
There 's little remaineth to cheer the lone-hearted
  Oppressed with the burden, "the loved one is gone!"

But *glad from the Grave* are our feet homeward tending,
  Though death's cold embraces our Brother restrain!
Hope springs from the hillock above which we 're bending,
  And whispers "Rejoice! you shall meet him again!
Death's midnight is sad, but there cometh the morning,
  The pathway is weary—its ending is nigh."
Then patient we wait till the glorious dawning,
  That 's told in our emblems of life in the sky!

TENNESSEE.–TEXAS.–VERMONT.

Tennessee.—*Grand Lodge*, established 1813; has now 210 lodges, 12.000 members. *Grand Chapter*,　; has 20 chapters, 868 members. *Grand Council*,　; has 10 councils, 385 members.

Texas.—*Grand Lodge*, established 1838; has now 210 lodges, 8400 members. *Grand Chapter*, 1850; has 60 chapters, 2250 members. *Grand Council*, 1856; has 12 councils, 500 members. *Grand Encampment*, 1855; has 6 encampments, 300 members.

Vermont.—*Grand Lodge*, established 1794; has now 44 lodges, 2063 members. *Grand Chapter*, 1822; has 11 chapters, 634 members. *Grand Council*, 1854; has 10 councils, 357 members. *Grand Encampment*, 1824; has 4 encampments, 160 members.

UNIVERSAL MASONIC LIBRARY, Vol. XXI.

The twenty-first volume of the series comprises the third volume of the History of the Knights Hospitallers, by De Vertot, 860 pages.

BETTER THAN HE LOOKED.

A good but young lodge, in Tennessee, had been terribly taken in and humbugged by various impostors, until, in their attempt to stand upon the perpendicular of caution, they rather *leaned backward*. They were in this condition, when a brother, passing through their village on his way home to Georgia, had the misfortune to lose his horse, and applied to the lodge for a little aid to help him on his way, promising faithfully to return it when he should reach the end of his journey. The lodge, stung with the recollection of their many losses, ordered him a "severe examination;" and, as he stood it without flinching, resolved, instead of lending him money, to "give him some work to do." This he mildly accepted, and went to work forthwith.

He was a blacksmith, and took a contract to shoe a company of horses belonging to a volunteer corps bound to the Mexican war. Like a real brother Mason, he hammered away. Up in the morning before the cock; up at midnight after the owl; under the bellies of horses; over the anvil; clinking with hammers; rasping with files—for six long days he labored uncomplainingly at his task. This was too much for the now conscience stricken lodge. They called a meeting; they forced the Tubal-cain before them, with his leather apron, bare and sinewy arms, begrimined and sweaty brow, blue and honest eye, modest and loving face; they compelled him to receive sufficient funds to purchase a horse and bear him home; and it is needless to add, their loan was promptly returned to them so soon as he touched Georgia soil.

DISCIPLINE TO THE REFRACTORY.

That Masons are bound to spread the mantle of charity over the failings of their brethren, remembering that the wisest have erred, and that each is liable to fall, does no conflict with the maxim that discipline must be dealt to the refractory. It is those who being often counseled, obstinately persist in error, who are the proper subjects of discipline in the lodge; and the lodge that neglects to reprimand, suspend, or expel, (the only grades of punishment known to the institution,) inflicts a fatal wound upon itself, and commits a wrong upon the Craft universal.

Offenses may be conveniently ranked under these fourteen heads : 1st. Secession from the Order; 2d. Skepticism; 3d. Profanity; 4th. Dishonesty; 5th. Falsehood; 6th. Licentiousness; 7th. Evil speaking; 8th. Covetousness; 9th. Violence; 10th. Conspiracy; 11th Sabbath-breaking; 12th. Indiscretion; 13th. Contumacy; 14th. Clandestine associations.

The preparing and presenting charges against an offending brother, is best done by the Junior Warden, and must be in the name of the lodge. A regular formula of charges applicable to all cases of discipline, is the following:

"The undersigned A—— B——, Junior Warden of C—— Lodge, No. ——, in the performance of his official duties, as specified in the By-laws, ——, ——, solemnly charges Bro. D—— E——, a (Master) Mason, and a member of (this) lodge, with unmasonic conduct, according to the following specifications: 1st. Etc., etc. And the undersigned, as the official prosecutor of the lodge, prays that the honor and dignity of Freemasonry may be vindicated by the due course of Masonic discipline upon the aforesaid Bro. D—— E——

(Signed)

A—— B——,
Junior Warden.

(*Date.*)

There is no form of offense but what can be presented through this medium.

Care must be taken that as many distinct specifications be presented as there are offense charged, and that time and place be noted with as much accuracy as possible, in every instance; but no charge must be made unless there is a reasonable prospect of conviction Mere public rumor, not based upon tangible fact, does not afford proper grounds for charges

The evidence is collected by a committee appointed for that purpose, who give the accused every opportunity to cross-examine, and to present counter-evidence. When all is prepared, it is laid before the lodge, and if satisfactory, the committee is then discharged. A free discussion of the case is then had before the lodge, during which the greatest liberty, consistent with good manners and decorum, is allowed the accused, and then he is directed to retire, that a verdict may be formed. If the decision is *guilty*, the vote is taken upon the proper class of punishment, commencing with that of *expulsion* A brother acquitted, retains the position he formerly occupied in the lodge, without any loss of dignity or credit.

UNIVERSAL MASONIC LIBRARY, Vol. XXII.

The twenty-second volume of the series comprises the fourth volume of the History of the Knights Hospitalers, by DE VERTOT, 395 pages.

12th Month. DECEMBER, 1860. 31 Days.

MOON'S PHASES.

	D.	H.	M.
Last Quarter,	5	0	53 eve.
New Moon,	12	7	40 mor.
First Quarter,	20	1	2 mor.
Full Moon,	27	10	9 eve.

Sun on Merid.

D.	H.	M.	S.
1	11	49	28.97
9	11	52	51.64
17	11	56	41.52
25	12	0	40.67

D. M.	D. W.	Sun's dec. S. °	′	″	Sun rises. H.	M.	Sun sets. H.	M.	Moon rises. H.	M.
1	Sat.	—	56	16	7	0	4	38	7	39
2	Sun.	22	5	4	7	1	4	38	8	46
3	Mon.	22	13	27	7	2	4	38	9	54
4	Tue.	22	21	25	7	3	4	37	11	2
5	Wed.	22	28	56	7	3	4	37	morn.	
6	Thu.	22	36	0	7	4	4	37	0	10
7	Fri.	22	42	39	7	5	4	37	1	19
8	Sat.	22	48	50	7	6	4	37	2	29
9	Sun.	22	54	35	7	7	4	38	3	43
10	Mon.	22	59	52	7	8	4	38	4	58
11	Tue.	23	4	42	7	9	4	39	6	13
12	Wed.	23	9	4	7	10	4	39	sets.	
13	Thu.	23	12	59	7	11	4	39	5	47
14	Fri.	23	16	26	7	12	4	40	6	51
15	Sat.	23	19	25	7	12	4	40	7	55
16	Sun.	23	21	56	7	13	4	40	8	58
17	Mon.	23	23	59	7	13	4	40	9	58
18	Tue.	23	25	34	7	14	4	41	10	56
19	Wed.	23	26	40	7	15	4	41	11	54
20	Thu.	23	27	19	7	15	4	42	morn.	
21	Fri.	23	27	29	7	15	4	42	0	51
22	Sat.	23	27	11	7	16	4	42	1	49
23	Sun.	23	26	25	7	17	4	43	2	52
24	Mon.	23	25	9	7	17	4	43	3	53
25	Tue.	23	23	26	7	17	4	44	4	52
26	Wed.	23	21	15	7	17	4	44	5	59
27	Thu.	23	18	36	7	18	4	45	rises.	
28	Fri.	23	15	28	7	18	4	46	5	27
29	Sat.	23	11	53	7	19	4	46	6	35
30	Sun.	23	7	50	7	19	4	47	7	45
31	Mon.	23	3	19	7	19	4	48	8	54

MASONIC EVENTS.

EXPLANATION OF SYMBOLS.—□ Lodge; ⌒ Chapter; △ Council; † Encampment.

3d. Grand □, N. C., Raleigh; Grand □, Ala., Montgomery; Grand □, Pa., Philadelphia.

4th. Grand ⌒, Ala., Montgomery.

5th. Grand □, N. B., Q. C., St. John; Grand †, Indiana.

6th. Grand △, Ala., Montgomery.

11th. Grand ⌒, Mass., Boston.

12th. Grand □, Mass., Boston.

27th. Grand □, N. B., St. John.

A Grand Lecturer should never leave the lodge he is instructing, until he has possessed them of the correct work, the correct lectures, and a knowledge of such disciplinary regulations, as are essential to their government.

To get at hidden truths in Masonry, three convenient rules are offered—diligent study, patient investigation, and unwearied conference with older brethren.

What is chiefly wanted in a Diploma, is clearness of style. There should also be space for names, good and correct diction, and the whole placed on material not easily worn out.

Let us ever surmise with charity. If obliged to "suppose," let us do it in the spirit of affectionate confidence, looking upon the brightest, not the darkest side of human character.

EARS OF CORN NEAR THE WATER FORD.

The landmarks of Masonry are not so much a fence or a wall, against which even the blind man may run, and which restricts even the most giddy and ignorant. They are rather posts and monuments, set at intervals, too great perhaps for the inexpert eye carelessly to see them, but not too great for science and skill to connect them with infallible certainty.......None see their own defects so clearly, as those who have labored most faithfully to remove them.

DECEMBER.

CHRONOLOGICAL EVENTS OF THIS MONTH.

FIRST.—

SECOND.—1813. Conv. Knoxville to est. G. L., Tenn.

THIRD.—

FOURTH.—1817. G. Ch., Ky., est.

FIFTH.—1813. Dempsey Carrell b.

SIXTH.—

SEVENTH.—1790. Wellington init. 1806. G. L., Del., est. 1835. Sixth Con. G. G. En. and Eighth Con. G. G. Ch., U. S., Washington, D. C. 1843. Cor. stone Lodge, Faith, Hope and Charity at Agra, India, pl.

EIGHTH.—1816. Geo. A. Baker, G. Sec., Pa., d.

NINTH.—1822. Conv. Vandalia to est. G. L., Ill.

TENTH.—1827. G. C., Ky., est.

ELEVENTH.—1809. Final Mas. Union, Mass. 1810. Conv. Washington to est G. L., D. C. 1821. G. L., Ala., est.

TWELFTH.—

THIRTEENTH.—1789. D. L. Potter b. 1838. G. C., Ala., est.

FOURTEENTH.—1799. Washington d. 1805. Western Star Lodge, No. 107, Kaskaskia, Ill., est.

FIFTEENTH.—1856. Hall, Woburn, Mass., ded.

SIXTEENTH.—1799. Washington interred. 1847. Honors to Generals Shields and Quitman by G. L., S. C.

SEVENTEENTH.—1757. First Lodge in New York est. 1825. Cor. stone Mon. Jonathan Maxcy, Columbia, S. C., pl.

EIGHTEENTH.—1786. G. L., N. J., est. 1841. Cor. stone Alms House, Calcutta, India, pl. 1843. G. L., Wis., est.

NINETEENTH.—

TWENTIETH.—1804. G. Ch., Vt., est. 1837. Conv. Houston to est. G. L., Texas. 1855. G. C., Ind., est.

TWENTY-FIRST.—

TWENTY-SECOND.—1820. Obsequies A. Lucas, G. Sec., N. C. 1836. Keystone, Bridge over Mersey, Warrington, England, inserted.

TWENTY-THIRD.—

TWENTY-FOURTH.—1746. First Lodge in Newfoundland chartered. 1754. Prov. G. L., S. C., est. 1793. DeWitt Clinton addressed Holland Lodge, N. Y.

TWENTY-FIFTH.—1522. Rhodes captured by the Turks. 1858. Morgan Nelson, P. G. H. P., Va., d.

TWENTY-SIXTH.—1799. Obsequies of Washington by G. L., Pa. 1831. Stephen Girard d.

TWENTY-SEVENTH.—1663. Earl St. Albans, G. M. England. 1749. First Lodge, Providence, R. I., chartered. 1802. Lexington Lodge, No. 1, Ky., addressed by Henry Clay. 1813. Grand Mas. Union, England. 1813. G. L., Tenn., est. 1817. Final Mas. Union, S. C. 1825. Lafayette visited G. L., Md. 1835. Grand Temple, Philadelphia, Pa., ded. 1844. Grand Mas. Festival, Kingston, C. W. 1854. Cent. Cel., G. L., S. C. 1854. Hall at Romeo, Mich., ded. Hall, Ft. Wayne, Ind., ded.

TWENTY-EIGHTH.—1778. Washington visited G. L. Pa. 1778. Gen. Varnum addressed G. L., Rhode Island.

TWENTY-NINTH.—1817. Harvey T. Wilson b.

THIRTIETH.—

THIRTY-FIRST.—1809. Cor. stone Covent Garden Theater, London, Eng., pl. 1831. Declaration by 1500 Masons, Massachusetts.

Each event above named has a strictly Masonic allusion.

THE MASTER'S POST.

The office of Master is one that few possess the age, experience, or abilities to fill. It is surrounded with difficulties and embarrassments. It requires promptitude of expression, quickness of thought, and presence of mind. It demands conciliatory manners, and instantaneous perception of character, and a considerable knowledge of mankind.

MISCELLANEOUS READING.

Speaking of the term *Raising*, so often used in Masonry, an anti-mason of great ferocity has given it as his opinion that the only thing that Masons can *Raise* properly, is *the Devil*, and that they *Enter* their lodges and *Pass* through their incantations for that express purpose........ The ripe old Mason is at last summoned away. His last night of grief is ended. His joy came like David's, *with the morning*. As a shock of corn fully ripe he submitted himself to death's sickle, and the harvest of his virtues has been gathered for the Divine Husbandman above........ All who would shape their moral and masonic edifice by the rules of W. S. and B., must do it upon the divine pattern. Man has found no way to divest himself of his vices, save as instructed in Divine Writ.

HISTORICAL AND STATISTICAL ITEMS.

There is no need to go to foreign countries, or quote the Battle of Waterloo, or the campaigns of Sir John Moore, for examples of Masonic fidelity upon the most trying occasions. Everyday life around us affords innumerable examples of that virtue, more practical, because better understood, than those with which Preston and Smith illustrate their subjects........No petition for Initiation can be prudently received by a lodge from any person, who has not resided at least a twelvemonth contiguous to the lodge, where his conduct and capacities have been scrutinized by and are well known to at least two of the members......The Holy Writings, "that great light in Masonry," contains 840,697 words, having 3,564,489 letters. With how many words of exhortation speaks that "guide to all truth," which "directs our paths to the Temple of happiness, and points out to us the whole duty of man !"......When Dr. Kane touched at St. Johns, Newfoundland, on his last Arctic voyage, he was presented by the Masonic lodge there with a silk banner........The arch was in use in the days of Sardanapulus, and probably much earlier. This is evidenced by recent explorations in Nineveh and elsewhere.

THE EMBLEMS OF THE CRAFT.

Who wears THE SQUARE upon his breast,
Does in the eye of God attest,
  And in the face of man,
That all his actions do compare
With the Divine, th' unerring square—
  That squares great virtue's plan :
That he erects his edifice
By *this design*, and *this* and *this !*

Who wears THE LEVEL says that pride
Does not within his soul abide,
  Nor foolish vanity ;
That man has but a common doom,
And from the cradle to the tomb
  A common destiny :
That he erects his edifice
By *this design*, and *this* and *this !*

Who wears THE G ; ah, type divine !
Abhors the atmosphere of sin,
  And trusts in God alone ;
His Father, Maker, Friend, he knows—

He vows, and pays to God his vows,
  As by th' Eternal throne :
And he erects his edifice
By *this design*, and *this* and *this !*

Who wears THE PLUMB, behold how true
His words, his walks ! and could we view
  The chambers of his soul,
Each thought enshrined, so pure, so good,
By the stern line of rectitude,
  Points truly to the goal :
And he erects his Edifice
By *this design*, and *this* and *this !*

Thus life and beauty come to view
In *each design* our fathers drew,
  So glorious, so sublime ;
Each breathes an odor from the bloom
Of gardens bright beyond the tomb,
  Beyond the flight of time :
And bids us build on *this* and *this*,
The walls of God's own Edifice!

VIRGINIA.—WISCONSIN.—WASHINGTON TER.

VIRGINIA.—*Grand Lodge*, established 1778 ; has now   lodges,   members. *Grand Chapter*,   ; has   chapters,   members. *Grand Encampment*,   ; has   encampments,   members.

WISCONSIN.—*Grand Lodge*, established 1843 ; has now 106 lodges, 3818 members. *Grand Chapter*, 1850 ; has 17 chapters, 600 members.

WASHINGTON TERRITORY.—*Grand Lodge*, established 1858 ; has now 7 lodges, 180 members.

UNIVERSAL MASONIC LIBRARY, Vol. XXIII.

The twenty-third volume of the series embraces three works: I. Use and Abuse of Freemasonry, by GEO. SMITH, 111 pages. II. Life in the Triangle, by ROB MORRIS, 170 pages. III. Historical Sketch of Knight Templary, by T. S. GOURDIN, 41 pages. In all 322 pages.

THE LOT.

The expressive and highly appropriate sentence that adorns the east of the lodge at St. ———, was selected by lot, under the following singular circumstances: When the Committee which had been appointed to purchase furniture, etc., met to settle the bills, it was found that a balance of a few dollars remained unexpended. This it was agreed should be devoted to painting a Scriptural motto over the Master's chair.

To select this, each member of the Committee, in his turn, submitted to be hoodwinked and open the Bible at a venture, and whatever Book his finger fell upon was noted down. This being done, lots were drawn which of the five should have the preference, and strange to say the result was the Second Book of Samuel. Each was again hoodwinked, and a search of the same sort made for chapters, brought them to the twenty-third, from which it was agreed the motto, if at all appropriate, should be taken. A hasty glance over the chapter brought them to this passage, which for propriety of sentiment can scarcely be paralleled in the whole Scriptures: HE THAT RULETH OVER MEN MUST BE JUST, RULING IN THE FEAR OF GOD. AND HE SHALL BE AS THE LIGHT OF THE MORNING WHEN THE SUN RISETH, EVEN A MORNING WITHOUT CLOUDS.

VISITING BROTHERS.

Visiting Brothers are the links that unite the ten thousand lodges of the world into one harmonious chain. They afford us the best means of testing our own Masonic charity and knowledge, and the integrity of the order in other jurisdictions. They give us objects for examination, objects for hospitality, and objects for relief. The lodge which has the most visiters, other things being equal, is the best-informed; they who give the most—the recipients being worthy objects—are the most ready to give again.

In the olden time this was the law of visiting brothers in distress: "If you discover him to be a true and genuine brother you are to respect him accordingly; if he is in want you are to relieve him if you can, or else direct him how he may be relieved; you must employ him some days, or else recommend him to be employed."

No where is the visiting brother so welcome, no where is he so well entertained, no where is his visit so productive of joy to all concerned, as in that lodge which understands the principles of an examination, and the courtesies due to him who presents the proper vouchers. There is an officer at hand to welcome and to clothe him. There is a seat in the lodge for him exactly graduated to his rank. There is a circle of cheerful faces looking radiantly upon him, and, at the proper moment a sheaf of glowing hands ready to grasp his own. Like the fall of needed rain upon the thirsty earth are these attentions to the heart of the lonely, homesick traveler, as he bows his head to receive them.

MEMORABILIA.

Our craft were called S. John's Brothers prior to the year 1440.......It is known that Masonry was diffused in Holland as early as 1731.......One of the oldest, if not the oldest Masonic medal extant, is the "Freemason's Ducat," made at Brunswick, Germany, about 1743.......The first legislation against Masonry was in England in 1425.......In 1825, Lodge No. 10, Clarksville, Tenn., commenced to make a library of Masonic matter.

MASONIC RULINGS.

A Diploma proves the holder at its date a member of the lodge; a Demit a nonmember.......The first duty of Masons in their relationship to the lodge is obedience. It is the first lesson taught.......All levity displayed in the preparation of a candidate is alike insulting to him and to the lodge.......The lectures should be given immediately following the ceremony.......No lodge can temporarily suspend its By-laws on any account.......A person while suspended is released from payment of dues, etc.......Upon the forfeiture of a charter or the lapse of a lodge, all its property real and personal, together with what accounts may be due it, reverts at once to the Grand Lodge.......The lodge can not change its minutes after they are approved and adopted.

UNIVERSAL MASONIC LIBRARY, Vol. XXIV.

The twenty-fourth volume of the series comprises Manual of Masonic Music, by J. B. TAYLOR, 336 pages.

MASONIC COLLEGES, SEMINARIES, Etc.

Many attempts have been made by Grand Lodges to found Colleges and Universities, and large expenditures of funds have been made to that end, but thus far with no results but disaster. The Grand Lodges of Kentucky, Missouri and Tennessee sunk heavy sums, and withdrew discouraged from the attempt. Those of Arkansas and North Carolina are now engaged in similar efforts.

But Academies and Seminaries, under the patronage of subordinate lodges, have been more successful. Many excellent institutions are now in existence, thus built up and sustained They honor the Institution that brought them into birth, afford a cheap and effectual method of providing educational advantages for the poor of the Order, and grace the towns and villages in which they are located.

ELI BRUCE, THE VICTIM OF ANTIMASONRY.

This unfortunate man, whose lot it was to head the column of masonic martyrs, was born in Massachusetts about the year 1795, and emigrated to Western New York near the age of twenty. At the time of Morgan's disappearance, he was sheriff of Niagara county, and resided at Lockport. He was accused by Hopkins, his deputy, of having provided a cell for the incarceration of Morgan; and although it is known that that individual was not brought to Lockport, yet this fact convicted him, in the minds of an antimasonic jury, of conspiracy in the abduction of Morgan, and he was sentenced to imprisonment in the jail at Canandaigua for the space of two years and four months. He served his whole term uncomplainingly, amid the sympathy of friends, and died of cholera in September, 1831, a year after his release. The diary of his sufferings, which he kept while in prison, is in the hands of Mr. Rob Morris, and presents a mournful picture of a noble heart, bowed down with poverty, anguish, and captivity.

THE MORGAN AFFAIR.

For a matter which produced so much excitement, and accomplished so much evil to masonry, this whole affair was very trivial. There was a drunken, worthless fellow living at Batavia, New York, in 1826, named William Morgan, who colleagued with another man but little better than himself, named David T. Miller, to publish an exposition of masonry. The Fraternity, at that place, fearing that evil results might follow such a publication, took steps to prevent it, but without effect. At last they conveyed Morgan, by his own consent, from Canandaigua to Niagara, a distance of eighty miles, and from thence assisted him, it is supposed, to leave the country. A hue and cry was raised, and as he was never heard of afterward, the hasty inference was drawn that the masons murdered him, and a general persecution was at once excited against the entire Order. This, for ten years, threatened its total downfall. The exposition, when published, however, was found to be but a reprint of others of similar character then extant, as false in the motives of their issue as in the facts of their invention and the whole Morgan excitement has passed away as one of those spasmodic exhibitions of public morality, so common in history, in which a scapegoat is made of one man or institution to expiate the sins of the many.

UNIVERSAL MASONIC LIBRARY, Vol. XXV.

The twenty-fifth volume of the series comprises three works: I. Masonry and Antimasonry, by Alfred Creigh, M. D., 333 pages. II. An Appeal, by Philip C. Tucker, 13 pages. III. An Address, by Jonathan A. Allen, M. D., 12 pages. In all, 358 pages.

VOL. XXVI.

The twenty-sixth volume of the series comprises The Freemasons' Monthly Magazine, London, January to June, 1855, 400 pages.

VOL. XXVII.

The twenty-seventh volume of the series comprises The Freemasons' Monthly Magazine, London, July to December, 1855, 380 pages.

ROB MORRIS AND HIS FAVORITE ODE.

This gentleman, whose name has become a password in masonic science only second to that of "the first known Artificer or cunning Workman in metals," was born August 31, 1818; initiated in Oxford Lodge, No. 33, Miss., April, 1846; and elected Grand Master of Kentucky, October, 1858. His masonic productions are numerous and valuable. In the departments of Masonic Law, History, Biography, and Belles Lettres, his productions were tho first in the field; his *Lights and Shadows of Freemasonry, Reminiscences of the Triennial Convocations of 1856, History of Freemasonry in Kentucky*, and *Code of Masonic Law*, respectively, being the earliest works upon those subjects emanating from American pens, and they have retained their places at the head of the catalogue. His fame as editor is chiefly associated with the *American Freemason*, conducted by him, for four years, with a vigor and research unparalleled in the history of masonic journalism; and by the *Voice of Masonry*, now under his well-practiced guidance.

It is to Mr. Morris that the masonic world is indebted for that mighty enterprise, the *Universal Masonic Library*, of which the *Almanac* contains the titles and descriptions. This is a compilation of fifty-two standard authors, upon all departments of masonic science, bound in the compass of thirty volumes octavo. The effect of this mighty undertaking has been to reduce the price of masonic literature to the Fraternity to one-third its former rates, and to render available to American readers works long out of print, and lost to the view. Of all human enterprises, the history of this is among the most interesting and curious.

As a poet, Mr. Morris is known by a large number of productions, of various degrees of merit, the most popular of which is the following:

THE LEVEL AND THE SQUARE.

We meet upon *the Level* and we part upon *the Square;*—
What words of precious meaning those words Masonic are!
Come, let us contemplate them, they are worthy of a thought,
With the highest, and the lowest, and the rarest they are fraught.

We meet upon *the Level*, though from every station come;
The rich man from his mansion, and the poor man from his home;
For the one must leave his wealth and state outside the Mason's door,
And the other finds his true respect upon the checkered floor.

We part upon *the Square*, for the world must have its due;
We mingle with the multitude, a cold, unfriendly crew,
But the influence of our gatherings in memory is green,
And we long upon *the Level* to renew the happy scene.

  * * * * * * * * *

There's a world where all are equal—we are hurrying toward it fast;
We shall meet upon *the Level* there, when the gates of death are past;
We shall stand before the Orient, and our Master will be there
To try the blocks we offer by his own unerring *Square*.

We shall meet upon *the Level* there, but never thence depart;
There's a *Mansion*—'t is all ready for each trusting, faithful heart—
There's a *Mansion* and a welcome—and a multitude is there,
Who have met upon *the Level*, and been tried upon *the Square*.

Let us meet upon *the Level* then, while laboring patient here;
Let us meet and let us labor, though the labor be severe;
Already in the Western Sky the signs bid us prepare
To gather up our Working tools, and part upon *the Square!*

Hands round, ye faithful Masons, form the bright, fraternal chain,
We part upon *the Square* below, to meet in heaven again.
Oh! what words of precious meaning those words Masonic are—
We meet upon the Level and we part upon the Square!

UNIVERSAL MASONIC LIBRARY, VOL. XXVIII.

The twenty-eighth volume of the series embraces three works: I. The Mystic Tie, by A. G. Mackey, M. D., 234 pages. II. Narrative of Anti-masonry, by Henry Brown, 190 pages. III. Oration, by Percy Morton, 12 pages. In all, 436 pages.

VOL. XXIX.

The twenty-ninth volume of the series comprises Philosophical History of Masonry, by A. C. L. Arnold, 284 pages.

VOL. XXX.

The thirtieth volume of the series embraces four works: I. Speculative Masonry, by Salem Town, LL. D., 155 pages. II. By-Laws Lodge of Antiquity, London, 11 pages. III. Ancient Poem, 41 pages. IV. The Egyptian and Hebrew Symbols, by Portal, 85 pages. In all, 292 pages.

UNIFORMITY OF WORK.

The various efforts made in Grand Lodges during the last twenty years, and since the revival of Masonry, to secure uniformity of Masonic work and lectures, form interesting and prominent episodes in the legislation of the period. The best minds of the craft have been engaged upon the subject, and divers plans, ingenious and plausible, have been devised to bring about results admittedly important in the highest degree. But these plans have generally failed. Not only have they failed, but in their developments they have too often introduced new and more complicated disorders, until innovations and "confusion worse confounded" reign in the Masonic Temple; and these are every day multiplying.

The secret of these failures in legislation is patent; it consists in this; that each Grand Lodge, when setting about to correct errors in the work of its jurisdiction, has looked only to its own boundary, forgetting that it forms but a part of a great family. Instead of inquiring, What is the original of the Masonic work? who has the ancient work? how can the former standard be discovered and set up? the question has been narrowed down to this: *How can we reconcile the various systems of work in vogue in our own State?* The result of such an investigation is, that a *compromise* has been adopted amongst the lecturers of its own jurisdiction; and so the number of bastard systems of work already in vogue has been increased.

The bounden duties of a Grand Lodge, in this respect, are to reject all innovations, by whatever authority introduced or maintained; to perpetuate the work as the fathers of Masonry in America taught it; and to refuse with abhorrence anything which would give a local cast to the work or lectures. Either Masonry is *general* or it is *nothing:* and a Grand Lodge is but wasting its time and influence teaching novelties which will never obtain friends outside of its own jurisdiction.

There is a system of Masonry yet extant which, being the origin of the other systems in vogue in the United States, forms one *touchstone* or *standard* by which all the others may be tried and corrected. This is called the "Prestonian" or "Webb Work." It was first arranged by that distinguished scholar and Freemason, WILLIAM PRESTON, about eighty years since, and communicated and adopted by the lodges of Great Britain with singular unanimity. In Scotland and Ireland the Prestonian system yet prevails without change. This system of lectures was brought to the United States about 1795, and eagerly adopted as the remedy for the conflicting systems then in use. Amongst those who became most famous in its dissemination was THOMAS SMITH WEBB, then (1795) a resident of Albany, N. Y.; afterwards successively of Rhode Island, Massachusetts, and Ohio: in which latter State he died, July, 1819, at Cleveland. From Mr. Webb's intelligence and zeal in this cause, and the fact that he published the first *Monitor* to correspond with the *Prestonian system*, that work in the United States took his name, and is familiarly entitled "The Webb Work."

This touchstone and standard of all that is correct in our numerous rituals was in general use in the lodges of the United States at the period of Mr. Webb's death, in 1819. His principal pupils, of which he had many,—Gleason, Barney, Cross, Fowle, Cushman, and others,—taught his work up to that time with literal exactness; and had he lived to the present day, the evils of innovation, which the craft are mourning over, might never have originated.

The "Webb Work" still exists in purity in the memories of many of the elders of the craft. In Vermont it has been the only system allowed for more than forty years, and is doubtless perpetuated there. In Rhode Island, Massachusetts, and other New England States, there may yet be found numerous individuals and lodges knowing no other system than this; and the same may be said, but with more or less reservation, of other States. But of all systems in vogue, however wide they may be from the true standard, the *basis and skeleton* of them are invariably found in the "Webb Work," and these constitute all that remains of *uniformity* amongst the four thousand six hundred lodges of the United States. In other words, a Brother traveling from one section of the Union to the other, and undergoing examination as a Mason, will find that *what he knows of the "Webb Work" will be universally recognized by the Fraternity, while anything else may or may not be acknowledged, as local peculiarities prevail.*

A great and united effort has been in progress during the past three years to bring about a discarding of all novelties, and a restoration of whatever is ancient and orthodox in the Masonic system. This effort has already secured the patronage of the best men amongst the craft. The Grand Lodges of Iowa and Kentucky have by solemn vote endorsed it and committed themselves as the adversaries of innovation and error.   Four sessions of a National "School of Instruction," numerously attended, have been held in different sections of Kentucky as preliminary to more extended operations throughout the Union.   Correspondence has been opened with Grand Lecturers in various jurisdictions, in which the different classes of innovations are discussed and the true remedies suggested.   Brethren of intelligence and zeal are preparing themselves to disseminate the ancient work in the spirit and devotedness of Webb and Preston.   All the signs of the times indicate that *the day of uniformity in Masonic work* is at hand.

The "Webb Lectures" far excel the others in strong, sensible language and a consistent interweaving of the operative and speculative, the ceremony and the explanation of the Masonic system.   A majority of the words, like the old Scriptures and the Pilgrim's Progress, are monosyllables of the Saxon tongue. Of *eighty-three* words, taken at random from the "Webb Lectures," *fifty-nine* are of this sort,—strong, nervous monosyllables,—roots of words,—each of which branches into various thoughts and suggestions.   This makes the "Webb Lectures" delightfully applicable to the use of the instructor: he may amplify any portion of them at his pleasure; the only limits to his ingenuity being the broad landmarks of the institution itself. The "Webb Lectures" are happily not found in the various expositions peddled from the baskets of low and vulgar dealers in periodical lore.   Morgan, Allyn, Bernard, Crafts, all fail in communicating the true light as our fathers taught it and fondly hoped to perpetuate it.   It is acquired only as Masonry should be acquired, from mouth to ear.   The *instructive tongue* communicates it; the *attentive ear* receives it; the *faithful breast* retains it; and thus from generation to generation it is preserved.

Every reader of this Almanac is invited to unite in a work the success of which is the interest, honor, and glory of Freemasonry. Every Mason must feel that until all speak the same tongue, perform the same work, and pursue the same end and aim, Freemasonry is not what it claims to be.   The noble institution has too long been left to the whims and crudities of unintelligent minds; and it is time that every one who loves Freemasonry should rally by the standard of Antiquity, Universality, Uniformity,—a motto worthy of the cause it indicates,—and give his influence to the right.   This done, and success is speedy and sure.

ADOPTIVE MASONRY—THE EASTERN STAR.

Few things have excited the curiosity of the Masonic brethren so much as the subject of Adoptive or Ladies' Masonry. In France many entire works are devoted to this theme, and great attention is given to cultivating the minds of the fair sex as partners in the work of Masonry. The theory of our brethren across the water is, that as ladies cannot be introduced into the Temple proper, as much grace as possible shall be bestowed upon "The Courts of the Women."

In the United States, even more than elsewhere, "Ladies' Degrees" are communicated, but not with the same attention to order and system as in France. They are usually given here merely as honorary compliments, with little or no ceremony, and of course with small impressiveness.

The names of the "Ladies Degrees" most in vogue in this country are the Eastern Star, the Good Samaritan, the Mason's Daughter, and the Heroine of Jericho; the second and fourth of these being confined to Royal Arch Masonry. The former is communicated by any Master Mason in good standing to the wife, widow, sister, or daughter of such. In the opinion of the writer, it is by every consideration the most graceful, interesting, and scriptural specimen of *Adoptive Masonry* extant, and as such the following "Signet" is given. In the hands of the enlightened Brother, it affords a lucid explanation to mysteries alike beautiful, interesting, and important.

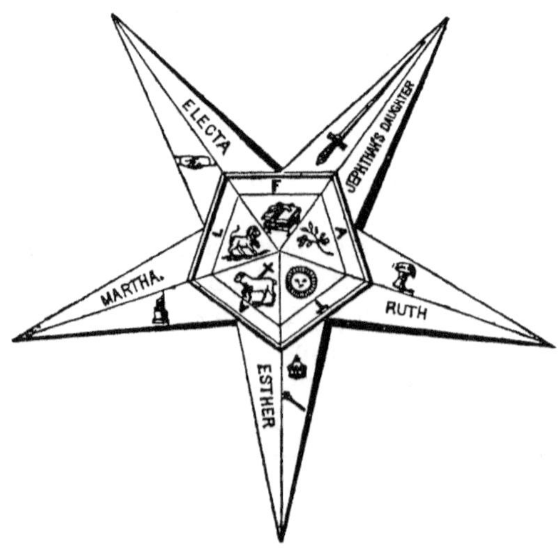

THE UNIVERSAL MASONIC LIBRARY.

A REPUBLICATION, in thirty large octavo volumes, of all the standard Masonic authors, fifty-three in number. The Library includes all the works of Dr. GEORGE OLIVER. It is an invaluable adjunct to a Lodge and to the parlor of a gentleman. A young Mason, seeking to acquire the knowledge of Masonic History, Jurisprudence, Philosophy, and Belles Lettres, in this series *has the whole,* and need look no further. Many hundreds of sets have been distributed with marked benefit to the Craft ; and although in the getting up of the enterprise, the private fortune of the projector has been hopelessly wrecked, yet the Craft is secured, at the lowest prices, in a perfect collection of all that is valuable in Masonic literature.

VOLUME FIRST.—1. Dictionary of Symbolical Masonry, including the Royal Arch. 2. The Book of the Lodge, or Officers' Manual.

VOL. SECOND.—3. Symbol of Glory. 4. Spirit of Masonry.

VOL. THIRD.—5. Illustrations of Masonry.

VOL. FOURTH.—6. Antiquities of Masonry. 7. Masonic Discourses.

VOL. FIFTH.—8. History of Freemasonry, from 1829 to 1841. 9. Mirror for the Johannite Mason. 10. Star in the East.

VOL. SIXTH.—11. Disquisitions of Masonry. 12. Masonic Manual.

VOL. SEVENTH.—13. Revelations of a Square. 14. Introduction to Freemasonry.

VOL. EIGHTH.—15. History of Initiation. 16. History and Illustration of Freemasonry.

VOL. NINTH.—17. Constitution Grand Lodge, England. 18. Constitution Grand Lodge, Ireland. 19. Constitution Grand Lodge, Scotland.

VOL. TENTH.—20. Theocratic Philosophy of Masonry. 21. Signs and Symbols of Masonry.

VOLS. ELEVENTH AND TWELFTH.—22. The Historical Landmarks of Masonry. By Oliver. Vol. I, 426 pages ; Vol. II, 450 pages.

VOL. THIRTEENTH.—23. Stray Leaves from a Freemason's Note Book. 24. Apology for the Order. 25. The Masonic Schism. 26. Insignia of the Royal Arch. 27. The Secret Discipline.

VOL. FOURTEENTH.—28. Lights and Shadows of Freemasonry.

VOL. FIFTEENTH.—29. Anderson's Ancient Constitutions. 30. History of Freemasonry, up to 1829.

VOL. SIXTEENTH.—31. Masonic Sermons. 32. Three Sermons.

VOL. SEVENTEENTH.—33. Principles of Masonic Law.

VOL. EIGHTEENTH.—34. History of Masonic Persecutions. 35. Masonic Institutes.

VOLS. NINETEENTH, TWENTIETH, TWENTY-FIRST, AND TWENTY-SECOND.—36. History of the Knights Hospitalers, of St. John of Jerusalem. 37. Statutes of the Knights Templar of England and Wales.

VOL. TWENTY-THIRD.—38. Use and Abuse of Freemasonry. 39. Life in the Triangle. 40. Historical Sketch of the Order of Knights Templar.

VOL. TWENTY-FOURTH.—41. Manual of Masonic Music.

VOL. TWENTY-FIFTH.—42. Masonry and Anti-Masonry. 43. An Appeal to the Inhabitants of Vermont on the Subject of the Anti-Masonic Excitement. April, 1829. 44. An Address to the Masonic Convention at Middlebury, Vermont. Apr. 7, 1829.

VOLS. TWENTY-SIXTH and TWENTY-SEVENTH.—45. The Freemasons' Monthly Magazine, 1855.

VOL. TWENTY-EIGHTH.—46. The Mystic Tie. 47. Narrative of the Anti-Masonic Excitement. 48. Oration at the Re-Interment of General Joseph Warren, 1776.

VOL. TWENTY-NINTH.—49. Philosophical Philosophy of Masonry.

VOL. THIRTIETH.—50. Speculative Masonry. 51. By-Laws of the Lodge of Antiquity. 52. Ancient Poem on the Constitutions of Masonry, 1325. 53. The Egyptian and Hebrew Symbols.

WM. M. ELLISON, GENERAL AGENT,

Louisville, Ky.

MORRIS & MONSARRAT will also take orders. $50 per set.

CONDENSING THE RAYS OF LIGHT.

MASONIC *light*, as the term is technically applied to knowledge, instruction, or illumination of the mind in Masonic things, is composed of rays or parts scattered most carelessly through the length and breadth of the land. But few and partial attempts have ever been made to gather them up. The authors of Masonic volumes, essays, and addresses have preferred to give theoretical views based upon fancy and adorned with eloquence, to gathering up with labor and pains the diffused rays of Masonic light, richly but negligently diffused. Therefore the rays yet fly as the gold lies in the mine, without value, until the hand of man collects and binds them together to proper uses.

In the management of the Masonic journal styled *The Voice of Masonry*, wherein a very large corps of stated and occasional contributors are concerned, the chief aim of the whole is *the collecting these scattered rays*. It is found that every Mason, and many who are not Masons, many ladies as well as gentlemen are in possession of well-authenticated facts in Masonry, some of a thinking character, some that fill a niche in history, some of the greatest possible importance, many only of passing and ephemeral interest. These rays are of the most varied hues and character. They range over every theme of aid in distress, assistance against violence, resisting temptation, recognition of brethren under interesting circumstances, honor to the dead—whatever enters nearest into social life, and makes the most indelible impressions upon the memory. It is found that the country is rife with traditions of this sort, worthy of collection, of condensation, of record in the standard journal of the Masonic craft.

This Almanac is largely made up by this kind of condensing the scattered rays. A year since and hundreds of these chronological details, most of which are historically of the greatest possible importance in Masonry, were flying carelessly and without value through the memories of those who knew nothing of their value, or in the uncut pages of addresses and proceedings. And now behold! when collected, condensed, and published, what a sheaf of rays, what a bright light does this little book emit! how every page excites the wonder of the reader, causing him to ask with surprise, " Whence hath this man these things ? "

The success that has attended the labor of the preparation of this Almanac, immense as that labor has been, is made the basis of an appeal to every reader for *more light*. It is urgently solicited of each who possesses himself of a copy of this work, that he look into his own heart and memory and examine these, if there is not some tradition, some incident, some little fact in the style of the numerous little facts contained in this book, which has never been published, but which, if laid before a hundred thousand readers, as the facts in this Almanac will be, would warm up some heart, or inform some mind, or fill some vacant place in Masonic history, or in some other way do good to the Craft. The result will be that not one only, but two, and three, and oftentimes six or more such traditions will come up to the light. Then note them down, regarding not any choice form of words, and send them to us, who busy ourselves in collecting these scattered rays of light, and thus do a good in the world at slight trouble, which may influence many hearts after yours has ceased to beat.

The Facsimile

THE NEW ENGLAND ANTI-MASONIC ALMANAC
FOR 1830

THE
New=England Anti=Masonic
ALMANAC,

FOR THE YEAR OF OUR LORD
1830.

A " poor blind candidate" receiving his obligation

" To all of which I do most solemnly and sincerely promise and swear, without the least equivocation, mental reservation, or self evasion of mind in me whatever; binding myself under no less penalty, than to have my throat cut across, my tongue torn out by the roots, and my body buried in the rough sands of the sea at low water mark, where the tide ebbs and flows twice in twenty four hours ; so help me God, and keep me steadfast in the due performance of the same."

BOSTON:

PUBLISHED AND SOLD BY JOHN MARSH, (*Proprietor of the Copy Right,*) No. 96 & 98 STATE STREET.
Sold also by most Booksellers and Traders in New-England.

ECLIPSES.

There will be *six* eclipses this year—4 of of the Sun, and 2 of the Moon, as follows.

I. Feb. 22, Sun eclipsed, invisible, ☌ at 11h. 52m. eve. ☽ lat. 1° 23′ 15″ N.

II. March 9, Moon eclipsed, invisible. ☍ at 8h. 48m. morn.

III. March 24, Sun eclipsed, invisible. ☌ at 10h. morn. ☽ lat. 1° 17′ 36″ S.

IV. Aug. 18, ☌ Sun eclipsed, invisible. ☌ at 7h. 9m morn. Moon's lat. 1° 23′ 30″ S.

V Sept. 2, Moon eclipsed, partly visible.

	H. M.
Ecliptic 8,	5 54 eve.
Moon ris. totally eclipsed,	6 29 do.
End of total darkness,	6 44 do.
Eclipse ends,	7 42 do.

VI. Sept 16, Sun eclipsed, invisible. ☌ at 9h. 44m. eve. Moon's lat. 1° 13′ 15″ N.

☞Venus ♀ will be evening star till March 7, and then morning star till Dec. 20.

Jupiter will be morning star till July 5, and evening star the rest of the year.

Chronological Cycles.

Dominical Letter,	C	Epact,	6
Lunar Cycle, or Golden No.	7	Solar Cycle,	19

Names and Characters of the Signs of the Zodiac.

♈ Aries,head.	♌ Leo, heart.	♐ Sagittarius, thighs.
♉ Taurus, neck.	♍ Virgo, belly.	♑ Capricorn, knees.
♊ Gemini, arms.	♎ Libra, reins.	♒ Aquarius, legs.
♋ Cancer, breast.	♏ Scorpio,secrets.	♓ Pisces, feet.

Names and Characters of the Aspects and Nodes.

☌ Conjunction.	Vc Quincunx, 150 degrees.
✶ Sextile, 60 degrees.	☍ Opposition, 180 degrees.
☐ Quartile, 90 degrees.	☊ Ascending Node.
△ Trine, 120 degrees.	☋ Descending Node.

☞The sun, moon, and planets, are denoted by the following characters ; ☉ Sun, ☽ Moon, ☿ Mercury, ♀ Venus, ⊕ Earth, ♂ Mars, ♃ Jupiter, ♄ Saturn, ♅ Herschell.

—⊷⊶—

TO PATRONS.

The New England Anti-Masonic Almanac of 1829, having met with an unexpected and unprecedented patronage, we issue this number with confidence. Considerable pains have been taken to render it worthy of the public approbation,and to those who are distrustful of the character, designs, and tendency of dark and mysterious SECRET SOCIETIES, we cannot but think it will be welcome. The cause of the People, the cause of Humanity, Justice, Liberty, and EQUAL RIGHTS, must and will prevail against all the arts and artifices of a *midnight combination.*

Entered Apprentice's Sign of Distress.

The Master (all the brethren imitating him) extends his left arm from his body so as to form an angle of about 45° and holds his right hand traversely across his left, the palms thereof one inch apart. This is called the *first sign of a Mason*—is the *sign of Distress* in this degree, and all alludes to the position a candidate's hands are placed in when he takes the obligation of an Entered Apprentice Mason.   *Light on Masonry, p. 22.*

	D.	H.	M.			D.	H.	M.
First Quarter,	1	9	50 A.		Last Quarter,	16	11	19 A.
Full Moon,	8	10	48 A.		New Moon,	24	0	10 A.
					First Quarter,	31	6	3 M.

D. M.	D. W.	Miscellaneous Matters	S. Rises & Sets.	Sun's dec'lS.	Moon Sets.	Moon South.	M. Pl.	High Water.
1	Fr	Norflk burnt '76 *cold*	7 31 5	23 1	morn.	5 47	♈	3 22
2	Sa	Anti M. Con. Dedham	7 31 5	22 56	0 12	6 38	20	4 17
3	Su	Bat. Princeton. ['29	7 30 5	22 50	1 21	7 31	♉	5 26
4	M.	♀ sets 8 28eve *rough*	7 30 5	22 44	2 30	8 24	18	6 52
5	Tu	7*s so. 8 31 eve.	7 29 5	22 37	3 36	9 18	♊	8 15
6	W.	*winds—some snow*	7 29 5	22 30	4 39	10 12	16	9 20
7	Th	♄ south 2 7 morn.	7 28 5	22 23	5 38	11 7	29	10 12
8	Fr	Battle N. Oreans '15	7 28 5	22 15	rises.	11 59	♋	10 57
9	Sa	*High Tides.—more*	7 27 5	22 6	5 33	morn.	26	11 35
10	Su	*mild with*	7 26 5	21 58	6 32	0 51	♌	ev. 13
11	Mo	Stamp act passed '65	7 26 5	21 48	7 32	1 39	22	0 47
12	Tu	♀ sets 8 30 eve.	7 25 5	21 39	8 32	2 26	♍	1 21
13	W	☌ ☿ ♅ *rain—*	7 24 5	21 29	9 29	3 11	16	1 55
14	Th	peace ratified '84.	7 23 5	21 18	10 25	3 53	28	2 27
15	Fr.	☽ in apogee. *look*	7 23 5	21 7	11 23	4 35	♎	3 3
16	Sa	7*s so 7 43 eve. *out*	7 22 5	20 56	morn.	5 18	22	3 44
17	Su	Franklin born 1706.	7 21 5	20 45	0 19	6 1	♏	4 33
18	M.	*for a driving storm.*	7 20 5	20 33	1 16	6 45	16	5 37
19	Tu	*Quite low Tides*	7 19 5	20 20	2 13	7 31	28	6 53
20	W.	♄ so. 1 11 morn. *fine*	7 18 5	20 7	3 11	8 19	♐	8 8
21	Th	☉ enters ♒ *for*	7 17 5	19 54	4 9	9 11	23	9 12
22	Fr	LouisXVI. beheaded	7 16 5	19 40	5 5	10 5	♑	10 6
23	Sa	[1793.	7 15 5	19 26	5 57	11 0	20	10 52
24	Su	♀ sets 8 32 eve. *sev-*	7 14 5	19 12	sets.	11 56	♒	11 33
25	M.	*eral days very rough*	7 13 5	18 57	6 20	ev. 52	19	morn.
26	Tu	☌ ☉ ♅ [*elon* ☿	7 12 5	18 42	7 32	1 47	♓	0 14
27	W.	☽ in perigee. Gr.	7 11 5	18 27	8 43	2 41	18	0 53
28	Th	Peter Gr. d. '25 *pleas*	7 10 5	18 11	9 53	3 34	♈	1 33
29	Fr	Geo. 4th crown'd '20	7 9 5	17 55	11 3	4 26	17	2 12
30	Sa	7*s so. 6 44 eve.	7 8 5	17 39	morn.	5 19	♉	2 55
31	Su	*ant for the season.*	7 6 5	17 22	0 12	6 12	15	3 45

Entered Apprentice's Due Guard.

The Master then draws his right hand across his throat, the hand open, with the thumb next to the throat, and drops it down by his side. This is called the due-guard of an Entered Apprentice Mason, (many call it the sign) and alludes to the penalty of the obligation.—[See penalty on title page.]

Light on Masonry, p. 22.

	D.	H.	M.			D.	H.	M.
Full Moon,	7	2	58A.	Last Quarter,		15	7	44A.
				New Moon,		22	11	52A.

D. M.	D. W.	Miscellaneous Matters.	S. Rises & Sets·	Sun's dec'lS·	Moon Sets.	Moon South.	M' Pl.	High water.
1	M.	*Low Tides.*	7 5 5	17 5	1 19	7 5	29	4 48
2	Tu	*now for a*	7 4 5	16 48	2 23	7 59	♊	6 9
3	W.	☍ ☉ ♄	7 3 5	16 31	3 24	8 53	26	7 38
4	Th	♃ rises 4 49 morn	7 2 5	16 13	4 19	9 45	♋	8 52
5	Fr	♀ sets 8 14 eve, *storm*	7 0 5	15 55	5 9	10 37	2 2	9 47
6	Sa	Gov. Eustis d. 1825 *of.*	6 59 6	15 36	55 3	11 27	♌	10 33
7	Su	Earthq. at Phila. '13	6 58 6	15 18	rises.	morn.	18	11 12
8	M.	*High Tides.* *snow*	6 57 6	14 59	6 13	0 14	♍	11 47
9	Tu	*with cold bleak winds.*	6 55 6	14 40	7 12	1 0	12	ev.20
10	W.	Jup. rise 4 32 morn.	6 54 6	14 20	8 9	1 44	24	0 51
11	Th	Inf. *more com-*	6 53 6	14 1	9 7	2 26	♎	1 21
12	Fr	☽ in apogee. *fortable.*	6 51 6	13 41	10 4	3 9	18	1 53
13	Sa	*colder*	6 50 6	13 21	11 0	3 52	♏	2 26
14	Su	♀ stat. Valen. day	6 49 6	13 0	11 57	4 35	12	3 3
15	M.	♀ sets 7 43 eve. *with*	6 47 6	12 40	morn.	5 20	24	3 46
16	Tu	*Tides Low.* *rain.*	6 46 6	12 19	0 54	6 7	♐	4 41
17	W.	Ghent Treaty. rat '15.	6 45 6	11 58	1 51	6 56	18	5 54
18	Th	☉ ent. ♓ *sudden chan-*	6 43 6	11 37	2 47	7 48	♑	7 20
19	Fr	♄ so. 10 53 eve. *ges*	6 42 6	11 16	3 41	8 42	14	8 38
20	Sa	♃ rises 4 morn. *mild*	6 40 6	10 54	4 31	9 37	28	9 39
21	Su	Masonic oaths disc. at	6 39 6	10 33	5 17	10 33	♒	10 29
22	M.	[Le Roy, '28	6 38 6	10 11	sets.	11 30	27	11 14
23	Tu	Sp. decl. war a. Pt '01	6 36 6	9 49	6 19	ev.26	♓	11 55
24	W.	☽ per. *for the season*	6 35 6	9 27	7 33	1 22	27	morn.
25	Th	♀ sets 7 eve. *much*	6 34 6	9 5	8 47	2 17	♈	0 35
26	Fr	*cooler again*	6 32 6	8 42	10 0	3 12	26	1 55
27	Sa	♄ so.10 22 eve. ['01	6 31 6	8 20	11 11	4 7	♉	1 55
28	Su	Fast throughout G. Brit.	6 29 6	7 57	morn.	5 2	21	2 39

Cursed be he that smiteth his neighbor SECRETLY. Cursed be he that taketh reward to slay an innocent person.‡ Deut. xxvii. 24, 25.—He sitteth in the lurking places of the villages. In the SECRET places doth he murder the innocent. Ps. x. 8.—We have RENOUNCED the HIDDEN things of dishonesty, not walking in craftiness. 2 Cor. iv. 2.

Fellow Craft's sign and Due-Guard.

The sign is given by drawing your right hand flat, with the palm of it next to your breast, across your breast from the left to the right side with some quickness, and dropping it down by your side; the due-guard is given by raising the left arm until that part of it between the elbow and shoulder is perfectly horizontal, and raising the rest of the arm in a vertical position, so that part of the arm below the elbow, and that part above it, forms a square. The two given together, are called *the sign and due-guard of a Fellow-Craft Mason,* and they are never given seperately; they would not be recognized by a Mason if given seperately.

	D.	H.	M.			D.	H.	M.
First Quarter,	1	3	18A.		LastQuarter,	17	0	52A.
Full Moon,	9	8	48M.		New Moon,	24	10	0M.
					First Quarter,	31	2	14M.

D. M	D. W.	Miscellaneous Matters	S. Rises & Sets.	Suns dec'lS.	Moon Sets.	Moon South.	M. Pl.	High Water.
1	M	*Storms at hand.*	6 28 6	7 35	0 17	5 57	♊	3 28
2	Tu	Bolieu died 1711.	6 27 6	7 12	1 20	6 51	23	4 28
3	W	*Low Tides,* cool	6 25 6	6 49	2 17	7 44	♋	5 47
4	Th	1st Cong: met, '89.	6 24 6	6 26	3 8	8 36	19	7 14
5	Fr	♃ rises ♂ 22 morn.	6 22 6	6 3	3 54	9 26	♌	8 31
6	Sa	Le Roy Con.'28. *winds*	6 21 6	5 39	4 35	10 13	14	9 28
7	Su	♄ s.9 52 e.[☌ ☉ ♀	6 19 6	5 16	5 10	11 0	27	10 13
8	M	♄ sets 4 57 m. *with*	6 18 6	4 53	5 43	11 44	♍	10 52
9	Tu	*Middling Tides.* sud	6 16 6	4 29	rises.	morn.	21	11 25
10	W	Gr. elon. *den chan-*	6 15 6	4 6	7 3	0 28	♎	11 57
11	Th	Sirnames used 1072	6 14 6	3 42	8 0	1 10	15	ev.27
12	Fr	☽ in apo. *ges.*	6 12 6	3 19	8 57	1 53	26	0 58
13	Sa	Plan. Her. dis.'81.	6 11 6	2 55	9 54	2 36	♏	1 29
14	Su	*a storm of snow*	6 9 6	2 32	10 50	3 21	20	2 2
15	M	♃ rises 2 51 m. *or*	6 8 6	2 8	11 47	4 6	♐	2 38
16	Tu	♄ sou. 9 13 eve. *rain*	6 6 6	1 44	morn.	4 54	14	3 20
17	W	♄ sets 4 22 morn. *is at*	6 5 6	1 21	0 42	5 44	27	4 13
18	Th	*Low Tides.* hand.	6 3 6	0 57	1 35	6 36	♑	5 23
19	Fr	☌ ♂ ♃ *more changa-*	6 2 6	0 33	2 26	7 29	23	6 49
20	Sa	☉ enters ♈ *ble, but*	6 1 6	S. 9	3 13	8 24	♒	8 15
21	Su	Benedict. *generally*	5 59 7	N. 14	3 57	9 19	20	9 21
22	M	*fine.——*	5 58 7	0 38	4 38	10 14	♓	10 14
23	Tu	♃ rises 2 26 morn.	5 56 7	1 2	5 16	11 10	20	10 59
24	W	☽ in perig. *Tides*	5 55 7	1 25	sets.	ev. 6	♈	11 41
25	Th	*Rainy.*	5 53 7	1 49	7 43	1 3	20	morn.
26	Fr	*quite high.*	5 52 7	2 12	8 57	2 0	♉	0 22
27	Sa	♀ stationary.	5 51 7	2 36	10 9	2 58	20	1 3
28	Su	*dull weather.*	5 49 7	2 59	11 16	3 55	♊	1 45
29	M	♄ sets 3 36 morn.	5 48 7	3 23	morn.	4 52	19	2 29
30	Tu	♄ south 8 31 eve.	5 46 7	3 46	0 18	5 47	♋	3 18
31	W		5 45 7	4 9	1 13	6 40	16	4 16

Master Mason's Due-Guard.

The due-guard is given by putting the right hand to the left side of the bowels, the hand open with the thumb next to the belly, and drawing it across the belly, and let it fall; this is done tolerably quick. It alludes to the *penalty* of disembowelling, &c.

☞ It would seem from these signs, that masons were taught to think more of the penalty of *death* for disclosing secrets, than of the guilt of *perjury*.

	D.	H.	M.			D.	H.	M.
Full Moon,	8	2	45M.	New Moon,	22	6	43A.
Last Quarter,	16	2	5M.	First Quarter,	29	3	10A

D.M.	D.W.	Miscellaneous Matters.	S.Rises & Sets.	Suns dec'lS.	Moon Sets.	Moon South.	M. Pl.	High Water
1	Th	*Low Tides.* *Much*	5 43 7	4 32	2 1	7 31	29	5 29
2	Fr	Jef. b. '43 *finer—*	5 42 7	4 55	2 43	8 19	♌	6 53
3	Sa	♃ rises 1 47 morn.	5 41 7	5 18	3 20	9 6	24	8 8
4	Su	♄ sets 3 12 morn. *fre-*	5 39 7	5 41	3 54	9 51	♍	9 7
5	M	Goldsmith d. 1774	5 38 7	6 4	4 25	10 34	18	9 53
6	Tu	♊ ☉ ♃ *quent showers.*	5 36 7	6 27	4 53	11 17	♎	10 30
7	W	♄ south 7 51 eve.	5 35 7	6 49	5 21	morn.	11	11 4
8	Th	☽ in apogee. *Rough*	5 34 7	7 12	rises.	0 0	23	11 36
9	Fr	Peace ratified by G.B.	5 32 7	7 34	7 55	0 43	♍	ev. 7
10	Sa	U.S.Bank icp '16. ['84.	5 31 7	7 56	8 53	1 26	17	0 38
11	Su	Bri. barges taken '12.	5 29 7	8 19	9 49	2 12	29	1 11
12	M	*with high winds,*	5 28 7	8 40	10 44	2 59	♐	1 45
13	Tu	♄ stat. *and some*	5 27 7	9 2	11 37	3 47	23	2 22
14	W	♃ rises 1 14 morn.	5 25 7	9 24	morn.	4 37	♑	3 4
15	Th	♄ sets 2 35 morn.	5 24 7	9 45	0 27	5 29	19	3 56
16	Fr	♄ south 7 18 eve.	5 23 7	10 7	1 15	6 22	♒	5 2
17	Sa	Franklin d. 1790.	5 21 7	10 28	1 59	7 15	15	6 26
18	Su	*snow—*	5 20 7	10 49	2 39	8 8	29	7 51
19	M	Bat. of Lex. 1775.	5 19 7	11 10	3 18	9 2	♓	9 2
20	Tu	☉ ent. ♉ *mild again,*	5 17 7	11 31	3 55	9 57	28	9 53
21	W	♀ rises 3 32 morn. *high*	5 16 7	11 51	4 32	10 52	♈	10 46
22	Th	☽ per. Sup. ☌ ☉ ☿	5 15 7	12 11	sets.	11 50	28	11 29
23	Fr	*Tides high.* *wind.*	5 13 7	12 31	7 53	ev.48	♉	morn.
24	Sa	♄ sets 2 6 m.	5 12 7	12 51	9 4	1 46	28	0 11
25	Su	*Very fine for*	5 11 7	13 11	10 10	2 45	♊	0 53
26	M	♃ rises 0 32 morn.	5 9 7	13 30	11 10	3 42	27	1 36
27	Tu	☌ ♂ ♅ *the season.*	5 8 7	13 50	morn.	4 39	♋	2 18
28	W	NapoleonEm. forElb.	5 7 7	14 9	0 2	5 31	25	3 6
29	Th	*Tides diminish-* ['14.	5 6 7	14 27	0 47	6 22	♌	3 58
30	Fr	*ing.* *Warm showers.*	5 4 7	14 46	1 27	7 9	20	5 2

SECRET things belong to God. &c. Deut. xxix. 29.—Hide me from the SECRET counsel of the wicked, etc. Ps. lxiv. 2, 3, 4.

Master Mason's Grand Hailing Sign of Distress.
The sign is given by raising both hands and arms to the elbows perpendicularly, one on either side of the head, the elbows forming a square. The words accompanying this sign in case of distress, are, ' *O Lord, my God, is there no help for the widow's son.*' As the last words drop from your lips you let your hands fall in that manner, best calculated to indicate solemnity. King Solomon is said to have made this exclamation on the receipt of the information of the death of Hiram Abiff. Masons are all charged never to give the *words* except in the dark when the sign cannot be seen.

	D.	H.	M.		D.	H.	M.
Full Moon,	7	7	18 A.	New Moon,	22	2	29 M.
Last Quarter,	15	11	34 M.	First Quarter	29	6	4 M.

D. M.	D. W.	Miscellaneous Matters.	S. Rises & Sets.	Suns dec'l N	Moon Sets.	Moon-South	M. Pl.	High Water.
1	Sa	*Somewhat cooler —*	5 3 7	15 4	2 2	7 55	♍	6 15
2	Su	□ ☉ ♄ *more*	5 2 7	15 22	2 34	8 39	15	7 31
3	Mo	♄ sets 1 28 m. *rain.*	5 1 7	15 40	3 3	9 21	27	8 35
4	Tu	Bonaparte d. 1821.	5 0 7	15 57	3 31	10 3	♎	9 23
5	W	♃ stat. ☽ in apo.	4 58 8	16 15	3 59	10 46	20	10 4
6	Th	♃ rises 11 51 eve.	4 57 8	16 32	4 29	11 30	♏	10 40
7	Fr	♀ rises 3 10 morn.	4 56 8	16 48	rises	morn.	14	11 14
8	Sa	⊡ ☉ ♂ *Fine again*	4 55 8	17 5	7 49	0 14	26	11 47
9	Su	*for planting.*	4 54 8	17 21	8 45	1 1	♐	ev. 21
10	M		4 53 8	17 37	9 39	1 49	20	0 55
11	Tu	♄ sets 0 58 m. *show-*	4 52 8	17 52	10 30	2 39	♑	1 31
12	W	♀ rises 3 2 m. *ers*	4 50 8	18 8	11 18	3 29	15	2 8
13	Th	Jup. rises 11 23 eve.	4 49 8	18 23	morn.	4 21	28	2 50
14	Fr	♃ so. 3 54 m. *with*	4 48 8	18 37	0 2	5 13	♒	3 39
15	Sa	Paper cur. es. '75.	4 47 8	18 52	0 42	6 4	25	4 37
16	Su	♅ stat. *thunder*	4 46 8	19 6	1 20	6 56	♓	5 54
17	M	*Low Tides* [elon ♀	4 45 8	19 19	1 56	7 49	23	7 21
18	Tu	♀ rises 2 52 m. *some*	4 44 8	19 33	2 31	8 42	♈	8 38
19	W	☽ perigon. *rain—*	4 43 8	19 46	3 7	9 36	22	9 38
20	Th	Columbus d. 1506.	4 43 8	19 58	3 44	10 31	♉	10 28
21	Fr	☉ ent. ♊ Gr. elon.	4 42 8	20 11	4 25	11 29	22	11 13
22	Sa	*High Tides.* [☿ *fine*	4 41 8	20 23	sets	ev. 28	♊	11 57
23	Su	*weather for a few*	4 40 8	20 35	8 56	1 27	21	morn.
24	M		4 39 8	20 46	9 53	2 25	♋	0 39
25	Tu	♃ rises 10 33 eve.	4 38 8	20 57	10 43	3 21	20	1 21
26	W	Gen. Elec. Bost.	4 37 8	21 7	11 26	4 14	♌	2 2
27	Th	♃ south 3 morn.	4 37 8	21 18	morn.	5 3	19	2 44
28	Fr	*days.*	4 36 8	21 28	0 3	5 50	29	3 29
29	Sa	*Low Tides. more*	4 35 8	21 37	0 36	6 35	♍	4 20
30	Su	*rain.*	4 35 8	21 46	1 6	7 18	23	5 21
31	M	*cooler with wind.*	4 34 8	21 55	1 33	8 0	♎	6 31

Mark Master's Ear Sgn.

He then clutches the third and little fingers of his right hand with his thumb, extends at the same time his middle and fore fingers, brings up his hand in such a manner as to have the side of the middle finger touch the rim of the right ear, then lets it drop.   [see next page.

	D.	H.	M.			D.	H.	M.
Full Moon,	6	9	35M.	New Moon,		20	10	19M.
Last Quarter,	13	6	5A.	First Quarter,		27	10	32A.

D. M.	D. W	Miscellaneous Matters	S. Rises & Sets.	Suns dec'lN	Moon Sets	Moon South.	M Pl	High Water.
1	Tu	*Fine weather*	4 33 8	22 3	2 1	8 43	17	7 39
2	W	☽ in apogee. *for*	4 33 8	22 11	2 30	9 26	29	8 40
3	Th	☿ stationary. *Far-*	4 32 8	22 19	3 0	10 10	♏	9 28
4	Fr	♀ ris. 2 29. morn.	4 31 8	22 26	3 32	10 55	23	10 10
5	Sa	*mers.*	4 31 8	22 33	4 6	11 43	♐	10 48
6	Su	Trin. Sun. *Signs of*	4 30 8	22 39	rises.	morn.	17	11 21
7	M	Art. E. B. *High tides.*	4 30 8	22 46	8 25	0 33	♑	ev. 0
8	Tu	♃ sou. 2 7 morn.	4 30 8	22 51	9 15	1 23	12	0 36
9	W	♃ rises 9 46 eve.	4 29 8	22 56	10 0	2 15	25	1 14
10	Th	♀ rises 2 21 m. *show-*	4 29 8	23 1	10 41	3 7	♒	1 52
11	Fr	♄ sets 10 56 eve. *ers.*	4 28 8	23 6	11 19	3 59	22	2 32
12	Sa	Rye House plot dis.	4 28 8	23 10	11 54	4 50	♓	3 16
13	Su	1683. *good weather for*	4 28 8	23 13	morn.	5 41	19	4 9
14	M	*Low tides.*	4 27 8	23 17	0 29	6 32	♈	5 17
15	Tu	Inf. ☌ ☉ ☿ *vegita-*	4 27 8	23 19	1 3	7 24	17	6 41
16	W	*tion. high winds.*	4 27 8	23 22	1 38	8 17	♉	8 4
17	Th	☽ per. B. Bunk. H. '75	4 27 8	23 24	2 15	9 11	16	9 12
18	Fr	Bat. of Waterloo, '15.	4 27 8	23 25	2 57	10 8	♊	10 8
19	Sa	☌ ☽ ☿ *remarkable*	4 27 8	23 26	3 43	11 6	15	10 56
20	Su	*fine for the season.*	4 27 8	23 27	sets.	ev. 4	♋	11 39
21	M	☉ enters ♋ *High*	4 27 8	23 27	8 26	1 1	14	morn.
22	Tu	♀ ris. 2 7 m. *tides.*	4 27 8	23 27	9 14	1 57	28	0 21
23	W	♃ rises 8 23 eve. *look*	4 27 8	23 27	9 55	2 49	♌	1 1
24	Th	Glass 1st made 1457.	4 27 8	23 26	10 29	3 37	24	1 38
25	Fr	♄ sets 10 3 eve. *out*	4 27 8	23 25	11 1	4 24	♍	2 14
26	Sa	♃ sou. 0 43 morn.	4 27 8	23 23	11 31	5 9	19	2 53
27	Su	*for showers*	4 27 8	23 21	11 58	5 51	♎	3 35
28	M	*Tides pretty low.*	4 27 8	23 18	morn.	6 33	13	4 21
29	Tu	☽ in apo. Tax on Tea	4 28 8	23 15	0 26	7 16	25	5 19
30	W	*pleasant.* [1767.	4 28 8	23 12	0 56	8 0	♏	6 27

God is light, and in him is no DARKNESS at all. If we say that we have fellowship with him, *and walk in* DARKNESS, we lie, and do not the truth, etc. 1 John v. 6. 7.

Hand Sign, and part of Due-Guard of a Mark Master.
As his hand drops, (as in last page) in falling bring the outward side of the little finger of the left hand across the wrist of the right, then lets them fall by his sides. These are the *sign and due-guard* of a Mark-Master, and alludes to the penal part of the obligation.

Light on Masonry, page 91.

	D.	H.	M.			D.	H.	M.
Full Moon,	5	9	40A.		New Moon,	19	7	30A.
Last Quarter,	12	10	52A.		FirstQuarter,	27	3	52A.

D.M.	D.W	Miscellaneous Matters.	S.Rises &Sets	Suns dec'l N	Moon Sets.	Moon South.	M. Pl.	High Water
1	Th	♃ rises 7 45 eve.	4 28 8	23 8	1 27	8 44	19	7 39
2	Fr	*Very warm*	4 29 8	23 4	1 59	9 31	♐	8 41
3	Sa	♄ sets 9 30 eve. *but*	4 29 8	22 59	2 37	10 20	13	9 33
4	Su	Adams & Jef. d. 1826.	4 29 8	22 54	3 21	11 11	27	10 19
5	M	☌ ☉ ♃ *fine growing*	4 30 8	22 49	rises.	morn.	♑	11 0
6	Tu	*High tides. weath-*	4 30 8	22 43	7 52	0 4	22	11 39
7	W	♓ sou. 11 47 eve.	4 31 8	22 37	8 36	0 57	♒	ev· 18
8	Th	☿ rises 1 56 m. *er.*	4 31 8	22 30	9 15	1 49	18	0 55
9	Fr	Gr. elon. ☿ *Now is*	4 32 8	22 23	9 52	2 41	Pi.	1 33
10	Sa	Columbus b. 1447.	4 32 8	22 16	10 26	3 33	16	2 11
11	Su	J. Q. Adams b. 1766.	4 33 8	22 8	11 0	4 24	♈	2 53
12	M	*the time for haying.*	4 33 8	22 0	11 35	5 15	14	3 41
13	Tu	Sat. sets 8 54 eve.	4 34 8	21 52	morn.	6 8	28	4 42
14	W	☽ in perigee. *Dry.*	4 35 8	21 43	0 12	7 1	♉	6 3
15	Th	Stony point taken.	4 35 8	21 34	0 51	7 55	27	7 31
16	Fr	*sign of showers,*	4 36 8	21 24	1 33	8 50	♊	8 48
17	Sa		4 37 8	21 14	2 21	9 47	25	9 49
18	Su	*with thunder*	4 38 8	21 4	3 15	10 44	♋	10 39
19	M	Geo. IV. crown'd '21.	4 39 8	20 53	sets.	11 40	23	11 22
20	Tu	*and lightning.*	4 39 8	20 42	7 45	ev.33	♌	morn.
21	W	Jup. sou. 10 43 eve.	4 40 8	20 31	8 23	1 24	19	0 0
22	Th	*Dull weather.*	4 41 8	20 19	8 57	2 12	♍	0 37
23	Fr	☉ enters ♌ *more fine*	4 42 8	20 7	9 28	2 58	15	1 11
24	Sa	♀ rises 1 55 m. *again.*	4 43 8	19 54	9 57	3 43	27	1 45
25	Su	Dog days begin. *A*	4 44 8	19 42	10 25	4 25	♎	2 18
26	M	St. Anne. *storm at*	4 45 8	19 29	10 54	5 8	21	2 54
27	Tu	☽ in apogee. *hand.*	4 46 8	19 15	11 24	5 51	♏	3 34
28	W	*Quite low tides.*	4 47 8	19 2	11 56	6 35	15	4 21
29	Th	*pleasant again.*	4 48 8	18 48	morn.	7 21	27	5 21
30	Fr	Wm. Penn d. 1718.	4 49 8	18 33	0 32	8 9	♐	6 36
31	Sa	Jup. sets 2 30 morn.	4 50 8	18 18	1 12	8 59	21	7 52

I spake openly to the world, etc. and in SECRET have I said nothing. John xviii. 20.

Mark Master's Grand Sign of Distress.
Representing the candidate with the key-stone held between his thumb and fore finger. (See Light on Masonry, p. 99.) On the key stone these letters are engraved so as to form a circle. H. T. W. S. S. T. K. S.— the initial letters of the words *Hiram, Tyre, Widow's son sent to King Solomon.*

	D.	H.	M.			D.	H.	M.
Full Moon.	4	8	13M.		New Moon,	18	7	9M.
Last Quarter,	11	3	24M.		First Quart.	26	9	19M.

D. M.	D. W.	Miscellaneous Matters.	S. Rises & Sets.		Suns dec'lN	Moon Sets.	Moon South.	M. Pl.	High Water.
1	Su	☍ ☉ ♅ *sultry*	4 51	8	13 4	1 58	9 52	♑	8 59
2	M	♂ sou. 3 21 morn.	4 52	8	17 48	2 51	10 45	17	9 54
3	Tu	♀ rises 2 7 m. *weath-*	4 53	8	17 33	3 50	11 39	♒	10 40
4	W	Sup. ☌ ☉ ☿ *er.*	4 54	8	17 17	rises	morn.	14	11 21
5	Th	A. M. Stat. Con. 1829	4 55	8	17 1	7 53	0 33	28	ev. 0
6	Fr	*Tides pretty high.*	4 56	8	16 45	8 29	1 27	♓	0 39
7	Sa	♈ south 9 30 eve.	4 57	8	16 28	9 3	2 20	26	1 17
8	Su	☽ in perigee.	4 59	8	16 11	9 38	3 12	♈	1 55
9	M	☌ ☿ ♄ *refresh-*	5 0	7	15 54	10 14	4 5	25	2 37
10	Tu	Royalty. abol. in Fr.	5 1	7	15 36	10 52	4 58	♉	3 24
11	W	♓ sets 1 44 m. [1792.	5 2	7	15 19	11 33	5 52	23	4 22
12	Th	Geo. IV. b. 1762.	5 3	7	15 1	morn.	6 46	♊	5 38
13	Fr	*ing showers, with*	5 5	7	14 43	0 19	7 42	21	7 10
14	Sa	☌ ☉ ♄ *thunder and*	5 6	7	14 24	1 10	8 38	♋	8 33
15	Su	10 Sun. aft. Trin.	5 7	7	14 6	2 6	9 33	19	9 35
16	M	*lightning.*	5 8	7	13 47	3 6	10 27	♌	10 25
17	Tu	♀ rises 2 30 morn.	5 10	7	13 28	4 7	11 19	15	11 5
18	W	♂ stationary.	5 11	7	13 8	sets.	ev. 8	28	11 42
19	Th	*High Tides.*	5 12	7	12 49	7 31	0 55	♍	morn.
20	Fr	♂ sou. 2 20 morn.	5 13	7	12 29	8 2	1 40	23	0 16
21	Sa	♓ sets 1 3 morn.	5 15	7	12 9	8 31	2 24	♎	0 48
22	Su	*evenings growing*	5 16	7	11 49	8 59	3 7	17	1 20
23	M	☉ enters ♍ *cool-*	5 17	7	11 29	9 28	3 50	29	1 52
24	Tu	☽ apogee. *er.*	5 19	7	11 9	10 0	4 34	♏	2 24
25	W	Jup. south 8 18 eve.	5 20	7	10 48	10 34	5 19	2 3	3 2
26	Th	*Low tides.*	5 21	7	10 27	11 12	6 5	♐	3 45
27	Fr	*changable with signs*	5 23	7	10 6	11 55	6 54	17	4 39
28	Sa	*of rain.*	5 24	7	9 45	morn.	7 44	29	5 52
29	Su		5 25	7	9 24	0 43	8 37	♑	7 14
30	M	♀ rises 3 2 morn.	5 27	7	9 2	1 39	9 31	25	8 32
31	Tu	*More pleasant.*	5 28	7	8 41	2 40	10 25	♒	9 33

Freemen, boldly take your stand   Wield the pen with willing hand,
Spread the truth throughout the land,   Down with masonry!

Past Master's Sign.

The sign (sometimes called the due-guard) is given by laying the edge of the thumb of the right hand, in a vertical position on the centre of the mouth, high enough to touch the upper lip. (*See Light on Masonry, p.* 111.

☞ These signs should become familiar to the eye, in order that they may be detected, should masons offer them in a court of Justice.

	D.	H.	M.		D.	H.	M.
Full Moon,	2	5	54A.	New Moon,	16	9	44A.
Last Quarter,	9	9	14M.	First Quart.	25	2	8M.

D. M.	D. M.	Miscellaneous Matters.	S. Rises & Sets.	Suns dec'lN	Moon Sets.	Moon South.	M. Pl.	High Water
1	W	*cooler with*	5 29 7	8 19	3 46	11 19	♒	10 23
2	Th	Lond. b. 1666. *high*	5 31 7	7 57	rises.	morn.	♓	11 5
3	Fr	*Very high tides.*	5 32 7	7 35	7 8	0 14	21	11 47
4	Sa	♓ sta. ☽ per. *winds.*	5 33 7	7 13	7 43	1 9	♈	ev.26
5	Su	Dog d. end. *warmer,*	5 35 7	6 51	8 20	2 3	20	1 5
6	M	LaFayette b. 1757.	5 36 7	6 29	8 58	2 58	♉	1 45
7	Tu	*but generally fine* [1829	5 38 7	6 6	9 40	3 53	20	2 27
8	W	Gt. A. M. meet. Bost.	5 39 7	5 44	10 25	4 49	♊	3 15
9	Th	♀ rises 3 25 m. [M.'26.	5 40 7	5 21	11 14	5 45	18	4 14
10	Fr	Miller's Of. fir'd by	5 42 7	4 58	morn.	6 41	♋	5 30
11	Sa	Morgan kidnap. 1826.	5 43 7	4 36	0 8	7 36	16	7 0
12	Su	At. to kidnap Miller	5 45 7	4 13	1 6	8 30	29	8 23
13	M	☌ ♀ ♄ Sat. [1826.	5 46 7	3 50	2 7	9 22	♌	9 24
14	Tu	*signs of a Storm.*	5 47 7	3 27	3 8	10 11	24	10 11
15	W	♂ sou. 0 30 morn.	5 49 7	3 3	4 8	10 58	♍	10 50
16	Th	*Middling tides.*	5 50 7	2 40	sets.	11 44	19	11 25
17	Fr	Gen. Wolf ta. Quebec	5 52 7	2 17	6 40	ev.28	♎	11 57
18	Sa	Jup. sets 11 18 e. ['59.	5 53 7	1 54	7 9	1 12	14	morn.
19	Su	Morgan mur. F. Niag.	5 54 7	1 31	7 38	1 55	25	0 28
20	M	☽ inapo. ☍ ☉ ♂ ['26.	5 56 7	1 7	8 9	2 38	♏	1 0
21	Tu	Fr. cal. a Repub. '92.	5 57 7	0 44	8 42	3 23	19	1 30
22	W	7*s sou. 3 41 m. *ve-*	5 59 7	N. 21	9 18	4 9	♐	2 3
23	Th	☉ enters ♎ *ry fine*	6 0 6	S. 3	9 58	4 56	13	2 40
24	Fr	♀ rises 4 6 m. *and*	6 2 6	0 26	10 43	5 44	25	3 22
25	Sa	♂ south 11 37 eve.	6 3 6	0 50	11 34	6 34	♑	4 13
26	Su	*pleasant.*	6 4 6	1 13	morn.	7 27	20	5 20
27	M	Jup. sets 10 48 eve.	6 6 6	1 37	0 32	8 20	♒	6 46
28	Tu	*A storm*	6 7 6	2 0	1 34	9 13	10	8 9
29	W		6 9 6	2 23	2 40	10 7	♓	9 14
30	Th	*is at hand.*	6 10 6	2 47	3 50	11 2	14	10 7

☞ The great National Anti-Masonic Convention will be held at Philadelphia, September 11th, 1830.

Most Excellent Master's Sign.

The sign is given by placing your hands one on each breast, the fingers meeting in the centre of the body and jerking them apart, as though you were trying to tear open your breast. It alludes to the penalty of betraying the secrets of this degree.

	D.	H.	M.			D.	H.	M.
Full Moon,	2	3	13M.	New Moon,		16	2	47A.
Last Quarter,	8	5	48A.	First Quarter,		24	5	36A.
				Full Moon,		31	0	34A.

D.M.	D.W.	Miscellaneous Matters.	S. Rises & Sets.	Suns dec'l S.	Moon Sets.	Moon South.	M. Pl.	High Water.
1	Fr	1st Steam Boat. 1807.	6 12 6	3 10	5 3	11 57	29	10 53
2	Sa	♊ ☉. ♓ *comfortable.*	6 13 6	3 33	rises	morn.	♈	11 34
3	Su	☽ per. *Very high*	6 14 6	3 57	7 1	0 53	29	ev. 14
4	M	♀ ris. 4 35 m. [*tides.*	6 16 6	4 20	7 43	1 50	♉	0 56
5	Tu	*weather for the*	6 17 6	4 43	8 28	2 48	29	1 38
6	W	*season.*	6 19 6	5 6	9 18	3 46	♊	2 21
7	Th	♂ south 10 43 eve.	6 20 6	5 29	10 13	4 44	28	3 11
8	Fr	Jup. sets 10 14 eve.	6 22 6	5 52	11 10	5 41	♋	4 9
9	Sa	Count Pulaski kil. '79.	6 23 6	6 15	morn.	6 36	26	5 23
10	Su	*with cool nights*	6 24 6	6 38	0 9	7 28	♌	6 48
11	M	*and mornings.*	6 26 6	7 1	1 10	8 18	21	8 6
12	Tu	♀ rises 4 55 morn.	6 27 6	7 23	2 11	9 5	♍	9 6
13	W	7*s. sou. 2 25 morn.	6 29 6	7 46	3 12	9 51	16	9 53
14	Th	♂ south 10 14 eve.	6 30 6	8 8	4 11	10 35	28	10 31
15	Fr	☌ ☽ ♀ *very*	6 31 6	8 31	5 9	11 18	♎	11 5
16	Sa	♅ stat. *changable,*	6 33 6	8 53	sets.	ev. 1	22	11 37
17	Su	*dull and*	6 34 6	9 15	6 18	0 44	♏	morn.
18	M	☽ in apo. B. Slp. Frol.	6 36 6	9 37	6 50	1 28	16	0 8
19	Tu	♂ stat. taken 1812.	6 37 6	9 59	7 25	2 13	28	0 40
20	W	Jup. sets 9 36 eve.	6 38 6	10 20	8 3	2 59	♐	1 12
21	Th	☌ ☿ ♃. ☿ stat. *clou-*	6 40 6	10 42	8 46	3 47	22	1 45
22	Fr	7*s. sou. 1 48 m. *dy.*	6 41 6	11 3	9 34	4 36	♑	2 22
23	Sa	☉ enters ♍ *wet weath-*	6 42 6	11 24	10 26	5 25	16	3 3
24	Su	Am. discov. 1492. *er.*	6 44 6	11 45	11 24	6 16	29	3 51
25	M	*fine for a few*	6 45 6	12 6	morn.	7 7	♒	4 53
26	Tu	*Low tides.*	6 46 6	12 27	0 26	7 59	25	6 12
27	W	♂ south 9 26 eve.	6 48 6	12 47	1 31	8 52	♓	7 38
28	Th	*days.*	6 49 6	13 7	2 42	9 45	22	8 50
29	Fr	Jup. sets 9 8 eve.	6 51 6	13 27	3 54	10 40	♈	9 47
30	Sa	♊ ☉ ♅ ☽ per.	6 52 6	13 47	5 9	11 36	22	10 35
31	Su	*now look*	6 53 6	14 7	6 25	morn.	♉	11 19

Royal Arch Mason's Due-Guard.

Raise the right thumb to the forehead, the hand and arm horizontal; thumb towards the forehead; draw it briskly across the forehead and drop it perpendicular by the side. It refers to the penalty (cleaing the skull.)

Light on Masonry, p. 139.

	D.	H.	M.		D.	H.	M.
Last Quarter,	7	6	9M.	First Quarter,	23	7	0M.
New Moon,	15	9	11M.	Full Moon,	29	10	34A

D.M.	D.W.	Miscellaneous Matters.	S. Rises & Sets.	Suns dec'lS.	Moon Rises.	Moon South.	M. Pl.	High Water.
1	M	*High tides.*	6 54 6	14 26	6 21	0 34	23	ev. 1
2	Tu	*out for a*	6 56 6	14 45	7 11	1 34	□	0 44
3	W	♃ se ts 8 52 eve	6 57 6	15 4	8 4	2 34	23	1 27
4	Th	♐ sou. 8 57 eve.	6 58 6	15 23	9 1	3 34	♋	2 12
5	Fr	Powder Plot, 1605.	6 59 6	15 41	10 2	4 31	22	2 59
6	Sa	7*s. sou. 0 53 morn.	7 1 5	16 0	11 4	5 25	♌	3 51
7	Su	*storm.*	7 2 5	16 17	morn.	6 17	18	4 55
8	M	*Low tides.*	7 3 5	16 35	0 6	7 6	♍	6 10
9	Tu	*grows fine*	7 4 5	16 52	1 6	7 52	23	7 26
10	W	♃ sets 8 30 eve.	7 5 5	17 9	2 6	8 36	25	8 31
11	Th	Dark d. N. E. 1819.	7 7 5	17 26	3 4	9 18	♎	9 20
12	Fr	7*s sou. 0 29 m.	7 8 5	17 43	4 2	10 1	19	10 2
13	Sa	☽ in apogee. *again.*	7 9 5	17 59	5 0	10 44	♏	10 39
14	Su	*more falling weath-*	7 10 5	18 15	5 56	11 27	13	11 12
15	M	*er, but*	7 11 5	18 30	sets	ev.11	25	11 45
16	Tu	*pleasant.*	7 12 5	18 45	6 2	0 56	♐	morn.
17	W	7*s. south 0 9 morn.	7 13 5	19 0	6 43	1 44	19	0 17
18	Th	Gr. earthq. 1755.	7 14 5	19 15	7 29	2 32	♑	0 51
19	Fr	♐ sou, 8 10 eve. *for*	7 15 5	19 29	8 19	3 21	13	1 26
20	Sa	♃ sets 2 58 eve. *the*	7 16 5	19 43	9 14	4 10	25	2 2
21	Su	*season.*	7 17 5	19 56	10 13	5 0	♒	2 41
22	M	☉ enters ♐ . *more*	7 18 5	20 9	11 16	5 50	21	3 26
23	Tu	*signs of a*	7 19 5	20 22	morn.	6 40	♓	4 20
24	W	♊ ☉ ♄ *Low tides.*	7 20 5	20 34	0 22	7 30	17	5 29
25	Th	☌ ☽ ♂ *storm.*	7 21 5	20 46	1 29	8 22	♈	6 51
26	Fr	7*s. so. 11 27 eve	7 22 5	20 58	2 40	9 15	16	8 12
27	Sa	♂ sou. 7 46 eve. *fine*	7 23 5	21 9	3 53	10 10	♉	9 16
28	Su	Earthq. in N. E. '14.	7 23 5	21 20	5 6	11 8	16	10 10
29	M	☽ per. *Tides high.*	7 24 5	21 30	rises	morn.	♊	10 58
30	Tu	*again for a few. days.*	7 25 5	21 40	5 44	0 8	16	11 42

By the blood of Morgan *slain !*   Masonry no more shall *reign !*
Victims shall not bleea in *rain !*   FREEMEN shall be FREE.

Royal Arch Mason's Grand Sign.

This is made by locking the fingers of both hands togeth-er, and carrying them to the top of the head, the palms up-wards, alluding to the manner in which the brother in the vault found his hands involuntarily raised to guard against the beating rays of the sun.

	D.	H.	M.			D.	H.	M.
Last Quarter.	6	10	32 A.	First Quarter,	22	5	58 A.
New Moon,	15	3	36 M.	Full Moon,	29	9	18 M.

D.M.	D.W.	Miscellaneous Matters.	S. Rises & Sets.	Suns dec'l N	Moon Rises.	Moon South.	M. Pl.	High Water
1	W	*Sudden*	7 26 5	21 49	6 38	1 9	♋	ev .26
2	Th	♂ sou. 7 32 eve. *chan-*	7 26 5	21 59	7 38	2 9	16	1 9
3	Fr	Sup. ☌ ☉ ☿ *ges—*	7 27 5	22 7	8 41	3 6	♌	1 51
4	Sa	7*s. so. 10 54 eve.	7 28 5	22 16	9 46	4 1	14	2 34
5	Su	*cool wind*	7 28 5	22 23	10 49	4 53	27	3 19
6	M	*with some*	7 29 5	22 31	11 50	5 41	♍	4 9
7	Tu	*Tides pretty low.*	7 29 5	22 38	morn.	6 26	22	5 8
8	W	*rain if not*	7 30 5	22 44	0 49	7 9	♎	6 15
9	Th	*snow—*	7 30 5	22 50	1 46	7 51	28	7 25
10	Fr	♄ sou. 5 9 morn.	7 31 5	22 56	2 43	8 33	16	8 27
11	Sa	☽ in apogee.	7 31 5	23 1	3 41	9 16	♏	9 18
12	Su	♄ stat.	7 32 5	23 6	4 36	9 59	22	10 0
13	M	*pleasant*	7 32 5	23 10	5 31	10 44	♐	10 39
14	Tu	Washington d 1799.	7 32 5	23 14	6 27	11 31	16	11 15
15	W	Hartford Con. 1814.	7 33 5	23 17	sets.	ev.19	28	11 51
16	Th	Tea des. Bost. 1773.	7 33 5	23 20	6 4	1 8	♑	morn.
17	Fr	*High tides.*	7 33 5	23 23	6 58	1 57	23	0 26
18	Sa	♐ south 7 eve. *for a*	7 33 5	23 24	7 56	2 47	♒	1 1
19	Su	*day or two—*	7 33 5	23 26	8 57	3 37	18	1 37
20	M	Cape Cod. 1st set. '20.	7 33 5	23 27	10 2	4 26	♓	2 14
21	Tu	Sup. ☌ ☉ ♀ *cool but*	7 33 5	23 27	11 7	5 15	14	2 54
22	W	☉ enters ♑. *healthy*	7 33 5	23 27	morn.	6 4	28	3 41
23	Th	*weather.*	7 33 5	23 27	0 13	6 54	♈	4 37
24	Fr	♄ so. 4 7 morn. *A*	7 33 5	23 26	1 22	7 46	25	5 52
25	Sa	Br. signed at Ghent	7 33 5	23 25	2 33	8 40	♉	7 16
26	Su	*storm is* [1816.	7 33 5	23 23	3 44	9 37	25	8 36
27	M	☽ in per. *near*	7 33 5	23 21	4 55	10 36	♊	9 39
28	Tu	*at hand.*	7 33 5	23 18	6 5	11 36	24	10 32
29	W	7*s. sou. 9 3 eve.	7 32 5	23 15	rises.	morn	♋	11 19
30	Th	Br. burnt Blackrock	7 32 5	23 11	0 36	6 8	24	eve. 2
31	Fr	*Tides High.* ['12	7 32 5	23 7	1 33	7 13	♌	0 43

COURTS.

United States Courts.

Supreme Federal Court. At Washington, to commence on the first Monday in Feb. annually.

Circuit Federal Courts in the First and Second Eastern Circuits.

In *Maine*—at Portland on the 1st of May, and at Wiscasset on the 1st of Oct. In *New Hampshire*—at Portsmouth, May 8th, and at Exeter, Oct. 8th. In *Massachusetts*—at Boston, May 15, and Oct. 15. In *Rhode Island*—at Providence, Nov. 15, and at Newport, June 15. In *Vermont*—at Windsor May 1, and at Rutland Oct. 3d. In *Connecticut*—at Hartford, Sept. 17, and at New Haven April 13. In *New York*—at New York April 1, and Sept. 1.

If any of the days happen on Sunday the Court commences on Monday.

District Federal Courts.

Maine—at Portland the 1st Tues. in June, and 1st in Dec. and at Wiscasset last Tues. in Feb. & 2d in Sept. In *New Hampshire*—at Portsmouth 3d Tues. in March & Sept. and at Exeter 3d in June & Dec. In *Massachusetts*—at Boston, 3d Tues. in March, 4th in June, 2d in Sept. and 1st Dec. In *Connecticut*—at Hartford, 4th Tues. in May & Nov. New Haven, 4th Tues. in Feb. & Aug. In *Rhode Island*—at Newport, 2d Tues. in May & 3d in Oct. Providence, 1st Tues. in Feb. & Aug. In *Vermont*—at Windsor, 21st May, and at Rutland on the 3d of October.

Courts in the State of Massachusetts.

Supreme Judicial Courts.

LAW TERMS. Suffolk & Nantucket; Boston, 1st Tues. March. Berkshire; Lenox. on week fol. 2d Tues. Sept. Hampshire, Franklin, & Hampden; Northampton, Mod. next preced. 4th Tues. Sept. Worcester; Worcester, 1st Tues. after 4th Tues. Sept. Middlesex; Cambridge, 3d Tues. af. 4th Tues. Sept. Bristol, Plymouth, Barnstable, & Dukes; Plymouth and Taunton, alternately, 4th Tues. after 4th Tues. Sept. New Bedford, Tues. next pre. 3d Mon. Nov. Norfolk; Dedham, 5th Tues. aft. 4th Tues. Sept. Essex; Salem, 6th Tues. after the 4th Tuesday of September.

NISI PRIUS TERMS. Norfolk—Dedham, 3d Tu. Feb. Middlesex-Concord, 2d Tu. April. Essex-Ipswich, 8th Tu. aft. 1st Tu. March. Worcester-Worcester, 6th Tu. aft. 1st Tu. March. Franklin-Greenfield, 6th Tu. aft. 1st Tu. March, and 2d in Sept. Bristol-Taunton, 6th Tu. aft. 1st Tu. March, and New Bedford, 2d Tu. Nov. Hampshire-Northampton, 7th Tu. aft. 1st Tu. March. Hampden-Springfield, 8th Tu. aft. 1st Tu. March, & 1st Tu. Sept. Barnstable & Dukes-Barnstable, 8th Tu. aft. 1st Tu. March. Berkshire-Lenox, 10th Tu. aft. 1st Tu. March, & 2d Tu. Sept. Plymouth-Plymouth, 10th Tu. aft. 1st. Tu. March. Suffolk & Nantucket-Boston, 7th Tu. aft. 4th Tu. Sept. Nantucket-Nantucket, 1st Tu. July.

Calender of Courts of Common Pleas.

Worcester-Worcester, 1st Mon. March, 3d Mond. June, Mo. aft. 4th Mo. Aug. & 1st Mn. Dec. Hampshire-Northampton, 4th Mo. March, 3d Mo. Aug. 3d Mo. Nov. Berkshire-Lenox, 4th Mo. Feb. June & Oct. Franklin-Greenfield, Tu. of week aft. 4th Mo. March, 2d Mo. Aug. & Nov. Hampden-Springfield, 3d Mo. March, 4th Mo. Aug. & Nov. Suffolk-Boston, 1st Tu. Jan. April, July, & Oct. Essex-Ipswich, 3d Mo. March & Dec. Salem 3d Mo. June; Newburyport, 3d Mo. Sept. Middlesex-Concord, 2d Mond. Sept. March, & June; Cambridge, 2d Mo. Dec. Plymouth-Plymouth, 2d Mo. April, & Aug. 3d Mo. Nov. Barnstable-Barnstable, Tu. aft. 3d Mon. April, & 1st Tu. Sept. Bristol-New Bedford, 2d Mo. June & Dec. Dukes -Edgartown, 3d Mo. May, & last Sept. Nantucket-Nantucket, 4th Mond. May. & 1st Mo. Oct. , Norfolk-Dedham, 4th Mo. April, 3d Mo. Sept. & Dec.

The Courts of Sessions are abolished, and their powers transferred to a *Board of Commissioners*, who meet as follows, viz.

Essex–Ipswich, 2d Tu. Apr. & Tu. 16th Jan. Salem, 2d Tu. July; Newburyport, 2d Tu. Oct. Milddlesex–Cambridge, 1st Tu. Jan. Concord, 2d Tu. May, & 3d Tu. Sept. Norfolk–Dedham, 3d Tu. April, & 4th Tu. Sept. Plymouth–Plymouth, 3d Tu. March, and 1st Tu. Aug. Bristol–Taunton, 4th Tu. March, & Sept. Barnstable–Barnstable, 2d Tu. in April, & Oct. Dukes–Edgartown, Wed. aft. 3d Mon. May. and Wed. aft. 2d. Mond. Nov. Nantucket–Nantucket, 3d Mo. April, 2d Mo. Oct. Worcester–Worcester, 4th Tu. March, 2d Tu. Sept. Hampshire–Northampton, 1st Tu. March & Sept. Franklin–Greenfield, at the same times. Hampden–Springfield, 1st Tu. April, 2d Tu. Sept. Berkshire–Lenox, last Tu. April, & Sept.

The Municipal Court of Boston, first Monday in every month. The Police Court, Boston, every day (except Sunday) 9, A. M. & 3, P. M. The Justices' Court for the Co. of Suffolk, every Wed. & Sat. at 9, A. M.

Courts in Maine.
Supreme Judicial Courts.
York–at York, on the last Tu. April; Alfred, 3d Tu. Sept. Cumberland–Portland, 1st Tu. May, & Nov Oxford–Paris, 3d Tu. May, and 2d Tues. Oct. Lincoln–Wiscasset, 4th Tu. May; and 3d Tu. Sept. Kennebec–Augusta, 1st Tu. next after 4th Tu. May, and 1st Tu. Oct. Somerset–Norridgewock, 2d Tu. after 4th Tu. May, and last Tu. Sept. Penobscot–Bangor, 3d Tu. after 4th Tu. May, and 4th Tu. Oct. Hancock–Castine, 4th Tu. after 4th Tu. May. Washington–West Machias, 5th Tues. after 4th Tues. May. Waldo–Belfast, 6th Tu. after 4th Tu. May.

☞The Law Terms are held in the Spring, in each County.

Court of Common Pleas.
York–at York, last Tu. in May; Alfred, 2d Tu. Feb. and 3d Tu. in Oct. Cumberland–Portland, 1st Tu. March, 3d Tu. June, and 1st Tu. Oct. Oxford–Paris, 4th Tu. Jan. 2d Tu. June, and 4th Tu. Sept. Lincoln–Wiscasset, 4th Tu. Dec. Warren, 4th Tu. April; Topsham, 4th Tu. Aug. Kennebeck–Augusta, 2d Tu. April, Aug. & Dec. Somerset–Norridgewock, 2d Tu. March, last in June, and 1st in Nov. Penobscot–Bangor, 1st Tu. Jan. June, & Oct. Hancock–Castine, 3d Tu. March, 2d in July, & 3d in Nov. Washington–West Machias, 1st Tu. March, & 3d Tu. Sept. Waldo–Belfast, 4th Tu. March, July, and Nov.

Courts of Sessions.
York–York, Tu. preced. last mon. May; Alfred, 2d Tu. Oct. Cumberland–Portland, 1st Tu. in June, and 3d in Dec. Oxford–Paris, 3d Tu. June & last in Oct. Lincoln–Wiscasset, 2d Tu. May; Topsham, 2d Tues. Sept. Kenebeck–Augusta, last Tu. April, 1st in Aug. & last in Dec. Somerset–Norridgewock, 3d Tu. in March, & 1st in Oct. Penobscot–Bangor, 1st Tu. April, & Sept. and 2d in Dec. Hancock–Castine, last Tu. April, & Thur. following 3d Tu. Oct. Washington–West Machias, 1st Wed. after 1st Tu. in Mar. & 1st Wed. af. 3d Tu. Sept. Waldo–Belfast, 3d Tu. Ap. Aug. & Nov.

Courts in the State of New Hampshire.
Superior Courts.
Rockingham–at Portsmouth, 1st tues. Jan. & at Exeter, 1st tues. Aug.—Stafford–Dover, 3d tues. Jan. & at Gilford, 3d tues. Aug. Merrimack–Concord, 1st tues. Feb. & Sept. Hillsboro'–Amherst, 3d Tues. Feb. & Sept.—Cheshire–Keene, 1st tues. April & Oct. Sulivan–Newport, 3d tues. April & Oct. Grafton–Haverhill, 1st tues. May and at Plymouth, 1st tues. Nov.—Coos–Lancaster, 3d tues. in May.

Courts of Common Pleas.

Rockingham–Exeter, 3d tues. March, and at Portsmouth, 1st tues. in Oct. Stafford Rochester, 1st tues. April, & at Gilmanton, 3d tues. Oct.   Merrimack–Concord, 3d tues, April & 1st tues. Nov.   Hillsboro'–Amherst, 1st tues. May, & 3d tues. Nov. Cheshire–Keene, 1st tues. Jan. & Aug.   Sullivan–Newport, 3d tues. Jan. & Aug. Grafton–Haverhill, 1st tues. in Feb. & at Plymouth, 1st tues. Sept. Coos–Lancaster, 3d tues. Feb. and Sept

Courts in the State of Vermont.
Supreme and County Courts.

All begin their sessions on *Tuesdays.*—Bennington–S. C. at Manchester in 1829, alternately at Manchester & Bennington, 2d after 4th tues. Jan. C.C. at Bennington, 4th in April ; Manchester, 4th in Sept. Windham–S. C. at Newfane, 3d after 4th tues. Jan.   C. C. 3d in April, & Sept. windsor–S. C. at Woodstock, 4th after 4th tues. Jan.   C. C. 1st in June, & Dec. Rutland–S. C. at Rutland, 1st after 4th tues. Jan.   C. C. 2d in April & Sept. Addison–S. C. at Middlebury, 4th in Jan. C. C. 2d in June & Dec. Orange –S. C. at Chelsea, 5th after 4th tues. Jan. C. C. 3d in June & Dec. Chittenden–S. C. at Burlington, 1st in Jan. C. C. last in March & Aug. Washington–S. C. at Montpilier, 6th after 4th tues. in Jan. C. C. 4th after 4th Tues April, & 1st after 3d tues. Sept. Caledonia–S. C. at Danville, 7th aft. 4th tues. Jan.   C. C. 4th in April, & Wen. after 1st tues. Sept.   Franklin–S. C. at St. Albans, 2d in Jan.   C. C. 2d in April & Sept. Orleans–S. C. at Irasburg, 9th after 4th tues. Jan.   C. C. 2d in April, & last in Aug. Essex–S. C. at Guildhall, 8th after 4th tues. Jan.   C. C. 2d after 4th tues. April, & 3d in Sept. Grand Isle–S. C. at North Hero, 3d in Jan.   C. C. 4th in April & Sept.

Courts in the State of Rhode Island.
Supreme Judicial Courts.

Newport, 1st Mond. in March, and 4th in Aug : at Providence, 3d Mond. in March & Sept. South Kingston, 4th Mond. in April, and 2d in Oct. Bristol 2d Mon. March & Sept. East Greenwich, 2d Mon. in April & 1st in Oct.
Courts of Common Pleas.

Newport, 3d Mon. May, & 1st in Nov. at Providence, 4th Mon. in May & Nov. at South Kingston, 1st Mon. in Feb. & 2d in Aug. at Bristol, 1st Mon. in Jan. and 1st in June ; East Greenwich, 3d Mon. in Feb. and Aug.

Courts in the State of Connecticut.
Supreme Court of Errors.

Hartford, 2d tues. in June. New Haven, tue. following 4th tues. in June. Fairfield, 4th tues. in June. Brooklyn, 4th tues. in July. Litchfield, 3d tues. in June. Tolland, tues. following 4th tues. in July. Middletown, 2d tues in July. New-London, 3d tues. in July.
Superior Courts.

Hartford, 2d tues. in Feb. & 4th in Sept. New Haven, 3d tues. in Jan. & 2d in Aug. New London, 1st tues in Oct. Norwich, 4th tues. in January. Danbury, 4th tues. in Sept. Fairfield, last tues. in Dec. Brooklyn, 1st tues. in Jan. & 2d in Sept. Litchfield, 3d tues. in Feb. & Aug. Middletown, 4th tues. in Feb. Haddam, 4th tues. in Aug. Tolland, 3d Tues. in Apr. and Oct.   #### County Courts.

Hartford, 4th tues. in March, 2d tues. in Aug. & Nov. New Haven, 3d tues. in March, 4th in June & Nov. Norwich, 1st tues. in March, and 3d in Nov. New London, 2d tues. in June. Danbury, 3d tues. in Nov. Fairfield, 2d tues in Feb. and 3d in April. Brooklyn, 3d tues. in March and Aug. & 2d in Dec. Litchfield, 1st tues. in April, 4th in Sept. and 3d in Dec. Middletown, 3d tues in Oct. Haddam, tues. after the 1st Mon. in April. Tollond, 4th tues. in March, August, and December.

MASONIC.

The following article is the KEY to certain names mentioned by Giddins in his almanac of last year. The names there given in *stars* are here disclosed in full. [See the Anti-Masonic Almanac of 1829.

THE MURDER OF MORGAN

FURTHER PARTICULARS. As mistaken notions exist, at a distance especially, respecting the names, standing, and characters of some of the individuals implicated in the Morgan abduction, as referred to in Giddins's "*statement of facts*," and published in his Anti-Masonic Almanac for 1829; it seems to be no more than an act of justice to them as well as to the public, to set this matter right ; for which purpose I send you the following, which may be relied on.

CAPT. DARROW and ORASMUS TURNER were the two men who first called on Giddins, as related in the beginning of his statement. Darrow was a respectable man, and superintendant of the canal. He lived in Lockport, and was a member of the Chapter in that place. Turner was also a member of the same Chapter, and at that time Editor of the Lockport Observatory.— These two men were indicted in August, 1827, and brought to trial in Aug. 1828 ; but Giddins being rejected as a witness, they both were acquitted. It is believed that Turner has since testified before a grand jury, that he *did* go to the fort for the purpose of providing a prison for Morgan, thus proving the first part of Giddins's statement.

Col. E Jewitt was the keeper of the fort and the person on whom the above two called, and was said, that " any building under his care was at their service," &c. He was a Lieutenant in the U. S. army during a part of the last war, has since been a Col. of Militia, and was appointed by the Quarter Master Gen. in 1826, to take charge of the fort, but he at that time held no commission in the army, having been arranged out, I think in 1815. He is now under indictment and has had his trial put over several times—he will probably be tried the 3d week in next month, in Lockport. He was the first to call on Giddins when he returned from York, and signify to him that Morgan had been murdered,—(see the 43d p. of the A. M. Almanac of 1829.) He was also one of the persons who requested Giddins to walk the beach and look for the body—(see p. 45, near the bottom.) He is also alluded to near the top of page 44, and twice below in the same p. He was one of those who tried hard to persuade Giddins, that he ought to say that he " knew nothing about the affair," and that when called upon he should testify that way.—He was called before a Grand Jury, and from what can be learned, he did testify the same that he had urged Giddins to, viz. "that he knew nothing about it."

Col. WM. KING, at that time resided in Youngstown, one mile from the fort. on the Lewiston road. He had been a member of the Legislature,—was, during the war, a 2d Lieut. in the U. S. Army, has since been a militia Col.

and more recently has been a suttler for the army—but has held no commission in the army since the war. He has long been a mason, and took very
much pride in its honors, which were bountefully bestowed on him. He was
uncommonly *bright* in its ceremonies, and had held the offices both of Master of different lodges and High Priest of Chapter—he was really what Colden calls "a very great mason." He was a particular friend of DE WITT
CLINTON, and felt a confidence in becoming one of the ——————— in
case Clinton become President. He was insinuating in his manners, and
proud spirited, but withal very vain. He was more zealous in the Morgan
affair than any other one of the conspirators in that quarter. He was the
one that called Giddins from his bed, when Morgan was brought to the fort.
and who said "*we have got the d—d perjured rascal*" &c. (see p. 32.) He
was one of the four that crossed the river with Morgan—he and Bruce were
the two that went into the town while Morgan remained on shore. He was
one of the seven that held the consultation on the plain, and went twice
into the Magazine on the night of the 14th, and also the one that proposed
that " *all should go together and do their duty*" &c. (see p. 39.) He conversed more with Morgan than any other one, and was bent on his destruction. He was the person who got in such a passion with Giddins on the
evening of the 15th, (see p. 40, near the bottom.) He was the one who received the key from Giddins and handed it to E. Adams ; he is the one who
received the letter from Clinton, respecting the suppression of the book, (see
p. 41.) Clinton wrote the letter to the western Lodges, as he states, (see p.
41. He was one of those who requested Giddins to search the shore for the
body, and who said the Knight from the east called on him, showed his dag-
ger, &c. He was also the one who got into so violent a rage, (see p. 45,
near the top.) He was always very violent against seceding masons, and
denied positively, any concern in the conspiracy, and expected to get clear
as no testimony of any consequence was against him but Giddins, and he
lived in hopes that he could succeed in having him rejected again ; but
when BRUCE testified on the trial of Whitney, his hopes of getting clear
must have been utterly lost ; and accordingly when he learnt the purport of
Bruce's testimony, he indirectly called him a perjurer, was soon after taken
in a fit of appoplexy, (as is said,) and died on the 28th ult. about 11 o'clock
in the village of Youngstown, and at the TAVERN HOUSE of O. Wells.—He
was buried the next day with military honors, at the *Fort Grave Yard*, close
by the gate of which *he*, and *Bruce*, and HAGUE, took Morgan from the
carriage, *bound* and *hoodwinked*, and from which they led him to the boat
on the morning of the 14th Sept. 1826. He has left a wife and 11 children
in indigent circumstances—He was formerly from Boston. A few days after Morgan's destruction, he shewed a letter he had received from MR. GIB-
BENS* of *Boston* ; the letter stated that he (Mr. Gibbens) was a delegate
from Massachusetts to the *Gen. Grand Chapter of the U. S.* in session in N.
York city, in August and Sept. 1826—he went on to state with what dignity Clinton presided, and said something about the Morgan affair, which is
not distinctly reccollected, and ended with a request for King to write him
particulars—King then took occasion to observe *that the affair was known to
that body.*

E. MCBRIDE and another were the two who came down to the boat from
the town. McBride was a member of parliament, and a *high*, *bright*, and
warm mason.

---

*•.Col. Gibbens is *Grand High Priest* of the Massachusetts GRAND ROYAL
Arch Chapter. From this circumstance, many have suppossed the masons
of this state know more of the Morgan outrage than they wish people to believe.

Hague, member of the Lockport Chapter, was the one who stopped with Giddins in the boat, and who used morgan so cruelly, by threatening to shoot him with the pistol, &c. The pistol belonged to Bruce. Hague was indicted at the same time of Turner and others; he was taken sick, and it has been said that the masons were suspicious of his *making disclosures;* be this as it may, he was hurried to New York under pretence of being doctored, *when he was unfit to go,* and there *died.* He was the one that Morgan called doctor, and the first express that came down from Lewiston on the 14th to still Morgan.

Lawson was one of the two that came down from Lewiston in the afternoon of the 14th to still Morgan, and who said, "*Morgan would make no more noise after he saw him,*" &c.

Gen. P. Whitney, N. Beach, Samuel Chubbuck, I. L. Bastow, T. Shaw, King, and Giddins were the seven who held the consultation on the plain—the three first and King were bent on Morgan's destruction; they went into the magazine twice that night and held long conversations with Morgan etc.—yet the first three have sworn in open court and the first five before a grand Jury, that they knew nothing of the affair, agreeably to what they tried to induce Giddins to do! Whitney is a Maj. Gen. of militia, and then kept a tavern at the *Falls:* he is high priest of the Lewiston Chapter, has been a long time a mason, and was a respectable man—Beach and Chubbuck live in Lewiston, and belong to that chapter—Shaw is Master of the Lodge in Lewiston—Bastow is a postmaster at black rock; he was at that time a professor of religion and a man very much respected by every body—he was master of that lodge, and I believe had an office in the chapter. He is the person alluded to in the 39th page of the narrative, who said, when called on by King to come along, "Gentlemen, if you insist, I *must go with you,*" etc. Giddins was the other who made a similar observation—Thus you see that religion does not prevent a mason from perjuring himself to save his masonry.

King and Wm. Miller were the two who went into the magazine on the 15th—King promised Morgan a Bible, and to see his wife and children.

King, Adams, and Miller were the three who met near the house of Giddins on the evening of the 15th. King got in a rage. Miller could prove from *scripture* that it was right to execute Morgan, etc. Miller lives near Lewiston—has sworn before a grand Jury that he "knew nothing about it." He is now under indictment on Giddins testimony alone. Adams is the man who stopped at Giddins's while he was gone to York, and had charge of M. —went to the magazine on the morning of the 20th, and found Morgan gone —told Giddins about giving King the key on the 19th, and being requested by King to take the boat round at midnight; he has also sworn before a Jury and open court that "he knew nothing about it!" He is now under indictment, and will probably be tried on the 3d week in July, as well as the others; but the chief testimony against him is Giddins.

Garside is the man referred to in page 41, near the bottom, who talked about inflicting penalties, etc. and said he would go up and see "King on *the* business"—that he "*caught a bass tother night,*" etc.—and offered to pull down Canandaigua Jail, see page 42—He lived in York; at that time he lived in Niagara, U. C. opposite to Fort Niagara, he is an Englishman by birth, a butcher by trade, and a *savage by nature.*—I firmly believed he had a hand in the Morgan murder.

Capt. Estus was the captain of the steam boat that run to York daily,— and who made frequent enquiry on 15th, 16th, and 17th, about the prisoner, (see p. 42) also who answered Giddins that "he guessed Morgan had gone where he would write no more books." etc. (see page 43, at the top.)

Adams was the man who was suspected, and who was sent for by King and others, and against whom King got in such a rage. *(See p. 45, top.)*

Judge Hotchkiss was the mason who enquired of Giddins, on 15th, how it was with the prisoner, and who spoke in favor of his releasement, (see p. 42.) Bruce and Hague led Morgan to the boat ; Bruce was the one who went into town with King after they crossed the river. Bruce has shown his wickedness by keeping back part of the truth in his testimony—he must have known that Morgan's arms were tied, as he led him—and he could not have been ignorant of the fact that his own pistol was there. Since his sentence he has been taken by *habeus corpus* before a Grand Jury at Bataiva where four have been indicted, he there refused to testify, knowing that he was not oblieged to! and thus has forfeited all public sympathy in his behalf.

MORGAN'S MURDER :—FURTHER PARTICULARS

Extract of a letter to Daniel B. Brinsmade, Esq by Avery Allyn—dated New York, 28th March, 1829.

" Morgan was kidnapped by the masons, pinioned fast, taken to a place of execution, where, after giving him to drink of some powerful composition of poisonous drugs, which failed to produce *death* as *anticipated*, they attemped to take life by letting blood, (under pretence that he was sick and needed the operation,) which reduced him very low and brought on a sort of derangement. On a second attempt to bleed him, he resisted with all his might, crying for mercy, and begging of them to allow him a bible to prepare for the awful realities of DEATH ; but with these requests they would not and did not comply. A second council sat on the wretched man and it was proposed and agreed to put the penalties of his masonic obligations in force upon him ; lots were cast for executioner, and it fell on Richard Howard, an Englishman by birth, a great villian, who fled from his country for crime, and came to America under an assumed name, where, like the unclean spirit, he took to himself seven other devils, who planned the murder of a peaceable citizen of this state. But Howard, as I said before, was made the executioner of masonic vengeance, and soon the work of death was done. Howard by the assistance of his masonic friends, evaded justice—and some months after made his appearance in St. John's Hall in this city, his mind agitated with the consciousness of the stain of a fellow creature's blood upon his soul. He sought the open Lodge of his masonic brethren, and confessed himself the executioner of masonic vengeance upon the traitor Morgan. In order to deliver their persecuted brother from his pursuers, they held a consultation, and agreed to send him to Europe, to forward which with all possible dispatch, they raised large sums of money, gave it to him, and procured his speedy departure."

The following statements coroborate the assertion of Mr. Allyn, in regard to Morgan's having been bled in the dungeon of Niagara and also to the fact of Richard Howard's participation in the crime.

Genesee County, } John Mann, being sworn, deposeth and saith—that
    ss.   } about the time that he heard and understood that William Morgan had been taken away from Batavia, he had a conversation with Richard Howard of Buffalo, book binder, (who works, or did work with Mr. Haskins,) who then informed this deponent that Morgan was confined in Fort Niagara ; and he believes in the same conversation with said Howard, he informed him that five persons had drawn lots to see who it would

fall upon to execute the laws of mansonry upon Morgan; that the lot fell upon him. He seemed much distressed, and clasped his hands together, and exclaimed, " My God ! must it be done !" or some words to that effect. He appeared to be under an impression that his masonic obligations, placed him under a necessity of submitting to do an act which seemed abhorrent to his natural feelings. In subsequent conversations, said Howard gave the deponent to understand that the *execution had been performed*, but said nothing more as to his own agency in the transaction. This deponent further saith, that until within a few days past, his mind has been very unsettled as to the course which he ought to have pursued in relation to the communications so made to him ; and he has been operated upon in some degree by fears for his personal safety ; and doubts as to the extent of his obligations to observe secrecy in respect to the statements so communicated to him ; that a few days ago, he held a consultation with a friend, as to the general duties of a person so situated, and he at last determined to communicate the facts to some persons who might feel bound to act upon them as public good should seem to require.   JOHN MANN.

Sworn the twenty first day of February, 1827, before me.

WM. H. TISDALE.
First Judge of Genesee.

Extract from Giddins's Narrative in allusion to this fact.

Soon after the boat left the wharf, my lodger and myself went to the magazine to see if Morgan wanted any thing to eat or drink, and we did not forget to take the pistol with us ; we opened the outside door, and were upon the point of unfastening the other, when Morgan spoke from within in the following manner, as near as I can recollect :—" Gentlemen, you had better not open this door ; I have got a barricade here that will astonish you ; I think there are but two of you, and, as I am situated I can master you both ; I am determined *not to be bled to death* by that doctor ; but here I will starve, rather than fall into his hands." We told him that we came to see if he was in want of any thing, not to hurt him ; but if he made any resistance he would fare worse. One of us then said to the other in a loud voice, for him to hear, "Here, give me the pistol."—Morgan on hearing this, began to cry murder, and we thought it prudent not to to go in.—I advised my lodger to hurry to Lewiston with all possible speed, and inform the masons that Morgan was very noisy, and that they must send down some one to silence him.

It was not long before one came down from Lewiston, a distance of seven miles, for that purpose ; he, however, did not succeed, for, on going to the magazine, Morgan was pounding, and making much noise ; he spoke to him after opening the outside door, and told him to be silent, or he would blow his brains out, he having the same pistol as before spoken of. We then began to unfasten the inside door, when Morgan spoke in the following manner :—" Gentlemen, I advise you not to come here ; I am prepared to defend myself, and am determined to starve in this prison, rather than *be bled to death by you, doctor*." He had frequently, previous to this, spoken to this man, and always called him doctor, although he was not. Morgan then made a good deal of noise ; and continued crying murder. He was threatened in severe terms, if he did not stop his noise, but all did no good ; he continued crying murder, and came away without entering the body of the building.   ------

City and County of New York, ss.

Avery Allyn, of Washington, Litchfield County, Connecticut, being sworn, saith that in the month of March, 1828, he visited Morton Encampment of Knights Templers, at their regular meeting in St. John's Hall, that while he the said deponent was in said Encampment, he conversed with several well informed Knights of the Order, for the purpose of obtaining a perfect knowledge of the lectures, and also of the duty of the several officers, particularly that of Junior Warden, which office the deponent then held in Clinton Encampment, Connecticut.

The deponent further saith, that while in said Encampment, previous to closing, a respite was ordered by the Sovereign Master ; during which time the deponent had a conversation with———, (who then acted as Prelate,) on the subject of the abduction and murder of Wm. Morgan ; the deponent then told said———he did not believe Morgan had been murdered by the masons; to which he replied, I can tell your more about it than you know ; for, (said he,) justice is done him—the penalty of his obligation has been put in force upon him ; the man that did the deed was in this room, and confessed that he was the man that executed the penalty of his obligation on Morgan.

And deponent saith that he believes that it was further said, that the masons held a consultation and agreed to send Richard Howard the murderer of Morgan, to Europe.

The deponent further saith, that on the same above mentioned evening, he held a conversation with another Knight Templar, who told him that he knew that Morgan was *dead :* for, said he, 1 saw the man in this room, who struck the blow ; and in open lodge he confessed *that it was he that struck the fatal blow ; that it was he that killed him !* by putting· the penalty of his obligation in force upon him.   And the masons agreed, said he, that he, (the assassin Howard,) should depart immediately for Europe ; to defray the expense of which, money was given by the masons, and he himself put fifty cents into the hat which was sent round the room to make a collection for the above mentioned purpose.

And the deponent further saith, that on that evening, or on the first or second evening following at another meeting of masons at St. John's Hall he attended said meeting, and had then a conversation with———, who said Morgan deserved death, and that justice had overtaken him.

The deponent further saith, that a knowledge of above facts gave him much uneasiness, fearing that the course which the masons of New York had taken, would result eventually in the destruction of an order, which the deponent then considered more virtuous than any other, and in the advancement of which he had spent much time and money.

The deponent further saith, that about the 10th of March he left New York for Augusta, Ga. and returned about the first of May following ; that he did believe for three or four months, that it was his duty to conceal the above facts, and to use every effort to protect Richard Howard. But on further deliberation he became convinced that the duty he owed to God, and to his country was paramount to any masonic obligation. He therefore felt himself at liberty and in duty bound to use every endeavor to persuade the masons to bring assassin Howard to justice, and set the public mind at rest.

The deponent further saith, that he conversed with a number of masons whose opinions were, that in case the masons had killed Morgan, they had done an act which duty imposed ; and in case any mason knowing who the executioners were, should expose them to the world, he would surely be *Morganized*.

Deponent further saith, he conversed with another Knight Templar, who said, I know that Richard Howard was concealed in St. John's Hall at the time his pursuers were in search of him in this city, (N. York,) and that there was a good deal of money raised, and many special meetings of the masons on his account, and that they sent him across the Atlantic.   And again, speaking of the death of Morgan, —— said, —— knows all about it ; he also said he was very sorry that the masons as a body had any thing to do about it.   AVERY ALLYN.

Sworn before me this 28th day of March, 1829.   HORACE HOLDEN,
Commissioner, &c.

☞In our Almanac of next year, we intend to designate such of our State and County officers as are masons, so far as they come to our knowledge. Communications post paid addressed to the publisher will be thankfully received, stating what county and state officers are known to be masons, and what sheriffs, judges, coroners, justices of the peace, &c. in Massachusetts, belong to the order.   Correctness is desired in such communications.

Secret Societies.

The Odd Fellows, is a new secret society got up by the masons, in which they hope to preserve their principles and advantages, after masonry is cloven down.   All *secret societies* are dangers to any government whether it be Monarchial or Republican.

Seceders.—It is calculated there are 2000 seceders from the masonic institution ; 100 of which are gospel ministers.

Masonic Poetry.
As men from *brute* distinguished are
A mason other men excels.
Ahemun Reason.

☞The masons to slur the the opposers of secret societies, advertise " *Anti-Masonic Itch Ointment for sale.*"   We recommend it.   It is a sure cure for the masonic *Itch.*

Mr. Hayden in his Report to the New York Senate, says it has been ascertained that masons for fifty years back, have held three fourths of all the public offices in New York State ; while their proportion according to number, is only one eighth.

The New York State anti-masonic convention ascertained that 40 high sheriffs out of 50 were masons.

The Pennsylvania State convention address, state that the masonic judges in Pennsylvania, are five to one.

☞The masonic combination could not be kept up so long if its members did not receive from it peculiar benefits.

Fruits of Masonry.

Some persons are surprised at the tenacity with which masons adhere to their *silly* and profane institutions, after its iniquity is exposed.   The BEN-EFITS and ADVANTAGES of the secret combinations are of such importance, that it will never be abandoned if masons can help it.   Read the OATHS and then read the following cases where the craft felt their benefit.—

Masonic incidents.
From Ward's Anti-Masonic paper.
The following comes from an honorable man, whose word is a safe guar-

anty for its truth.   Moreover it is Masonry to the very letter ; and other anecdotes might, and may hereafter be told, of similar import.

New York, April 23, 1829

DEAR SIR.—I was a few days since invited to become a member of the
Fraternity of Free-masons, by a gentlemen of partial acquaintance—he did
not urge by any direct means, but said it would be of great utility to a man
of my turn of mind, and would help me in my business ; and if perchance I
should ever become involved in difficulty, it would oftentimes furnish a
speedy and miraculous escape ; relating at the same time, instances, to elu-
cidate what he had advanced ; and among which was one, that during the
late war, wherein an individual was concerned in smuggling goods, and when
the CUSTOM HOUSE OFFICERS had arrested him, he by certain *masonic
signs,* made known his situation, and had his property restored and his per·
son set at liberty.   Thus recommending it to me as good and profitable, because that by it unlawful acts can be committed, and the felon evade the
justice of the law.

Another.

From the same.

At a public meeting in the city of New York, on the 20th of April, the
following statement was made.

To illustrate the malign nature of masonic oaths, Mr. L. L. RICE, being
requested, related that a respectable CALVANISTIC CLERGYMAN had this
day apprised him, with deep regret, and with serious apprehensions of the
consequences, of the following facts ; That he had within a few months been
called upon by the master of a lodge in this city of which he was a member,
to administer the marriage ceremony to a bride on her death bed.   That
when he shrunk from the office, the sign of masonic distress, with the re-
membrance of his oath, constrained him in conscience to aid his brother mason in a matter against conscience.   The only witness was another mason.
Seven days after the marriage ceremony, the bride died ; and a few weeks
following, the bridegroom called for a certificate of marriage, and when this
was refused, he gave the magic sign of masonry, and the clergyman feeling
bound to keep his *oath, and abhorring perjury,* wrote for him the certificate
as required, *without date.* The widower took it, and immediately himself
wrote the date five years back ! at which time the clergyman was not in the
ministry. The mason had lived five or six years with the woman without being
married ; and the object of this untimely marriage was to secure property,
which is now being contested, and concerning which the clergyman is in
daily expectation of being called as a witness.

This, said Mr. R. shows the facility which masonry affords to acts of deception and fraud ; and it likewise shows the influence of masonic oaths
over even the best of men.   It is Freemasonry's fearful and practical comment upon her own unhallowed oaths.

GREAT MEN.—" Beware of Secret Associations.—*George Washington.*
" I am decidedly opposed to all Secret Societies, whatever."—*Samuel
Adams.*
" I am opposed to all Secret Associations."—*John Hancock.*
" I am not, never was, and never shall be a Free Mason."—*John Quincy
Adams.*
" That Masonry is sometimes applied to the acquisition of political power,
CANNOT BE DENIED."—*De Witt Clinton,* (a high mason.)
" I have long entertained my present opinion, that a man *wishing to es-
chew all evil,* should *not be a Free Mason.—Cadwallader D. Colden.*

3

From the Morristown Palladium.

☞ We here present to the State of New Jersey, a document of the most commanding interest—the RENUNCIATION of *Mr. John R. Mulford.* Mr. Mulford resides within four miles of this town. He is a member of the Christian church; a farmer and mechanic; independent, virtuous and intelgent,—no partizan in politics, or at elections—no seeker of office; but a modest, retired, and industrious citizen, of unquestioned probity and respectability, whom no interest but that of his country, and of religion, could have induced to stand forward as he now does, the open accuser of a powerful and vindictive association. Let the following be perused with deep attention.

TO THE PUBLIC.

In making the following statement of my views and disclosures on the subject of Speculative Free Masonry, I am not conscious of being governed by any motives except a desire to discharge my duty as a member of civil society, and of the church of Jesus Christ, and also to promote the cause of truth and justice in our social relations; but above all, the cause of a pure and undefiled religion, as it is taught in the living oracles of God, without the corrupt mixtures of human invention.

I joined Whippany Lodge, in this county, about thirteen years ago, and took the first three degrees of Masonry, and continued to visit the Lodge about five years—then I silently withdrew, and have since had no fellowship with masonry

My reasons for thus forsaking the Lodge, and why I feel it my duty publicly, and forever to renounce the order of Free Masonry, are as follows, viz:

That the principles of Masonry inculcate neither religion, morality, truth nor justice, but the contrary of all these, which I have both experienced and witnessed.—While I continued a lodgegoing member, a mason told me he did not believe there was any better religion than masonry. This alarmed me; and I began to look at the institution with a more jealous eye. Since that time I have seen and felt its pernicious influence in many ways, some of which I will mention.

I have seen a Grand Jury selected by a Masonic Sheriff, with an express view to prevent an indictment against a brother Mason, and was told by the foreman of that jury, that had it not been the case of a brother that was coming before them, *he* should not have been there I have also seen a Mason brought up to be tried on an indictment, and observed him make the masonic signal of distress, and another sign to the jury, which latter sign of the hand drawn across the throat, two of the jurors answered; and these same jurors when out, refused to conviction a clear case of guilt. I have also seen masonic signs exchanged between the bar and bench. I have also seen its influence in the choice of public officers, having heard it mentioned in the lodge that such a brother was to be run for Assembly man, by which I understood that we (the brethren) were to support him, and he was run and elected. I have seen three editions of Morgan's Illustrations of masonry, and to guard the public against deception in so important a matter, I feel it my duty to state that the first one is a true and genuine exposition of masonry as I was taught it in the lodge; whereas, the two last have been altered; the one in many particulars, and the other in pass words and in changing the signs, no doubt to deceive the people. For these reasons, and many more that I could name, I consider masonry as a corrupt and awfully wicked system, and unfit for the society of Christians or honest men; and considering the pretensions it makes of republicanism, charity, the handmaid of religion, &c. I view it as one of the greatest impositions ever practised upon mankind, that of Mahomet not excepted. I am perfectly satisfied from what I have seen, that had the masons the reins of power in their hands, or in the hands of men whom they could, as they say, "MAN-

AGE," we should soon be reduced to a state of "hewers of wood and drawers of water," they our "Grand Masters, Most Worshipful's," &c. and we *the people their* SLAVES.   I would here forewarn all persons, especially the youth from entering the lodge to find the secrets of masonry, or any thing good; they will only find a scene of folly and wickedness, and purchase this at the expense of both money and credit.

Of this latter class, I have known individuals to enter the lodge with correct morals and steady habits; and in a few years become dissipated and worthless members of society.   Such is its corrupt and corrupting influence.

If such persons wish to know the true secrets of masonry, and will take the trouble to call on me, I will communicate to them as far as I have gone in this "mystery of iniquity," "without money and without price."

As a member therefore, of the church of Christ, and of civil society, I do hereby publicly, "solemnly, and sincerely" renounce free masonry forever, and can, and will hold myself no longer bound by its horrible and bloody oaths.   JOHN R. MULFORD.

Genungtown, Chatham Township, Morris Co. July 31, 1828.

TESTIMONY.

We the undersigned, inhabitants of the township of Chatham, N. J. take this opportunity of expressing and making known to the distant public, our feelings of esteem and approbation of the moral and religious good character of Mr. John R. Mulford.   His relative standing in society, until his renunciation of masonry, was equal to our best citizens; since which time his character has been most wantonly traduced by the votaries of that institution.   MR. JOHN R. MULFORD is a very independent farmer, a man of punctuality, integrity, and fair Christian character.   In order to do justice to the feelings, and save the reputation of the above named gentleman from unmerited censure, unsolicited, and without consultation, we most cheerfully subscribe our names in testimony of our undiminished confidence and esteem.

John B. Miller, Abraham Britten, Henry Hopping, A. Sayer, Jeremiah H. Browning, Jas. F. Hopping, Ebenezer Sayer, E. C Thompson, Amaza W. Genung, Ashbel Carter, James Glover, E. B. Genung, Barz's Campfield, Abram Sampson, David L. Carter, Stephen Dickinson, Ashbel Bruen, David Howell, Jos. O. Hedges, Charles Ross, Laure Burnet, Lewis Carter, Isaac B. Lee, William Thomson, Jas. H. Woodruff, Gabriel Johnson, John Young, Abraham Magie, Calvin Howell, Aaron Genung, L. M. Browning, Edwin Marsh, W. H. Genung, Samuel Woodruff, Charles Carter, Luke Miller, Alex. Sayer, Jona. Richards, Cyrenus Bruen, Geo. M. Hopping, Cyrus Richards, Isaac H. Bruen, Robert Albright, Adna Thomson.

BRIBERY IN CONGRESS.

The only *known* case of bribery in our national councils was attempted under the *secresy* and *shield* of masonic obligations.— John Anderson, a mason, wished to defraud the government out of a sum of money for pretended claims, and applied *masonically* to a "worthy brother," as he thought, but the man he wished to practice roguery with was not a mason, and the thing was blown.

☞ See the document. ☜

From a Volume of Congressional Records.

WASHINGTON, JAN. 6, 1818.

The Hon. Lewis Williams,

Honored Sir : I return you thanks for the attention I received to my claims to pass so soon. Mr. Lee will hand you some claims from the River Ralsin, which will pass through your Honorable Committee ; and I have a wish that the conduct of the British in that Country may be related in full, on the floor of Congress ; which will give you some trouble in making out the Report and supporting the same. *I have now to request that you will accept of the small sum of* FIVE HUNDRED DOLLARS as *part* pay for the extra trouble I give you ; *I will present it to you as soon as I receive some from Government* (!) This is CONFIDENTIAL, that *only you and me may know any thing about it* ; or, in OTHER WORDS, I *give* it to you as a man and a MASON ; and *hope you belong to that society.* Sir, should it happen that you will not accept of this small sum, I request that you will *excuse* me ; if you do not accept, I wish you to drop me a few lines ; if you accept, I wish no answer. I hope you will see my view on the subject, that it is for extra trouble. [!!!!!!!!!!]

I will make a statement and present the same to the committee, which will be supported by Gen. Harrison, Col. Johnson, Mr. Hubbard, Mr. Meigs, Post Master General, Gov. Cass's Report as Commissioner, and others. *I rely on your honor in keeping this a SECRET*, and your exertion in passing these claims as soon as possible. I need not inform you that we are as poor unfortunate orphan children, having no representation in Congress—so must look on your honorable body as guardians. Pardon this *liberty* from a *stranger.* I am, with high esteem, your most humble and obedient servant.   JOHN ANDERSON.

The Hon. Cadwallader C. Colden of New York, formerly mayor of the city and member of Congress, who has taken all the masonic degrees, says one hundredth, nay, a *thousandth part* of the money of the masonic Institution, is not devoted to charity, but spent in gewgaws, parades, and feasting.

If masonry contains any thing good, why conceal it from mankind? The Scriptures are given to man " without money and without price." Is masonry more valuable ?

Important Questions.

First. Do we want SECRET SOCIETIES among us ? *Second.* Are they of any *public* use ? *Third.* Are they not *dangerous* to our political Institutions ? *Fourth.* Have we not been duly warned of the danger, in the *murder* of an unoffending citizen ? *Fifth.* Ought they to be permitted to exist among us ?

Let every citizen deliberate on the above questions—weigh them well in his mind, and be guided by the result.

☞Masonry is now taught gratis in Massachusetts by Jacob Allen; in New York by Jarvis Hanks; in Ohio, and Pennsylvania, by other seceding masons almost gratis.

A Bad Sign. Masons consider any disposition on the part of the public, to investigate the objects and tendency of their institution as an affront.

A Sign. Masonic tavern keepers frequently have a *square and compass* on their signs to decoy masons from other public houses, Two travellers rode up to an inn in New York lately, but observing this *mystic character* on the sign, turned away. The host seeing it called out, " *Gentlemen I am not a mason, I disapprove of it. The sign was put up by Major Mah-hah-bone, who kept the house before me.*" But the travellers suspecting masonic *craft* would not come back. The landlord much vexed had the masonic sign taken down and an AMERICAN Eagle put up in its place, and henceforth found his account in going for *fair play* and Open Competition instead of Secret Signs and Dark Combinations.

OATHS OF FREE MASONRY.

☞The following are some of the penalties under which masons bind themselves, or (with more propriety) under which they blindly have thought themselves bound, to keep inviolate the secrets of the order.

The Entered Apprentice's penalty is, to have his throat cut across, his tongue taken out by the roots, and his body buried in the sea.

Fellow Craft's Penalty.—To have his left breast torn open, his heart and vitals taken from thence and thrown over his left shoulder, and carried into the valley of Jehosephat, there to become a prey to the wild beasts of the field and the vultures of the air.

Master Mason's Penalty.—To have his body severed in two in the midst, and divided to the north and south, his bowels burned to ashes in the centre, and the ashes scattered to the four winds of heaven.

Mark Master's Penalty.—To have his right ear smote off, that he may be forever unable to hear the word, and his right hand chopped off as an imposter.

Past Master's Penalty. To have his tongue split from tip to root, or cleave to the roof of his mouth, that he might forever hereafter be unable to speak the word.

Most Excellent Master's Penalty.—To have his breasts torn open, his heart and vitals taken therefrom and exposed to rot on the dunghill.

Royal Arch Mason's Penalty—To have his skull struck off, and his brains exposed to the scorching rays of a meridian sun.

3*

Knight of the Red Cross's Penalty.—To have his house torn down and the timber thereof set up, and be hanged thereon ; and when the last trump shall blow, that he be forever excluded from the society of all true and courteous knights.

Knight Templar's Penalty.—To have his head struck off, and placed on the highest spire in Christendom—he then drinks wine from a human skull, and says, may this libation appear as a witness against me, both here and hereafter ; and as the sins of the whole world were laid upon the head of the Saviour, so may all the sins committed by the person whose skull this was, be heaped upon my head in addition to my own, should I ever knowingly or wilfully violate any obligation heretofore taken, take at this time, or shall at any future period take, in relation to any degree of masonry or order of knighthood—to die the death of a traitor, by having a spear, or other sharp instrument, thrust in my left side.

Illustrious Knight of the Cross' Penalty. For the violation of the least matter or particle of any of the here taken obligations, he is to be made the silent and mute subject of the displeasure of the illustrious order, and have their power and wrath turned on his own head, and to his dishonor and DESTRUCTION ; which, like the nail of Jael, may be the sure end of an unworthy wretch, by piercing his temples with a true sense of his ingratitude ; and for a breach of silence in case of such an unhappy event, that he will die the infamous death of a traitor, by having a spear, or other sharp weapon, thrust into his left side, bearing testimony even in death of the power of the mark of the Holy and Illustrious Cross, before I, H. S. our three Illustrious Counsellors in Heaven.

Perfect Master.—Being *dishonored*, and to receive the penalties of all former obligations.

Intimate Secretary.—Body dissected, bowels taken out, heart cut in pieces, and the whole thrown to the wild beasts of the field.

Provost and Judge.—That of all the former obligations.

Intendant of the Buildings or Master in Israel.—Body severed in two, and bowels taken out.

Elected Knights of Nine.—*To be struck with the dreadful poignard of vengeance,* and to have the head cut off, and stuck on the highest pole, or pinnacle in the eastern part of the world as a monument of villany !

Elected Grand Master or illustrious elected of Fifteen.—To have the body opened perpendicularly and horizontally, and exposed to the air for eight hours that the flies may prey on the entrails, also to have the head cut off and placed on the highest pinnacle in the world, and *to be ready to inflict the same penalty in all who disclose the secrets of this degree.*

Illustrious Knights or Sublime Knights Elected. The body cut in quarters.

The degree of Knights of the Ninth Arch.—Penalties of all former obligations, and in case of failure, the body to be exposed to the beasts of the forests as a prey.

The degree of perfection or Grand Elect perfect and Sublime Mason.—To have the body cut open, and the bowels torn out, and given to the vultures for food !

The degree called nights of the East and West.—Severe wrath of almighty creator of Heaven and Earth.

Degree called Knight of the Eagle and Sovereign Prince of Rose Croiz de Heroden.—Being forever deprived of the true word ; to be perpetually in darkness ; my blood continually running from my body ; to suffer without intermission ; the most cruel remorse of soul ; that the bitterest gall, mixed with vinegar, be my constant drink ; the sharpest thorns for my pillow, and death of the Cross complete my punishment !

Venerable Grand Master of all Symbolic Lodges Sovereign Princess of Masonry, Master Advitiam, or Grand Pontiff.—Being forever despised and dishonored by the craft in general.

Knights of the Royal Axeor or Hache, (Hatchet) sometimes called *Grand Patriarch,* by the name of Prince of Labanus.

This meeting is called a college.

Chiefs of the Tabernacle.—Violating the obligation I perjure myself, and I consent that the earth should be opened before my eyes, and that I should be engulfed, even to my neck, and thus miserably perish.

Prince of the Tabernacle.—To be stoned to death and the body left above ground deprived of burial.

Knights of the Brazen Serpent.—To have the heart eaten by the most venomous of Serpents, and thus perish most miserably !

Prince of Mercy or Scotch Trinitarian.—to be condemned, cast out and despised by the whole universe.

Sovereign Commander of the Temple at Jerusalem.—To have the several wraths of almighty God inflicted !

THE KEY OF MASONRY. PHILOSOPPICAL LODGE. KNIGHTS ADEPTS OF THE EAGLE OR SUN.*

Requisitions to make good masons. You must shake of the yoke of infant prejudice, concerning the mysteries of the reigning religion, which worship has been imaginary, and only founded on ,the spirit of pride, which envies to command and be distinguished, and to be at the head of the vulgar, in affecting an exterior purity, which characterizes a false piety, joined to a desire of acquiring that which is not its own, and is always the subject of this exterior pride, and unalterable source of many disorders, which being

---

* This degree should be read by every Christian ; it is aimed at the heart of every Christian.—Light on Masonry, p. 253.

joined to gluttonness, is the daughter of hypocrisy, and employs every matter to satisfy carnal desires, and raises to these predominant passions, altars, upon which she maintains, without ceasing, the light of iniquity, and sacrifices continually offerings to luxury, voluptuousness, hatred, envy, and perjury. Behold, my dear brother, what you must fight against and destroy, before you can come to the knowledge of the true good and sovereign happiness! Behold this monster which you must conquer—a serpent which WE detest as an idol that is adored by the idiot and vulgar under the name of RELIGION!!!

Penalty.—Tongue thrust through with a red hot iron, both eyes plucked out, deprived of smelling and hearing, and both hands cut off, and exposed in that condition in the field, to be devoured by voracious animals.

Knight of Kadesh.—All the penalties of former obligations to be inflicted.

Chronology of Masonic Events.

Origin of speculative free masonry (in England,)	1717
First book of constitutions published,	1723
Masonry introduced into the East Indies,	1729
Its secrets exposed by Prichard, 1st martyr to M. vengeance,	1730
Masonry introduced into Ireland,	1730
Masonry introduced into France,	1731
Masonry introduced into North America (Boston,)	1733
Masonry introduced into Africa,	1736
Masonry introduced into Scotland,	1736
Degrees above the 3d or master, began to be added (in Fra.)	1740
Higher degrees modified by Frederick, Voltaire, and others, and introduced into America, by a Jew from France,	1760
Masonic secrets exposed, and author missing soon after,	1770
First chapter of Royal Arch Masons established,	1787
Masonic secrets exposed by Smith, who suddenly died, believed to have been poisoned by masons, about	1798
Age of the first three degrees of speculative freemasonry	113 y.
Age of Royal Arch Masonry,	43 years.

Liberty of the Press.

Extract from Mr. A. Walker's address before the Anti-Masonic Meeting, at the Council Room, Boston.—

" I well know that a certain editor in Boston, who *presumed* to insert a series of communications *for* and *against* masonry, both *ably* and *fairly* written, immediately suffered the loss of a great number of masonic subscribers. I think he told me seven withdrew at one time; and another, who ventured to mention that an anti-masonic meeting was held in Dedham on a certain day, received a call from an agrieved *brother* the next morning, ordering him to stop his paper for that high and unpardonable offence against the institution."

MASONIC SIGNS AND GRIPS.

This is the grip of the Entered Apprentice, and it is called *Boaz.* It is by this grip that masons who are strangers discover each other.—Morgan thus describes it. "The right hands are joined together as in shaking hands and each sticks his thumb nail into the third joint or upper end of the fore finger." If a reader in shaking hands with a person should feel him pressing his thumb against the upper joint of his fore finger, he may know him to be a mason. It would be well for all to get into this way of shaking hands. It is easy to be learned and it would be a compliment to the masons. The children could learn it easily.

A MASONIC  EMBLEM.

ENTERED APPRRNTICE'S PASS GRIP.

Pass Grip.—Take each other by the right hand, as if to shake hands, and each put his thumb between the fore and second fingers, where they join the hand, and press the thumb between the joints. The name of the pass-grip is *Shibboleth,* and is the password. ☞In the cut the three fingers are made to drop down instead of *clentching,* this is done to shew the grip plainer.

FELLOW CRAFT'S DEGREE.—*From Morgan's Book.*

Real Grip.—Take each other by the right hand, as if to shake hands, and put the thumb on the joint of the second finger where it joins the hand, and crooking the thumb, so that each can stick the nail of his thumb into the joint of the other. *Word.* JACHIN —given in the same manner as in the first degree.

☞These things are learned quickly by practice.

MASTER MASON'S DEGREE.

This is the *Pass Grip* of the Master's Degree. *Captain Morgan* thus describes it :—Press the thumb between the joints of the second and third fingers, where they join the hand. The name of it is *Tubal Cain,* and it is the pass word. We let the two fingers be separated here to shew the grip ; the hand properly should be closed. ☞Let the children learn these grips and signs. It will amuse them.

Due Guard. " Draw the right hand across the throat, the hand open and the thumb next to the throat, and then let it drop down by the side."—*Morgan.* Many call this *a sign.* It alludes to the penalty of the Apprentice's obligations—having the throat cut across, &c. This sign seems more appropriate for a gang of robbers or pirates than a *Religious and Charitable Society.*

MASTER MASON'S DEGREE.

Real Grip.—Take hold of each other's right hand as if to shake hands, and stick the nails of each of your fingers into the joints of the other's wrist where it unites with the hand. This is what the masons call the *Lion's Paw.* It was by this grip that Solomon pulled Old Hiram out of his grave after he was rotten, according to Masonic Chronicles.

MASTER MASONS'

Sign of Distress. Raise both hands and arms perpendicularly, one on each side of the head, the elbow forming a square. The accompanying words are, " *O Lord, my God, is there no help for the Widow's Son.*" At the last words, let the hands slowly fall.—The words are not spoken except in the dark when the sign cannot be seen.

MASONRY AND INTEMPERANCE GO HAND IN HAND.

How many youth who sipped the intoxicating bowl of masonry in the name of Friendship and Brothely love have found the Serpent of Intemperance lurking at the bottom. In masonic language, swearing is called "*labor,*" and tippling " *refreshment.*" The less one has to do with either the better.

Those who applaud Masonry without knowing any thing about it, are called *Jack Masons.* They are likened to this poor animal, for like him they tug and sweat under a heavy burthen without knowing what it is. The Jacks are very annoying, being generally set on by the craft. You may know them by the introductory observation—" I am not a mason, but I know it to be a noble institution."

JOHN MARSH, Stationer, and Account Book Manufacturer, No. 96 and 98 state st. sign of the large Leger, Boston, has for sale at the lowest prices, Writing paper—Binders Board—Gold Leaf—School and Account Books, &c. with every description of *Stationary articles*, at Wholesale or Retail.

☞ J. M. is agent for the *Byam's Blacking and Opodeldoc*, Gordak's Medicine, *Kidder's Indelible Ink*, and Parker's Panacea, can supply dealers with any quantity wanted on the best terms.

☞ Country merchants and traders generally, will find it particularly advantageous to purchase at this establishment, as particular attention is taken to keep every article in the line wanted by them, and of such qualities and prices as will suit their trade.

*** Strict personal attention to all orders. Light Goods sent to any part of the City free of expense. Store open until nine o'clock evenings.

GORDAK'S MEDICINE.

Prepared only by WILLIAM GORDAK, from Germany.

JOHN MARSH,

Sole Agent for the United States, No. 96 and 98, State Street,
SIGN OF THE LARGE LEGER.

All orders for any quantity, addressed as above, will receive immediate attention. Also may be had, at retail, by most of the Apothecaries, and generally at the Country Stores throughout the United States.

☞ 12th Edition of 10,000 copies each ☜

GORDAK'S GENUINE PHYSICAL DROPS,

Made entirely of Roots and Herbs—Preventative against Fevers.

This Medicine will cure Colds, Coughs, Jaundice, Bile and Weakness at the Stomach. It will purify the Blood, Create an Appetite, and Cure the most inveterate Headache. For Worms in Children it is a most efficacious Medicine.

Price per Bottle 25 cents.

☞ Thousands of certificates could be offered of its wonderful efficacy, but the very rapid sale and general satisfaction it has given in all cases, is a sure test of its virtues. Upwards of 90,000 bottles have been sold in less than eighteen months.

ANTI-MASONIC BOSTON FREE PRESS.

Be just and fear not.—*Shakspeare.*

This paper is published every Friday evening at No. 13, Merchants' Hall (over the Post Office) at 3,00 a year, if paid at the end of six months, or 2,50 in advance, 1,50 six months, 1,00 three months. It is a paper of large size, and contains in addition to the general news of the day, much matter shedding light on the dark and mysterious subject of *MASONRY.*—It is emphatically a FREE PRESS. It is not subject to the power and influence of any *SECRET SOCIETY.* At this crisis, when the energies of the public press are bound down by the *cable tow* of masonry, this paper professes to be free from all influence, but that of the public voice, and its motto is, the people " *the whole people, and nothing* BUT *the people.*"   Boston, 1829.

Appendix A

ALMANACS—HISTORY & EVOLUTION

Early History

As with many of man's early discoveries, it is impossible
to fix the exact point in time when man first employed the
calendar. We do know that from the dawn of civilization until
the end of the Old Stone Age, man was primarily a hunter and
gatherer of food. It was during the Neolithic Period (10,000
to 2500 B.C.) that man started to tame nature, and his world
was transformed by a new discovery; farming. Man ceased to
wander and tied himself to the land. The walls went up and
the first city-states were formed. Food supplies became more
stable and population increased. Wheat and barley, formerly a
scarce commodity, became more abundant as cultivated grain
fields, starting in southwest Asia, spread to most of the earth
except the inhospitable polar regions and remote islands such
as New Zealand.[1] Man, "the farmer," now dependent upon
agriculture and animal husbandry, began to concern himself
with the changing seasons, the management of which was
vital to the successful tilling of the soil, the sowing of seed,
and the harvest of crops. Moreover, as a bountiful harvest became more important to the growing population, surplus
crops were used for barter and became an economic asset to
the community. A more exacting prediction of the seasons
was necessary to produce the food supply and manage the
surplus until the next harvest. An almanac was the answer.

No doubt, man's first concept of time was based on the
movement of the sun, but the early farmer had little concern

---

[1] *The Last Two Million Years*, ed., The Reader's Digest Association
(London: 1974), p. 29.

for an eight-hour workday at some predetermined union scale. He worked long and hard. He was successful, or he went hungry. His day started when the sun came up and ended when he ran out of daylight, and it was just that simple. Consideration of the conditions under which early man worked and the primitive means by which he measured the seasons leads us to suspect the earliest time count must have been by the moon or month. While the visual aspects of the sun were more or less constant to the observer, the appearance of the moon in its visible phases changed according to a regular pattern. History credits the Babylonians with having first figured this out and having divided the month, roughly, into four seven-day periods. However, most historians agree it was the Egyptians who invented the calendar, and in turn, developed the first almanac.

Cheops, The Almanac of Stone

If the sun was man's first clock, then the mysterious pyramid was probably man's first almanac. The word mystery, when applied to the pyramid, is an appropriate adjective. Without question, the Great Pyramid of Cheops, the last remaining of the Seven Wonders of the World, is one of the most magnificent and multi-faceted landmarks in all history. However, the original purpose and subsequent function of this impressive structure has been the subject of many theories and controversies throughout the ages.

Men from all walks of life have played detective and the list is long and impressive. It includes astronomers, geologists, mathematicians, architects, historians, and engineers. Many were dedicated scientists, eminent scholars, and even obscure dilettantes. Collectively, they make up a group of Egyptologists who have worked to unravel the many threads of the Egyptian handiwork, each lining up on either side of an issue to establish a pet theory and either prove or disprove those of others. From a professional approach or as a matter of personal interest, these zealots have tried to determine the "why, when, and where" of the pyramid. The "where" is obvious. It is the "when and why," along with the "by whom," that causes the continuing debates.

For years, because of the lack of definite proof, it has been argued by some that the inhabitants of Egypt 5000 years ago were incapable of the precise astronomical calculations and mathematical solutions required to locate, orient, and erect the Great Pyramid where it now stands. Certainly, someone had the necessary talent, because it was located, oriented, and erected where it now stands. If it was not the Egyptians, then who were the brilliant sojourners? Where did they come from? Where did they go when they finished their task? We continue to guess.

Another problem receiving a great deal of attention is the matter of original intent. Many historians continue to adhere to the belief that the original purpose of the pyramid was that of a tomb to memorialize some vainglorious Pharoah who believed his journey into the Land of the Sun would be enhanced by the degree of preservation of his earthly body and the amount of worldly goods buried with him.

About ten years ago, Peter Tompkins wrote a book about the secrets of the pyramid.[2] In this beautifully illustrated volume, Tompkins analyzed the many theories on the true purpose and functions of the pyramid and its relationship with the other structures such as Stonehenge, the ziggurats of Babylon, and the lesser pyramids. He delved into the influence of the pyramid in the fields of astronomy, astrology, deodesy, and history. The core of Tompkins' literary exercise centers around the controversial theory that the pyramid was constructed as a highly sophisticated scientific instrument. Of course, his conclusions are subject to argument, but the book does conclude that the pyramid was and is a great deal more than just another musty tomb.

According to Tompkins, recent studies of Egyptian hieroglyphs and ancient cuneiform tablets of the Babylonians and Sumerians show that advanced science did flourish in the Middle East at least 3000 years before Christ. Tompkins

---

[2] Peter Tompkins, *Secrets of the Great Pyramid*, (New York: Harper & Row, 1971).

suggests the Great Pyramid was designed on the basis of hermetic geometry, most of which was lost and did not emerge until centuries later. He says that recent findings make it possible to reanalyze the pyramid and establish considerable scientific import to the project. Evidence is weighted in favor of the pyramid having been erected first as an astronomical, deodetic, and mathematical instrument, its use as a tomb coming at a much later date. Like Stonehenge and other megalithic calendars, the pyramid has been shown to be an almanac by means of which the length of the year (365.2422 days) could be measured as accurately back then as it can be today with a modern telescope. It probably served as a celestial observatory from which maps of the stellar hemisphere were drawn. It is very possible that whoever built the pyramid knew the precise circumference of the earth, and the length of the year to several decimal places. The architects must have known the mean length of the earth's orbit around the sun and the 26,000 cycle of the equinoxes.

Regardless of the original intent, length of time in development, and ultimate functions of the pyramid, those who study the theories in Tompkins' book can believe that the pyramid was man's first splendid almanac.

The Rational Almanac

One of the modern investigators mentioned by Tompkins was an obscure Yorkshireman, Moses B. Cotsworth, who wrote a fascinating book entitled *The Rational Almanac*. Tompkins described Cotsworth as a legislative enthusiast whose lifelong ambition was to reform what is called our "barbarous" almanac.[3]

Cotsworth considered the present calendar unacceptable.[4] It is derived from the early Romans who had a ten-month year of 334 days. There was no January or February, these months being added in the 7th century B.C. when a lunar year

---

[3] Ibid, p. 121.

[4] The calendar of Cotsworth's day and the current calendar are the same.

of 354 days was established. The eleven-day shortage caused the seasons to converge in time, so in 46 B.C., Julius Caesar added ninety-one days. Although closer, the difference between the civil calendar and the actual solar year resulted in an extra day every 128 years. Pope Gregory tackled the problem and decided to drop ten days in 1582. The Catholic world accepted the solution, but Protestant England refused to go along. There were riots in the streets of London with the people crying, "Give us back our ten days." Of course, the English accepted the plan eventually, and now by employing the use of leap years, it is assured that the present calendar is good for the next 20,000 years. This should have satisfied those living during Cotsworth's time as well as anyone living today, but Cotsworth was convinced there was a need for a revised calendar. He mounted his campaign and persisted in an impassioned plea for reform.

Cotsworth was greatly influenced by two of his contemporaries, both intrepid pyramid sleuths, Robert T. Ballard, an engineer for the Australian railroad, and Piazzi Smyth, Astronomer Royal for Scotland. Ballard published a small volume in 1882 which was titled *The Solution of the Pyramid Problem*. Smyth had developed the theory that the pyramid had been intentionally located, oriented, and sloped for the phenomenon to occur in the latitude at the spring equinox, when at noon, the sun was directly over the equator. At the same time Ballard was espousing his theory, and without his knowledge, a French astronomer, Jean Biot, backed Ballard's position, noting "with or without intention by the Egyptians who built the Great Pyramid, it has, since it existed, functioned as an immense sundial which has marked annually the periods of the equinoxes with an error of less than a day and three quarters."

All of this had an impact on Cotsworth, and he managed several conversations with Smyth before setting out for an on-the-spot investigation of the pyramid. Eventually, Cotsworth became convinced that the designers of the pyramid intended the finished product to serve as a perfect calendar to determine the seasons and the exact length of the year by regular graded and recurring shadows: an almanac, the original purpose of which was to "ensure food supplies and enable the rules to regulate their stores to last until harvest, whilst preventing famine from endangering the public welfare."[5]

Clogs

Eventually, almanacs made the exodus from Egypt and showed up in other developing nations in the form of smaller copies of the gigantic megalith at Cheops. They were far less sophisticated and not nearly as durable, but some have survived in crumbling ruins, such as Xochimilco in Mexico and Stonehenge in the United Kingdom. During the transition, the purpose was the same, but the size, shape, and scope of the almanac began to change.

A link in the evolutionary chain is the clog or notched stick. Before the invention of printing, and perhaps before the introduction of writing, square-edged, oblong wooden clogs with hieroglyphic and symbolic devices cut along their edges were used as calendars. It has been suggested they were patterned after the obelisk and might have been used as early as the time of Abraham.[6] Perhaps there is a relationship, the pyramid or obelisk having been used to make the actual sighting and calculation and the clog as a handy, portable record.

Clogs were the original calendars of the Norwegians and Danes. They were used to designate church and state festivals in northern Europe until the early 12th century when the first calendars were published on the Continent, but their use continued in some parts of England until as late as the end of the 17th century.

Manuscripts

While the almanac is unquestionably one of the earliest of all publications, the exact date is uncertain. The British

---

[5] Moses B. Cotsworth, *The Rational Almanac*, (London: The Stationers' Company, 1905) No page number. See Forward.

[6] Ibid, p. 27.

Museum houses an almanac which dates from the time of Rameses II who ruled Egypt from 1290 to 1223 B.D. It shows lucky and unlucky days in black and red, notes religious festivals, and predicts the fate of children born on certain days.[7] The Greeks and Romans had listings of days for legal and public business. However, the earliest expressed mention of published almanacs, in a more modern sense, pertains to those of Solomon Jarchus around 1150 A.D.[8]

In his *Opus Majus*, 1267, Roger Bacon used the term *almanac*, possibly for the first time, in his tables recording the movement of the heavenly bodies. The Savilian Library at Oxford has a manuscript copy of an almanac published by Patrus de Dacia in 1300 A.D. Examples of the first so-called *standard* almanac were issued at Oxford by John Somers and Nicholas de Lynne, 1380 and 1386 respectively.[9] Superstition and the appeal of astrology created a popular interest in almanacs, consequently printers, astrologists, and even fakes fed upon the public demand. In England, for a time, prognostications were forbidden, so English readers had to rely on translations until 1431, the date of the first almanac written in English.

The British Museum has a 1431 manuscript in English which contains a calendar and rules for its computation along with predictions of eclipses for a period of time. Such early almanacs were not printed of course, but they were written on long strips of vellum with pictorial calendars of saint's days. They contained mostly astronomical and weather information, but they also recorded religious observances and seasonal data, serving both church and state as compendiums for use by the nobility. The common man was left out, because he could not read, and he could not afford to purchase manuscripts. However, with the advent of the Gutenberg press, printed matter became more accessible to the general public which was gaining on illiteracy, and there was a new market for all forms of printed matter.

---

[7] *Encyclopedia Americana*, Volume 1, 1977 ed., s.v. "Almanac," p. 612.

[8] *Encyclopedia Americana*, Volume 1, 1973 ed. s.v., "Almanac," p. 656.

[9] Ibid.

The dates assigned to the first printed almanacs in Europe and England are 1457 and 1497 respectively, and these are unnamed. The first printed almanac of real importance was *Ephemerides Ab Anno* by Regiomontanus (Johann Muller), a German astronomer and mathematician in Nuremberg. The date was around 1472.[10] In addition to the usual astronomical calculations, this almanac also contained data for navigators, and it is said that *Ephemerides Ab Anno* was used by Columbus. Also, it contained predictions for the future, and considering the price tag of ten golden crowns per copy, soothsayers must have been worth their weight in gold in those days.

As almanacs became more accessible, they became more comprehensive and scientific, and between the 16th and 17th centuries, the almanacs included anniversaries, home medical advice, navigational data, statistics, jokes, fiction, and any number of interesting facts.

Publishers of early printed almanacs seem to have been title conscious and came very close to including the entire table of contents in the title. A typical example is:

> Prognostycacyon of Mayster John Thybault, medycyner and astronomer of the Emperyall Majestie, of the yere of our Lorde God MCCCCCXXXIJ., comprehending the iiij. partes of this yere, and of the influence of the mone, of peas and warre and of the skyenesses of this yere, with the constellacions of them that be under the vij planettes, and the revolucions of kynges and princes, and of the eclipses and comets.[11]

In England, the almanac became a monopoly. After 1571, Elizabeth I granted exclusive rights to Watkins and Roberts, two members of The Company of Stationers. Later, James I granted a new patent extending the rights to Oxford and

---

[10] Moses B. Cotsworth, *The Rational Almanac*, (London: The Company of Stationers, 1905), p. 27. Cotsworth sets the date of *Ephemerides* at 1472; J. E. Behrens, "The Farmer's Almanac," *Knight's Templar*, Volume XXIX, No. 1, January 1978, p. 5. Behrens gives the dates of *Ephemerides* as 1474 to 1506.

[11] *Encyclopedia Britannica*, Volume 1, 1949 edition, s.v., "Almanac," p. 668.

Cambridge, the king's interest in almanacs resulting, no doubt, from increased royalties. The Company, attuned to the potential profits, tailored their predictions to fit the wishes of the sovereign and eventually won back the exclusive rights. The Company has published a number of almanacs, the most famous of which was *Vox Stellarum* by Francis Moore, which started for the year 1701 and continues today under the title *Old Moore's Almanac*. The Company of Stationers enjoyed exclusive rights until well into the 19th century when the monopoly was challenged in court and was terminated. Even so, The Company has not suffered and has continued to be a dominant factor in the publication of English almanacs.

The early 19th century saw considerable improvement in the quality of this class of publication, to some extent through the efforts of the society for the Diffusion of Useful Knowledge which issued the *British Almanac for the Year 1828*. The Company of Stationers kept their hand in, and since 1870, their principle work has been *The British Almanac* and *The Companion*. *Whitaker's Almanac*, started in 1868, is one of the better known English almanacs, and Ireland has *Thom's Irish Almanac*, continuing since 1843. There are other important almanacs in Scotland, France, and Germany that date back from the 17th to the 19th centuries.[12]

American Almanacs

The first American almanac was *An Almanac Calculated for New England*, 1639, by William Pierce, Mariner. It was printed by Stephen Day who bore the title of first printer in America, so its first-place position seems secure. In 1687, William Broadford's press in Philadelphia published a single-leaf almanac by Daniel Leeds. His son, Titan, continued the publication, off and on, and it was one of six almanacs in Philadelphia when Benjamin Franklin launched his famous *Poor Richard's Almanac*. Franklin must have considered Leeds his more serious competitor, because he engaged in a humorous rift between himself and Titan Leeds through his fictional

---

[12] Ibid, p. 668.

character, Richard Saunders, no doubt stimulating reader interest in *Poor Richard.*

From 1725 to 1775, outstanding almanacs were compiled by Nathaniel Ames, physician and innkeeper of Dedham, Massachusetts, who has been described as a scholar, wit, orator, and one of the brightest stars in the constellation of the famous Ames family. The almanac was the *Astronomical Diary and Almanak*, and it is believed to have influenced Franklin's *Poor Richard*. Ames' son continued the publication until 1775 when it had reached an annual circulation of 60,000, far exceeding that of Franklin.

During the 1700's and 1800's, there were around 2000 almanacs printed. They were published for various trades, organizations, and military and religious groups. During the 18th century, the almanac departed from the newspaper format which was essentially one sheet of paper folded twice to that of several pages stitched together, and in this manner, the almanac became the forerunner of the modern magazine.

The Old Farmer's Almanac

Benjamin Franklin's *Poor Richard* might be considered the most famous of all American almanacs, but the one with the best track record is the *Old Farmer's Almanac*, first published in Boston by Robert Bailey Thomas in 1793. This 189-year-old *Old Farmer's Almanac* is not to be confused with the 164-year-old *Farmer's Almanac*, both of which started with the same name (*Farmer's Almanac*), and both of which are around today. The *Old Farmer's Almanac* was edited by Thomas for over fifty years, and he took personal charge of all the astronomical calculations. His success is reflected in the fact the annual circulation had reached over 200,000 copies by the time of his death. Following the death of Thomas, his heirs took charge and ran things with little change until 1939, when a man named Sagendorph took charge, adding the word "Old" to the original title which had been, simply, *Farmer's Almanac*. Today, it is published by Rob Trowbridge, and the editor is Jud Hale. The circulation is over 2,725,000, and it is considered the oldest continuous publication in America.[13] Today's 197-page *Old Farmer's Almanac* is a far cry from the 48-page first edition of Thomas in 1792. It contains more stories, miscellany, and information; and, in keeping with the trend, it contains a great deal of advertising. The improvement, expansion, and modernization is desirable, but it is a little sad to have lost those nostalgic tidbits of wisdom found in earlier versions. For example, one of the "Rules for Long Life" appearing in an early edition is:

> After coming out of bed, you should never go to and look out of the window.

One interpretation of this advice is that if one did rise and go to the window and look out into the yard, one might be confronted with the sight of wild Indians and thus have ten years scared off his life.[14]

Another jewel is a recipe to kill worms in horses:

> Give the horse . . . three mornings together, a pint of strong rue tea; in it bruise and squeeze the juice of three or four heads of garlicks; dissolve in it a handful of salt.

It has been suggested this sort of thing was discontinued because it probably killed more horses than it did worms.[15]

The current edition contains a number of amusing articles which appeal to the reader interested in trivia. Even the titles bring about a smile or a chuckle.[16] There is an article about the earthworm which is said to be the only potentially immortal creature on earth. In a section about medical oddities, there is an account of the first case of artifical insemination by a bullet. There are "Old and New Mathematical Puzzles," "Rainy Day Amusements," and a world-shaking article on "Why and How Do Kitty-Cats Purr."

In "Anecdotes and Pleasantries," there is "How the Doughnut Was Invented for Sure," "Living the Good

---

13 J. E. Behrens, "The Farmer's Almanac," *Knight Templar*, Volume XXIX, No. 1, January 1978, p. 6.

14 Ibid.

15 Ibid.

16 *The Old Farmer's Almanac*, 1981, (Dublin, N.H., 1980: Yankee, Inc.)

Life on about 44¢ a Day," "How to Collect and Preserve a Snowflake," and an article which is headed, "Fortune Cookies Are Chinese. Right? Wong!" [Sic] As a matter of fact, the fortune cookie was invented in California.

Advertisement is aimed at those primarily interested in agriculture and health, with emphasis on the do-it-yourselfer. One ad appeals to action-minded men who need a super potency tonic. Another product of this ilk is called a formulated "rooster" pill, designed to get one up in the morning "bright eyed and bushy tailed, and crowin'." There are advertisements for preparations to remove Father Time's brown spots from the hands, a miracle skin cream containing cucumber, and some sure cures for baldness. In full color, inside the back cover, there is a witch hazel ad which says Americans have been depending on the product just about as long as on the *Old Farmer's Almanac.*

There are classified ads, fishing advice, outdoor planting guides, tide information, time correction tables, weather by areas, and a spooky article on doomsday which begins with the nerve-racking assurance that, "A supernova will explode near the earth or we'll all drown in the floods from melting polar ice caps. Maybe we'll collide with a large asteroid. Whatever—mankind invariably seems to have the urge to bring on a day of reckoning."

The 176-page *Old Farmer's Almanac,* still going strong, is a delight to read and provides both entertainment and valuable information. There are those farmers and home gardeners who will not make the first move without first consulting this guide. The almanac deserves to continue for another 189 years.

The Farmer's Almanac

Several attempts to obtain a copy of *The Farmer's Almanac* at bookstores or libraries proved not only frustrating but futile. The mystery was solved upon finding a copy of the 16-year-old *American Farm & Home Almanac,* 1981 edition. This little 96-page almanac, selling for $1.25, is void of advertising except for an opening statement to the reader and an editorial statement on the back cover, either of which could be classified as advertising for the almanac itself or for its sister publication, *The Farmer's Almanac.* The publisher and editors are the same for both, and the cover of the *American Farm & Home Almanac* explains that *The Farmer's Almanac* cannot be bought on the newsstands but is given out as a "valued gift by sponsors as a public relations offering."

The policy statement on the back cover of *American Farm & Home* is interesting. It is titled, "Almanacs: A Nostalgic Way of Life," and explains that since the days of the early Romans, the almanac reflected a way of life, the messages being written on the temple walls or on papyrus brought from Egypt. Almanacs became popular in England in the 15th century and were started in America in 1639 by Captain Pierce. Over the years, there have been hundreds of almanacs, some political in nature, some religious, some patent medicine oriented, and some even x-rated. Reflecting policy, the editor says that *The Farmer's Almanac* is known for its "high moral content and excellent humor—sometimes called corny, but never porny—its anecdotes and amazingly accurate weather forecasts." With the *Farmer's Almanac* restricted from general sales on the newsstands, the editors express their feelings for the need to publish an almanac that reflects a high moral tone coupled with a nostalgic look at early Americana and they say that the *American Farm & Home Almanac* fills the bill, "disdaining," as they say, "the dream book motif and keeping it void of advertising." This almanac lives up to its editorial policy, presenting bits of logic, recipes, weather predictions, humor, poetry, and nostalgic odds and ends. All of this is presented free of smut and void of tiresome advertising of phony miracle cures for physical ailments, financial problems, or general unhappiness. Assuming the same guidelines apply to the *Farmer's Almanac*, both almanacs should appeal to anyone interested in the predictions, advice, and entertainment found within their covers.

The World Almanac and Book of Facts

A johnny-come-lately, compared to the two farmer's almanacs, is the 113-year-old *World Almanac and Book of Facts,* and this young upstart competes successfully for its share of today's market.

Through direct mail advertising to its customers, one of the major oil companies offers the current edition free; free, that is, for the small sum of $2.99 to cover postage, processing, and handling. It is a bargain, particularly in view of the fact that the subscriber may use a special toll-free telephone number at any time, twenty-four hours a day, for assistance in finding any topic or fact in the almanac. The advertising flier explains that the special edition, a $9.95 value, is not sold in bookstores and is available only via the mail offer to the company's credit card holders. There is some confusion about this, because another major oil company offers its customers exactly the same proposition under identical circumstances.[17]

According to the advertisement, the 976-page information-packed book is an indispensable one-volume reference book with five sections of about 190 pages, sixteen of which are in full color. There is a calendar section, a metric conversion table, and basic first aid advice.

The editorial statement contains a brief history of the publication which began in 1868 as as 120-page, hand-set volume with twelve pages of advertising, a feature missing from the current edition. It was first published by the *New York World*, and it ran until 1876 when it was suspended. It was revived in 1886 by Joseph Pulitzer who set a goal to make it a "compendium of universal knowledge." It was acquired by Scripps-Howard in 1931 and it bore the imprint of *The New York World Telegram* until 1967 when the imprint was changed to *The New York Telegram and Sun*. It is now published by the Newspaper Enterprise Association, Inc., all of which clearly establishes its realtionship with newspaper publishers.

The scope of this almanac is so extensive that the 30 page General Index is preceded by a Quick Reference Index. Some of the topics are Actors and Actresses, Animals and Plants, Awards and Prizes, Business Directories, Consumer Affairs, Disasters, Energy, Environment, Flags of the World, Geog-

---

[17] Direct mail advertising by major oil companies.

raphy, Health, History, Maps of the World, Money and Economy, Movies, Nations, Population, Vital Statistics, Religion, Sports, Taxes, Television, and Zip Codes. There is a listing of NFL champions, a chart of temperatures in eighty-four cities for thirty years, and a "time line" chart of history for 6,000 years. The almanac claims to be the best selling of all the world's books with the exception of the Holy Bible. Truly, as the ad claims, there are tens of thousand of up-to-date facts covering just about every conceivable topic. Even so, in presenting these facts, important to some, trivia to others, the editors share a smile in their statement, attributed to Henry Adams, grandson of presidents and noted historian, who observed, "Nothing in education is so astonishing as the amount of ignorance it accumulates in the form of inert facts."

The editor, acknowledging correspondence either critical or complimentary, promises that all such letters will be read by him, and he closes the gate on a potential problem with an emphatic statement that, "The World Book does not decide wagers."

Appendix B
BENJAMIN FRANKLIN'S,
POOR RICHARD

The Colonial almanac was the "mirror of the American mind between 1700 and the American Revolution."[1] During this era, almanacs were primarily calendars, but they were also "road books," containing descriptions of the highways, and a list of places the traveler could rest along the way. Usually, there were lists of the British kings and rulers of Europe, dates of the eclipses, and dates of courts and fairs. Additionally, they contained a chronicle of "remarkable things" such as the founding of the city of Philadelphia and the date when three bullocks were roasted on the ice of the Thames. Of course, they contained the changes of the moon and prognostications about the weather and often had a sprinkle of recipes, jokes, maxims, and cautionary rhymes thrown in for good measure.

Peddlers carried almanacs in their packs and offered them for sale along with their other wares. If they could not make a sale for cash, they might accept wheat, potatoes, a handful of nails, or even a bottle of rum in payment. For those who could pay anything, the almanac was virtually indispensable; and once purchased, the little booklet found itself occupying a prominent place in the home, generally strung on a stick and hung by the fireplace along with the family records.[2]

One can hardly contemplate the socio-economic progress of Colonial America without realizing the many contributions made by Benjamin Franklin. By the same token, one can hardly recount the many achievements of Benjamin Franklin

---

[1] Benjamin Franklin, *Poor Richard's: The Almanacks for the Years 1733-1758*, (New York: Bonanza Books, 1979), p. vii.

[2] Ibid.

without remembering his remarkable success with the almanac.

Benjamin Franklin was truly a jack-of-all-trades, and he mastered most of them. However, he started and finished, in his own mind, as a printer. That he considered himself a printer, first and foremost, is revealed in his will, when he began with these simple words, "I, Benjamin Franklin, printer . . ." He started as a printer's apprentice at the age of twelve, and by the time he was twenty-four, he had started his first newspaper, "The Philadelphia Gazette." During the following three years, he managed to get out of debt and reach some level of financial stability. His print shop had been printing almanacs of others, but at that point, he decided to print one of his own, in which he advanced his personal, religious, political, and philosophical views. His first edition was for the year 1733, and it was titled, *Poor Richard's Almanack*.[3]

Poor Richard had no rival among the publications of the American colonies. It ran for twenty-six issues and is estimated by Franklin himself, to have sold at the rate of 10,000 copies annually, reaching approximately one person in every hundred of the population. Franklin was both author and publisher, but while he used his name as the publisher, he wrote the almanac under the pseudonym of Richard Saunders.[4] An early feature of Franklin's almanac was an imaginary account of Richard Saunders' relationship with his wife and subsequent experiences, and this made Richard the first character in American fiction. Also, Franklin was among the first to employ the use of cartoons.

Much of the popularity of *Poor Richard* came about as a result of Franklin's proverbs. These little gems gleam as brightly today as they did when they were published. They are just as applicable too. Remember these? "God helps them that help themselves." "Fish and visitors stink after three

---

[3] *The World Book Encyclopedia*, Volume 7, 1968, s.v., "Benjamin Franklin." p. 416.

[4] *American Farm & Home Almanac*, (Lewiston, Maine: Simon & Schuster & The Almanac Publishing Company, 1981). In this it is pointed out that "Though not generally known, Franklin took his pseudonym, Richard Saunders, from the popular English Saunders almanac of the early 1700's. Thus, names lived, died, and were recycled."

days." "He that lies down with dogs shall rise up with fleas." Finally, there is the famous saying, "Early to bed and early to rise makes a man healthy, wealthy, and wise." Although written for the colonists, who Franklin called "middling people," as a result of the broad appeal of his maxims, the almanac made several trips across the Atlantic. There were constant new editions in England, Scotland, and Ireland, and there were fifty-six different editions translated into French.

The proverbs were not all Franklin's own of course. By his own admission, he assembled the wisdom of many ages and nations, borrowing freely from Dryden, Pope, La Rochefoucauld, and Rabelais, and he exercised his literary license as he saw fit. He would rewrite a particular adage when he chose, and he was not above using it again, revised, in a later edition. His "A Penny saved is a penny earned" started out in an earlier edition as "A Penny sav'd is a Twopence clear." In the 1758 edition of *Poor Richard*, Franklin printed a collection of his proverbs in the front of his almanac under the title, "The Way to Wealth." He described it as "the harangue of a wise old man." This collection was reprinted in America, Britain, and France, and if judged by itself would lead one to conclude that all of Franklin's aphorisms were moral or prudential. However, reading a number of others, probably less widely known, will show he could be equally caustic and cynical.

Franklin had an intense interest in all facets of human existence, and he was constantly seeking ways to make life more healthy, productive, comfortable, and convenient. He founded the Junto, a club which met in taverns and which discussed such topics as "What is Wisdom," and "Can a Man Arrive at Perfection." Out of this group sprang the American Philosophical Society. He was the first to import certain seeds for planting and he introduced the yellow willow to America. His concern for improved health conditions led to his discovery and warning that disease flourishes in a poorly ventilated room, and he helped to organize the first city hospital in America. He helped found the academy which later became the University of Pennsylvania, he vastly improved the postal system, and he set up a subscription library, the first of its kind in the world. His many contributions to the quality of life include the Franklin stove, the lightning rod, and bifocal glasses. All of these concerns for his fellowman were reflected in his almanac, and the experience Franklin gained with *Poor Richard* led to other publications. A survey of the twenty-six issues shows, to some extent, the progressive development of Franklin as a printer, publisher, civic leader, scientist, inventor, statesman, and philosopher. Of course the issues contained the usual meterological and astronomical material, but Franklin showed his devotion to matters of health in the first issue in a drawing of "The Anatomy of Man's Body as Governed by the Twelve Constellations," which he presented as a guide "when to purge, to bleed, or cut, thy Cattle, or—thyself." The first issue also contained a "Catalogue of Principal Kings and Princes of Europe, Date of Birth, Age, and Zodiac."

In the next issue, Franklin added the eclipses for 1734, and the 1739 edition contained: 1- Prognostication for 1739, 2-Of the Golden Number, 3- of the Eclipses for this Year, 4- Of the Diseases of This Year, 5- Of Fruits of the Earth, and 6- Of the Conditions of Some Countries (Drought.) In 1742, Franklin listed the Courts, Rules of Health and Long Life, and Rules to Find out a Fit Measure of Meat and Drink.

In the 1752 edition, Franklin discussed the calendar, beginning with, "Since the King and Parliament have seen fit to alter our Year by taking eleven days out of September . . ." He recounted the beginning of the calendar in Egypt, traced its development through the years, and explained the difference between a Tropical Year and a Civil Year, ending with the explanation that "to keep pace with the heavens," it requires "every four years to be 366 days."

In 1753, *Poor Richard* had a section on "How to Secure Houses, etc., from Lightning." This was one year after Franklin had conducted his most famous electrical experiment which resulted in his invention of the lightning rod. He urged his fellow citizens to use the device as a "means of securing the habitations and other buildings from mischief from thunder and lightning."

The 1758 issue was the last prepared by Franklin, and unfortunately, it contained no specific statement of resignation, and no reason for discontinuing the project. For a number of years, Franklin had been working toward greater leisure. That is "leisure," not retirement, which Franklin saw as the prerequisite to the pursuit of higher goals.[5] By 1758, he had bought his farm in New Jersey and started his electrical experiments. His civic responsibilities had increased, and from about 1750 on, he spent a great deal of time abroad. It is entirely possible that Franklin felt the almanac had served its purpose, having brought the fame and fortune necessary to free him for bigger and better things.

The only hint that Franklin prepared the 1758 edition as his last lies in the Preface which includes the collection of a hundred or so of his proverbs, all rewritten and restated, as his harangue of Father Abraham, a wise old man. This "tour de force" may or may not have been intended as the swan song of Franklin the Sage, but it was definitely, by virtue of its many reprints, an annuity of Franklin the Capitalist. For whatever reason, however, Franklin did retire as author and publisher of *Poor Richard*, and this unit of Colonial literature serves as an 18th century connecting link in the evolution of the almanac. It was, and still is, an informative and entertaining piece of journalism and a valuable contribution to Americana, the author's wit and wisdom just as pertinent as ever. All of the benefits Benjamin Franklin derived from *Poor Richard* are most deserving, and Franklin may have summed it up with these words; "Learning is to the Studious, Riches to the Careful, Power to the Bold, and Heaven to the Virtuous."

---

[5] On the subject of leisure, Franklin said, "Leisure is Time for doing something useful; this Leisure the diligent Man will obtain, but the lazy Man never; so that as Poor Richard says, 'a Life of Leisure and a Life of Laziness are two Things.' "

Appendix C

BITS AND PIECES

The Scope

Considering the fact that diagnostic or classic definitions of the almanac include meteorological calculations, astronomical data, some sort of calendar, and prophecies, it is amazing to find so many almanacs that take a different approach. Most modern almanacs are designed to serve the needs or interests of specific groups which may be church, professional, business, fraternal, or hobby related. They may contain political, religious, or idealistic opinions. They serve as a means of communication within the organization, acting as a source of specific information or a forum for the exchange or dissemination of ideas. While serving the interests of a particular group, within a specific time frame, they also reflect the customs, moods, trends, and ideology of both the group and the era. The almanac has come a long way from the original purpose of supplying the necessary information needed to produce and manage food supplies and prevent economic disaster or famine. From its early form, it has evolved into a literary horse of a different color, and today a concise definition of the almanac is nearly impossible, its use multi-varied, and it shows up in the strangest places.

Abraham Lincoln

Most attorneys know the story of Abraham Lincoln, and his use of the almanac in the courtroom. As the story goes, Abe was defending a man charged with murder.[1] The man, Duff Armstrong, was patronizing a bar and had been drinking

---

[1] Carl Sandburg, *Abraham Lincoln, The Prairie Years*, (New York: Charles Scribner's Sons, 1949), Volume II, p. 54.

there for two or three days. One evening, Armstrong was sleeping it off on a dry goods box when a man named Metzker came in and dragged Armstrong off the box by his feet. Armstrong took issue, but Metzker suggested they have a drink together rather than a fight. As they stood to drink, Metzker, obviously still in a hostile mood, threw his drink into Armstrong's eyes and Armstrong knocked Metzker down. The bartender stepped in and calmed the situation, and Armstrong returned to his dry goods box to finish his nap. At this point, a friend of Armstrong, Jim Norris, came into the bar and before long, Norris and Metzker got into a fight. Again the peacemaker, the bartender bribed Metzker with a pint of whiskey to leave the premises. Metzker went home and became ill for a period of five days, at the end of which, he died. The doctors and coroner's jury decided that Metzker had died from a blow over the eye caused by a blunt instrument.

A house painter, Charles Allen, swore that he saw the fight between Armstrong and Metzker, between eleven o'clock at night by the light of the moon, and that Armstrong hit Metzker with a sling shot. Based on this, Armstrong and Norris were arrested. Norris, who had killed a man previously and had been tried and acquitted, was brought to trial on the new charges involving Metzker. This time, he was convicted and sentenced to prison for eight years. At this point, Lincoln joined the defense of Armstrong.

The most damaging evidence against Armstrong seemed to be that of Allen, the house painter, who said he saw Armstrong by the light of the moon overhead hit Metzker with a sling shot. While examining the evidence pertaining to the sling shot, Lincoln sent out for an almanac, and at the opportune time, Lincoln showed that instead of the moon being in the sky at "about where the sun is at ten o'clock," as the witness testified, a well known family almanac showed that on the night of the murder, the moon had gone out of sight at exactly three minutes before midnight, or at 11:57 P.M. Thus, the almanac raised the question of whether there was sufficient moonlight by which the murder could have been witnessed. He was found not guilty.

Later, the rumor started that Lincoln had altered the almanac he used in the courtroom, but upon checking several of the popular almanacs, all agreed that there would not have been enough moonlight for any witness to see.

Occult Miscellany

The appeal of superstitition and astrology which created a popular interest in almanacs in the 14th century exists today, as witness the 1981 edition of *The Astrologer's Almanac and Occult Miscellany*. It has an astrological calendar showing 365 daily horoscopes plus personal forecasts for the complete astrological year, constituting advice on romance, marriage, business, health, family, and the basic needs of daily living.

No doubt there are persons who take this sort of thing seriously, but some of the astrological advice and predictions border on the humorous, if not actually ridiculous. If there is not enough amusement in the astrological section of this almanac, there is plenty to go around in the advertising section. One advertisement is that of the miracle power of the "omni-cosmics," that hidden power which "responds at once to help you gain endless streams of wealth . . . control the thoughts of others . . . achieve protection from evil . . . make illness and pain disappear . . . and much more!" Another amazing product is an item of jewelry, the Mystic Maga Cross, the original of which came from Ethiopia, the rulers of which are described as direct descendents of King Solomon and the Queen of Sheba. For the nominal sum of ten dollars, one may obtain the magic amulet, and it is promised that after just twenty-four hours of wearing the cross, instant big-money miracles will occur. The advertisement reads, "Suppose someone was to tell you this—a new Cadillac with a full tank of gas can be moved right from the dealer's showroom into your garage, without it costing you a cent!" Another "suppose" is, "Money locked away in a bank vault where it is doing nobody any good can be made to appear in a jar on your kitchen table." Instant miracles result from wearing the cross, according to the ad, and these are "worry and trouble ended, money, new cars, love powers restored, jobs, promotions, and one free credit card after another." Also, there is an advertisement from the promoters of "youth nutrients" which can help one keep looking beautiful and feeling great up to and beyond the age of sixty-five. It works very simply. It resets the aging control center and makes time march backwards. A twenty-one day supply of the miracle costs only $5.95 plus 90¢ postage. For those who feel the need of counsel, there is an advertisement by an "internationally known unitology forecaster" who will supply individual analysis, based on birthdate information. The analysis will assist in money matters, romance, changes, opportunities, and avoiding potential hazards. All of this costs only $6.95, plus postage and handling charges.

The "Gardner's Astrological Guide" is an article of some substance, and the religious calendar, along with a civil calendar, is useful. The "Legend of Mother Shipton" is interesting, and the "Fisherman's Astrological Guide" is honest. It presents itself only as an instrument for the fisherman to use according to his ability, intelligence, knowledge, and determination, concluding that a fisherman must make his own decisions, neither science nor astrology being capable of guaranteeing a full creel.

Almanacs and Corporations

In the Business Section of two local newspapers, there are reviews of an almanac, *Everybody's Business: An Almanac*, which bears the subtitle of "The Irreverent Guide to Corporate America."[2] It has three editors and a staff of forty-nine persons and employs three topographic companies. This $9.95 paper-back edition of 916 pages is a compendium of 317 large companies, most of which take in at least a billion dollars a year, 50% of which show annual volume of more than two billion dollars. The book answers a number of questions about the companies in everyday language, giving the history of the company and the "keys" to the corporate personality. The editor's statement explains the approach of

---

[2] *Dallas Morning News*, 11 May 1981, and *Fort Worth Star-Telegram*, 17 May 1981.

the publication by pointing out that the sales figures tell one thing about a company while the presence, or absence, of minorities and/or women on staff tells another. The down-to-earth approach is further reflected in the editors' explanation that a list of brand names shows an important aspect of the company, but the time that company spends in court sheds light from a different slant.

According to the reviews, there are 110,000 copies in print, but the almanac has not made the *New York Times* bestseller list, because "the book doesn't squarely fall into the nonfiction category." The explanation is, "how would you characterize a guide to corporate America which discusses Amtrak by noting the system's public relations expertise is demonstrated by the fact that 6 million of the people who called Amtrak in June 1979 got a busy signal?"

There is a statistical chart on each company discussed which shows sales, profits, Forbes 500 Ranking, industry ranking, date of founding, number of employees, and addresses. The text breaks down in sections as follows:

> 1-What They Do
> 2-History
> 3-Reputation
> 4-What They Own
> 5-Who Owns and Runs the Company
> 6-In the Public Eye
> 7-Where Are They Going
> 8-Stock Performance
> 9-Access (addresses)
> 10-Consumer Brands

The editor's irreverence toward corporations is shown in the statement, bemoaning the fact his book had not received the proper reviews, "Publishing is an industry known for its lack of market intelligence." Speaking of one of the giants of the drug industry, the editor concluded that the company is "a lethargic corporation ripe for takeover by someone who knows what to do." The headquarters building of a major airline is described as a "drab, windowless building with no pictures on the walls and no doors on the men's toilet stalls."

Sprinkled throughout the almanac are individual charts and articles which take a peek behind the scenes in Executive Suites. The book names names, and the titles are clever. There is a chart titled, "Who Sleeps the Most," which lists the major hotel chains, showing annual sales, number of units owned, and the number of rooms or beds. "Miss Hot Kiss Sells the Bomb" is a report on a military aerospace trade exhibition at which top armed forces officers are hosted by companies using women in skin tight jump suits to hand out advertising gimmicks. "The Ten Toughest Corporate Bosses" comes down hard. One executive is described as a galley master who, hearing that the rowers would die if the beat were raised to forty, would order, ",Make it forty-five."

The almanac contains historical data on the companies, and it is presented in a humorous and even nostalgic manner. For example, it is said that only two changes have been made in Levi's model 501 jeans since they first appeared in 1873. The company removed the copper rivet on the crotch seam in 1933 after the president of the company fell victim to the "Hot Rivet Syndrome" while crouched in front of a campfire. The other change was made after schools complained that rivets on the back pocket scratched the furniture. The rivets were moved to the front pockets.

"The Lamb's Larynx and a Dead Man's Ear" is a short article on the evolution of the telephone. In it there is a macabre description of one of Bell's early experiments when he built a speaking machine using an artificial skull and a lamb's larynx and a description of another device that used a dead man's ear connected to a lever.

The editor, Milton Maskowitz, is credited as having "done for big business what Rita Jenrette did for Congress." Moskowitz and his associates have produced an amusing and witty new book which "disintegrates with colorful detail the myth that big business is run by gray, pin-striped business-men in oak-paneled boardrooms."[3] *Everybody's Business* is an almanac with a purpose and it accomplishes its goals. It

____

[3] *Fort Worth Star-Telegram*, 11 May 1981, Robert H. Bork, Jr., Business Writer.

supplies hard facts on corporate America in an interesting manner, and the information is of value to investors, consumers, and those considering employment by the corporation discussed.

Embellishment and Fragmentation

In many cases, modern almanacs are radical departures from the old standbys such as *Poor Richard*, the *Old Farmer's Almanac*, and the *World Almanac and Book of Facts*. They lack some or all of the features usually associated with the old prototypes such as monthly calendars, astronomical calculations, important dates, health advice, demographics, ecology, and prophecy. Contemporary almanac-makers, taking any combination of these special features, embellish them and the publication becomes more specialized.

In celebration of the nation's 200th birthday, there was a *Bicentennial Almanac* which was a historical account of the political development of America, more of less in diary form, covering the Revolution of 1776 and ending with the Watergate Affair of 1975. The format of this book is that of a calendar.

In a technical magazine for handgun and rifle enthusiasts, there is an advertisement for a publication titled *The Handloaders Almanac*. It offers technical data for those involved in the hobby of reloading ammunition.

In 1975, the A. H. Belo Corporation, a newspaper publisher, prepared *The Texas Almanac and State Industrial Guide*. This publication is an almanac specializing in information pertaining strictly to Texas.

On the shelves of various book stores, the publications in the almanac section show the specialization of modern almanacs. There are almanacs for fathers, almanacs for mothers, almanacs for specific church groups, and almanacs for business. Also, the titles are interesting. There was found in one book store, in the almanac section, a publication titled *A List of Books*. Beside it was another titled *A Book of Lists*.

At the same time the almanac-makers have been narrowing the scope of these publications, the almanac of days gone by has become fragmented. It is no longer necessary to subscribe to an annual publication in order to obtain short and long term weather predictions, gardening advice, horoscopes, first aid tips, and suggested best times to try one's luck at the old fishing hole. The media supplies this information, well founded upon the scientific manipulation of various electronic devices. Television incorporates weather information in its newscasts, including current conditions and forecasts; and sometimes the phases of the moon, gardening tips, and the hours of the day best suited to wildlife activity. Severe weather warning may come at any time, and the media often offers advice to homeowners to exercise care to protect outside waterpipes and plants that might be affected by extremes in the weather.

Daily newspapers contain much of the information formerly presented in almanacs. There is generally a business section covering markets, personnel, and general economic trends. The section covering items of local interest contains news of the courts, universities, and important dates. The women's section usually carries horoscopes, advice to the lovelorn, and prophecies from modern day soothsayers.

On the surface, it seems that magazine has replaced the almanac in its pristine form. This is not surprising, considering the fact the almanac, forerunner of the magazine, is difficult to separate from the magazine in the field of journalism. Current magazines contain the general topics which were presented in earlier almanacs. For example, there are magazines which act as guides and offer both advice and insight in matters of health, money matters, human relationship, and prophecy. There are magazines of specific interest to homeowners, gardeners, travelers, hobbyists, and professionals. All of this would lead one to feel the almanac has faded from the scene. However, in spite of the specialization and embellishment of the almanac of by-gone days, the nearly 200-year track record of the almanac has to be considered. Accepting the subscription figures of such publications as *The Old Farmer's Almanac*, *The Farmer's Almanac*, and *The World Almanac and Book of Facts*, the reading public continues to support, obviously, the almanac as a journalistic entity.

Using a portion of an earlier quote, perhaps more than is realized, the almanac in some form is, ". . . the one universal book of modern literature, the supreme literary necessity in households . . ." The almanac occupies a place of distinction in the field of journalism.

Appendix D

THE FREE-MASON'S CALENDAR
OF 1812

The Free-Mason's Calendar of 1812 is a small 7½ by 4¼ inch
almanac with a gorgeous Masonic binding. The dark blue
cover is genuine leather, embossed in gold with Masonic
emblems, including the Compasses, Squire, Trowel, Level, 24
Inch Gauge, V.S.L., Sun, Moon, Stars, and the All Seeing
Eye. This 47 page book contains:

1	p.	Title Page
1	p.	Preface and Table of Contents
12	pp.	Almanac: One month per page, one line per day. Sunrise & Sunset. Moonrise and Moonset. High water mark at London Bridge. Saint's Days. Royal Birthdays. Dates of university and law days. Religious holidays, etc.
1	p.	Eclipses, Seasons, and Movable Feasts in 1812.
1	p.	Genealogical List of the Royal Family.
1	p.	Sovereigns of England, from 1066 (William the Conqueror) to 1812 (George III).
1	p.	Chart of Law and University terms.
1	p.	Table of Interest (How to figure interest rates).
1	p.	Commercial Stamps (Charges on legal documents).
10	pp.	Officers of the Grand Lodge of England in 1811. Also list of Grand Lodge officers from 1717.
1	p.	List of Subscribers to the Hall-Loan.
1	p.	Remarkable occurrences in Masonry. (Begins with the legendary founding of the first Grand Lodge by St. Alban in 287 A.D.).

12   pp.   Listing of Lodges with their new numbers,
                granted in 1792, and dates of meetings. In-
                cludes Lodges erased for non-conformity.

3   pp.   Town and Provincial Lodges, listed by towns.

The title page and Preface are interesting. Showing the purpose and scope of this Masonic almanac, these two pages prove Grand Lodge involvement in the publication of almanacs as a means of communication and they show the synonymity of the terms "calendar" and "almanac."

The formal title used the word "calendar," not "almanac," but immediately following the title is the statement that it also contains, ". . . the usual Matter in other Almanacs . . . and a great Variety of Articles concerning Masonry." Next is the statement that the almanac is, "published for the benefit of the Charity-Fund," and that it is "under sanction of the Grand Lodge of England." The printer was W. P. Norris and the publisher was The Company of Stationers, accomplished old hands, by 1812, in the field of almanacs. The almanac was priced at Two Shillings and Threepence.

The Preface points out the "flourishing state of the Society of Free-Masons, and the consequent necessity of a more general communication of its public . . . induced the Grand Lodge, in the year 1777, to publish a Calendar, which has hitherto been continued." There is mention of a Committee "under whose whole management it (the almanac) has been conducted." The Preface reiterates the charitable purpose of the almanac, and it ends with the statement that the publication, along with its useful lists, etc. "likewise contains a very comprehensive and correct Almanac, and as much matter of general utility as any other Calendar extant."

In step with the poet who said that a rose by any other name is still a rose, it might be said that an Engraved List is a Calendar is a Year Book is an Almanac.

ROB MORRIS' LIST OF ALMANACS

NOTE: This is a copy of page 61 in the 1862 edition
of the Rob Morris Almanac.

1862.   ROB MORRIS' FREEMASON'S ALMANAC.   61

Almanacs, Masonic and Unmasonic.

In Europe, the dissemination of Masonic intelligence by means of yearly Books (Almanacs and Annuaries) began in olden times. In Morris' collection are German Masonic Almanacs of 1776. But in this country the practice is more recent. The following are all the American Almanacs, Masonic and Antimasonic, in Morris' Masonic Collection at La Grange, Ky. They are given in order of dates.

1802   Catalogue Mas. Lodges, S.C. and Geo.
1807   "   "   "   , six Northern States
1824   Hardcastle's Mas. Calendar, N.Y.
1825   Permanent Lodge Calendar, N.Y.
1827   Masonic Register, N.Y.
1828   N.E. Almanac and Mas. Calendar, Boston, MS.
1841   Masonic Register, N.Y.
1850   "   "   "
1851   "   "   "
1851   Freemason's Directory, N.Y.
1852   Masonic Vade Mecum, Ky.
1854   Masonic Register, Pa.
1855   "   "   "
1855   Masonic Register, N.Y.
1856   Am. Dutch Jahrbucker, N.Y.
1857   Am. Dutch Jahrubker, N.Y.
1857   Universal Mas. Record, Pa.
1859   "   "   "   "
1859   Am. Dutch Jahrbucker, N.Y.
1860   Universal Mas. Record, Pa.
1860   Masonic Register, Pa.
1860   Cincinnati Mas. Directory, O.
1861   Masonic Register, Pa.
1860   Rob Morris' Freemason's Almanac, Ky.
1861   "   "   "   "
1862   "   "   "   "
1829   Giddins' Antimasonic Almanac, N.Y.
1830   "   "   "   "
1830   Antimasonic Almanac, Pa. (German)
1830   Giddins' Penn. Ant. Almanac, Pa.
1831   Sun Ant. Almanac, Pa.
1831   New England Ant. Almanac, Boston
1831   Giddins' Ant. Almanac, N.Y.
1832   "   "   "   "
1832   New England Ant. Almanac, Boston
1833   Giddins' Ant. Almanac, N.Y.

Appendix F

A LIST OF ALMANACS

Date	Example	Compiler/Publisher	Comment
1150	Unnamed	Solomon Jarchus	Earliest date of an almanac in a more modern sense.
1276	Opus Majus	Roger Bacon	Possibly the first use of the term "almanac."
1300	Unnamed	Patrus de Dacia	Manuscript. At the Savilian Library at Oxford.
1380 1386	Unnamed Unnamed	John Somers Nicholas de Lynne }	First so-called "standard" almanacs. Manuscripts.
1431	Unnamed		First almanac in English. At the British Museum.
1457 1497	Unnamed Unnamed }		Dates of "first" printed almanacs in English.
1472	Ephemerides ab Anno	"Regiomontanus" (John Muller)	First "important" almanac. Believed to have been used by Columbus.

Date	Example	Compiler/Publisher	Comment
1540	A Newe Almanacke and Prognostication For the Yere of our Lord 1540	Elis Bomelius, Doctor in Physicke	Example of almanac written by practitioners of Astronomy or Astrology or Doctor with treatment of human ailments as a feature.
1639	An Almanac Calculated for New England	William Pierce, Mariner	Believed to have been the first almanac in America. Printed under the supervision of Harvard College.
1687	Unnamed	Daniel & Titan Leeds, Wm. Bradford's Press	Daniel Leeds son (Titan) was a competitor of Benjamin Franklin.
1700	Vox Stellarum	Francis Moore	Continues today as *Old Moore's Almanac*.
1712	Traveler's Almanac	The Company of Stationers	For travelers and merchants. Contains method of telling time "sun-dial fashion. Information on markets, distances, weights & measures.
1714	Farmer's Almanac	N. K. Whitamor	First almanac using the name "Farmers."
1723	*Lists of Lodges	Grand Lodge of England	First lists proper. Official.
1724	*Engraved Lists of Lodges	John Pine, Engraver	Official engraved lists of lodges. John Pine, principal engraver. Other engravers: Emanuel Bowen, Benjamin Cole, and William Cole.

Date	Title	Author	Notes
1725 to 1775	*Astronomical Diary and Almanack	Nathaniel Ames	Probably the forerunner of Benjamin Franklin's *Poor Richard*. Said to have contained Masonry.
1728	Rhode Island Almanac	James Franklin	Compiled by the brother of Benjamin Franklin.
1732 to 1758	Poor Richard's Almanack	Benjamin Franklin	See Appendix.
1741	**Almanac des Cocus		France. Earliest anti-Masonic publication using the term "almanac."
1752 to 1778	*Almanach des Franc-Masons en Ecosse		The Hague. Earliest (?) Masonic almanac abroad.
1775 & 1776	*Freemason's Calendar	William Preston(?)	First English Masonic almanac (calendar). Printed in ordinary type. Not under Grand Lodge authority. Some feel Preston was responsible for the publication.
1777 to 1814	*Freemason's Calendar	Grand Lodge of England	First official English Masonic almanac. Appeared from 1777 until the time of the Union.

Date	Example	Compiler/Publisher	Comment
1778	*The Freemason's Calendar, or an Almanac	Grand Lodge of England	Title page pictured in the Transactions of the American Lodge of Research. Said to be in possession of the Grand Lodge of Massachusetts.
1793	Old Farmer's Almanac	Robert B. Thomas	Oldest continuous publication in America.
1802	*Catalog of Masonic Lodges, S.C. & Ga.		Listed as a Masonic almanac in the Rob Morris Collection.
1805	Citizen's and Farmer's Almanac	David Young	Forerunner of the *Farmer's Almanac of 1818*.
1807	*Catalog of Masonic Lodges, six northern states		Listed as a Masonic almanac in the Rob Morris Collection
1812	*The Free-Mason's Calendar of 1812	The Company of Stationers	Example of later English official Masonic almanac. See Appendix.
1814	Event		At this time, the format of the English Masonic calendar was changed to a "pocket book."
1818	The Farmer's Almanac	David Young	Continuous American publication for 164 years.

Year	Title	Source	Notes
1824	*Hardcastle's Masonic Calendar	New York	Listed as a Masonic almanac in the Rob Morris Collection.
1824	*No. 20: Howe's Genuine Almanac	"Philo Astronomie" (Howe)	Earliest American Masonic almanac discovered for use in commentary.
1824	*Permanent Lodge Calendar, N.Y.		Listed as a Masonic almanac in the Rob Morris Collection.
1826	*No. 22: The Free-Masons Almanac for 1826	"Philo Astronomie" (Howe)	Formerly *Howe's Genuine Almanac*.
1826	Event		Disappearance of William Morgan.
1827	**Illustrations of Masonry	William Morgan	Masonic exposure.
1828	*New England Almanac and Masonic Calendar	Marsh & Capen, Boston	Housed in the library at the House of the Temple.
1829	**Light on Masonry	Bernard	Masonic exposure.
1829	**Giddins' Antimasonic Almanac	Edward Giddins, New York	Rob Morris Collection. Drake listed Giddins' almanacs for the years 1828 through 1933.±

Date	Example	Compiler/Publisher	Comment
1830	**Giddins' Antimasonic	Edward Giddins,	Rob Morris Collection.
1830	*Reference	Isaiah Thomas	Series of Masonic almanacs by Thomas to which Morris referred in the opening statement of his 1860 almanac.
1830	**Antimasonic Almanac (German)	Pennsylvania	Rob Morris Collection.
1830	**Giddins' Pennsylvania Antimasonic Almanac	Edward Giddins	Rob Morris Collection.
1830	**Sun Anti-Masonic Almanac for	William Collom (Avery Allyn?)	It is possible that Avery Allyn was involved in the publication of this almanac in cooperation with an anti-Masonic newspaper, the *Sun*.
1830	**New England Antima-sonic Almanac for 1830	John Marsh, Boston	THE FACSIMILE. Housed in the library of the Grand Lodge of Texas.
1831	**New England Antima-sonic Almanac for 1831	John Marsh, Boston	Housed in the library of the Grand Lodge of Texas.
1831	**Vermont Anti-Masonic	Samuel Hemmenway, Jr.	Listed by Drake.±
1831	**Giddins' Antimasonic Almanac	Edward Giddins	Rob Morris Collection.

1832	**No. II: Anti-Masonic Sun Almanac for 1832	Avery Allyn & William Collom	This almanac bore the name of Avery Allyn as compiler.
1832	**The Ohio Anti-Masonic Almanac	Jenkins & Glover, Publishers	Listed by Drake.±
1832	**Giddins' Antimasonic Almanac	Edward Giddins	Rob Morris Collection.
1832	**New England Anti-Masonic Almanac doe 1832	John Marsh, Boston	Rob Morris Collection.
1833	**The Anti-Masonic Sun Almanac	William Collom	Listed by Drake.±
1833	**Anti-Masonic Almanac	Edward Giddins	Picture of the title page in the *Transactions* of the American Lodge of Research.
1834	**Eaton's Antimasonic Almanac	E. Eaton, Vermont	Xerox copy from the Vermont Historical Society. Listed by Drake along with 1833 and 1835 editions.±
1834	**The Anti-Masonic Almanac	S. J. Sylvester, Pennsylvania	Listed by Drake.±

Date	Example	Compiler / Publisher	Comment
1834	**Giddins' Antimasonic Almanac	Edward Giddins	Picture of title page in the *Transactions* of American Lodge of Research
1834	**New England Anti-Masonic	John Marsh, Boston	Picture of title page in the *Transactions* of the American Lodge of Research.
1838	*Masonic Kalendar for 1838	Grand Lodge of Texas	Probably the first thing published along the lines of Texas Grand Lodge Proceedings.
1841, 1850, & 1851	*Masonic Register, N.Y.	Samuel Maverck & William W. Nexsein	Rob Morris Collection. Also listed by Drake.±
1849	*Marsh's Masonic Register	Marsh, New York	Listed by Drake.±
1850	*A Masonic Register	R. R. Boyd, New York	Listed by Drake.±
1851	*Freemason's Directory	Kentucky	Rob Morris Collection.
1852	*Masonic Vade Mecum	Kentucky	Rob Morris Collection.
1854 & 1855	*Masonic Register	Pennsylvania	Rob Morris Collection
1855	*Masonic Register	New York	Rob Morris Collection.

1856, 1857, & 1858	*American Dutch Jahrbucher	New York	Rob Morris Collection.
1857 & 1859	*Universal Masonic Record	Pennsylvania	Rob Morris Collection.
1859/60	*American Dutch Jahrbucher	New York	Rob Morris Collection.
1860	*Universal Masonic Record	Pennsylvania	Rob Morris Collection.
1860	*Masonic Register	Pennsylvania	Rob Morris Collection.
1860	*Cincinnati Masonic Directory	Ohio	Rob Morris Collection.
1860 to 1878	*The Masonic Register & Almanac	Thomas Adams	Several editions housed in the library of the House of the Temple.
1860	*Freemason's Almanac	Rob Morris	THE FACSIMILE. The complete series of the Rob Morris almanacs (1860, 1861, 1862, 1863, and 1865) are in a bound volume at the library of the House of the Temple.

Date	Example	Compiler / Publisher	Comment
1861	*Masonic Register	Pennsylvania	Rob Morris Collection.
1863	*Calendar for the Hebrew Years 5622-5560 (1861-1900)	Nathaniel B. Shurtleff,	Housed in the library of the House of the Temple.
1964	*American Masonic Almanac	R. McMurdy	Housed in the library of the House of the Temple.
1868	World Almanac and Book of Facts	New York World	Continuous publication for over 110 years.
1874	*Keystone Masonic Almanac	The Keystone, (Masonic newspaper,) Philadelphia	Housed in the library of the House of the Temple.
1875	*Masonic 1875 Directory & Almanac	E. Y. Bronlow	Housed in the library of the House of the Temple.
1876	*The Keystone Centennial Masonic Almanac for 1876	The Keystone, Philadelphia	Housed in the library of the House of the Temple.
1908	Event	England	Date when the Masonic Calendar, in pocket-book became the Masonic Year book.

1920   *The Masonic Year Book   Robert I. Clegg   Variant type of Masonic year book.

---

* Masonic almanac
** Anti-Masonic Almanac
± Milton Drake, *Almanacs of the United States*, (New York: The Scarecrow Press, Inc.)

COLOPHON

Masonic Almanacs

AND

Anti-Masonic Almanacs

Thirteen hundred copies of this limited edition were manufactured by Pantagraph Printing Company of Bloomington, Illinois.

This book was photocomposed on an AM Comp/Edit System using the type face known as Janson.

The facsimile pages were reproduced from *Rob Morris' Freemason's Almanac, 1860* on loan from the Library of the House of the Temple, Washington, D.C. and from *The New England Anti-Masonic Almanac for 1830* on loan from the Texas Masonic Library, Waco, Texas.

The text paper is 60 lb. basis cream white Hammermill Opaque Offset manufactured by the Hammermill Paper Company. The book covers are made of Holliston Sturdite over board and stamped in gold.

All volumes issued by The Masonic Book Club are designed and prepared by Alphonse Cerza, Michael and Barry Weer and Fred Dolan.

Related Titles from Westphalia Press

Ancient Mysteries and Modern Masonry: The Collected Writings of Jewel P. Lightfoot, Edited by Billy J. Hamilton Jr.

Jewel P. Lightfoot. Former Attorney General of the State of Texas. Past Grand Master of the Masonic Grand Lodge of Texas. From humble beginnings in rural Arkansas, he worked to become an educated man who excelled in law and Freemasonry. He was a gentleman of his time, well-known as a scholar, public speaker, and Masonic philosopher.

Essay on The Mysteries and the True Object of The Brotherhood of Freemasons
by Jason Williams

This isn't a reprint of a classic. It's a new rendition with new life breathed into it, to be enjoyed both by the layperson trying to understand the Craft and Masonic scholars taking a deeper dive into the fraternity's golden years—when the concepts of liberty and equality were still fresh.

Female Emancipation and Masonic Membership:
An Essential Collection
By Guillermo De Los Reyes Heredia

Female Emancipation and Masonic Membership: An Essential Combination is a collection of essays on Freemasonry and gender that promotes a transatlantic discussion of the study of the history of women and Freemasonry and their contribution in different countries.

Freemasonry, Heir to the Enlightenment
by Cécile Révauger

Modern Freemasonry may have mythical roots in Solomon's time but is really the heir to the Enlightenment. Ever since the early eighteenth century freemasons have endeavored to convey the values of the Enlightenment in the cultural, political and religious fields, in Europe, the American colonies and the emerging United States.

Masonic Myths and Legends
by Pierre Mollier

Freemasonry preserves the teachings of a primitive Judeo-Christian gnosis. In order to better understand these legends and myths and their significance, Pierre Mollier has studied their origins and attempted to find their sources.

Exploring the Vault: Masonic Higher Degrees 1730–1800
by John Belton and Roger Dachez

The study adopted a forensic approach to the available evidence, and the discoveries exceeded expectations. The book details their 'archaeological finds' and offers a novel perspective on the development of the Higher Degrees during the eighteenth century.

Étienne Morin: From the French Rite to the Scottish Rite by Arturo de Hoyos and Josef Wäges

All extant Masonic records have been consulted and using this meta-data, a comprehensive reconstruction emerges, revealing that Étienne Morin was a founding masonic figure in Saint Domingue and creator of his own high degree system, that operated for a time as a defacto Grand Lodge.

The Impact of Freemasonry on the Secular and Liberal Discourse in Mexico
by Guillermo De Los Reyes, Translated by Bradley L. Drew

In this thought-provoking book, De Los Reyes argues that Freemasonry, through its lodges, played a decisive role in shaping Mexico's national thought, contributing to the creation of a liberal and secular State and fostering anticlerical sentiments among the laity that endured well into the twentieth century.

The French Rite: Enlightenment Culture
Cécile Révauger, Editor

This book, focused on the French Rite, covers the founding principles of the Enlightenment and their influence on the birth of modern Freemasonry as we know it today. The authors revisit the fundamental values of the Enlightenment, from a rational approach to religious tolerance and cosmopolitanism.

The Great Transformation: Scottish Freemasonry 1725-1810
by Dr. Mark C. Wallace

This book examines Scottish Freemasonry in its wider British and European contexts between the years 1725 and 1810. The Enlightenment effectively crafted the modern mason and propelled Freemasonry into a new era marked by growing membership and the creation of the Grand Lodge of Scotland.

Getting the Third Degree: Fraternalism, Freemasonry and History
Edited by Guillermo De Los Reyes and Paul Rich

As this engaging collection demonstrates, the doors being opened on the subject range from art history to political science to anthropology, as well as gender studies, sociology and more. The organizations discussed may insist on secrecy, but the research into them belies that.

Freemasonry: A French View
by Roger Dachez and Alain Bauer

Perhaps one should speak not of Freemasonry but of Freemasonries in the plural. In each country Masonic historiography has developed uniqueness. Two of the best known French Masonic scholars present their own view of the worldwide evolution and challenging mysteries of the fraternity over the centuries.

Worlds of Print: The Moral Imagination of an Informed Citizenry, 1734 to 1839
by John Slifko

John Slifko argues that freemasonry was representative and played an important role in a larger cultural transformation of literacy and helped articulate the moral imagination of an informed democratic citizenry via fast emerging worlds of print.

Why Thirty-Three?: Searching for Masonic Origins
by S. Brent Morris, PhD

What "high degrees" were in the United States before 1830? What were the activities of the Order of the Royal Secret, the precursor of the Scottish Rite? A complex organization with a lengthy pedigree like Freemasonry has many basic foundational questions waiting to be answered, and that's what this book does: answers questions.